# THE GUN DEBATE

## WHAT EVERYONE NEEDS TO KNOW®

# THE GUN DEBATE

## WHAT EVERYONE NEEDS TO KNOW ®

### PHILIP J. COOK
### and
### KRISTIN A. GOSS

OXFORD
UNIVERSITY PRESS

# OXFORD
UNIVERSITY PRESS

Oxford University Press is a department of the University of Oxford.
It furthers the University's objective of excellence in research, scholarship,
and education by publishing worldwide.

Oxford   New York
Auckland   Cape Town   Dar es Salaam   Hong Kong   Karachi
Kuala Lumpur   Madrid   Melbourne   Mexico City   Nairobi
New Delhi   Shanghai   Taipei   Toronto

With offices in
Argentina   Austria   Brazil   Chile   Czech Republic   France   Greece
Guatemala   Hungary   Italy   Japan   Poland   Portugal   Singapore
South Korea   Switzerland   Thailand   Turkey   Ukraine   Vietnam

Oxford is a registered trademark of Oxford University Press
in the UK and certain other countries.

"What Everyone Needs to Know" is a registered trademark of
Oxford University Press.

Published in the United States of America by
Oxford University Press
198 Madison Avenue, New York, NY 10016

Library of Congress Cataloging-in-Publication Data

Cook, Philip J., 1946-
The gun debate : what everyone needs to know / Philip J. Cook and
Kristin A. Goss.
pages cm. — (What everyone needs to know)
Includes bibliographical references and index.
ISBN 978-0-19-933898-6 (hardcover : alk. paper) —
ISBN 978-0-19-933899-3 (pbk. : alk. paper)
1. Gun control—United States.   2. Firearms ownership—United States.
3. Firearms—Law and legislation—United States.   I. Goss, Kristin A.,
1965-   II. Title.
HV7436.C657 2014
363.330973—dc23

2013042614

1 3 5 7 9 8 6 4 2
Printed in the United States of America
on acid-free paper

# CONTENTS

# 6  How America Regulates Firearms                                89

# 7  Effectiveness of Firearms Policy                              132

# ACKNOWLEDGMENTS

We are indebted to a number of experts whose research and advice we sought in writing and re-writing this book. Despite our combined 60 years of experience studying gun violence and gun policy, we needed and greatly appreciated the help. We are also deeply grateful for the extraordinary research assistance provided by Julia Quinn. Her efforts in tracking down sources, organizing them, and producing annotated drafts, greatly facilitated the effort to create a well-documented and comprehensive treatment of this subject in relatively short order. Perhaps most impressive was her ability to coordinate our separate efforts and make sure that never once did we work on the same chapter at the same time. She did all this with good humor and unflagging enthusiasm for the project itself. Thank you, Julia.

# THE GUN DEBATE

WHAT EVERYONE NEEDS TO KNOW ®

# 1

# AMERICA AND ITS GUNS

## What Is a Gun?

A more precise term for the subject of this book is firearm, which is a portable weapon that shoots projectiles from a metal tube, propelled at high speed by expanding gas that is generated by the explosion of gunpowder in a confined space. So we will not be discussing water pistols or BB guns or pricing guns, or for that matter cannons or catapults or rocket launchers. The focus is on the weapons owned by households for hunting, target shooting, and self-defense, and by police and private security as tools of their trade. There are a great variety of firearms, the most common of which can be categorized as rifles, shotguns, pistols, or revolvers.

## What Is the Problem with Guns?

Like so many commodities, firearms serve a variety of useful purposes but are also subject to misuse. The misuse, whether accidental or intentional, accounts for more than 30,000 deaths per year in the United States and something like a half million deaths worldwide.[1] Probably the greatest concern is in conjunction with interpersonal violence—criminal assaults, robberies, spousal abuse. When the perpetrator uses a gun rather than a knife or club or bare fists, the likelihood that the victim will die is greatly increased. The same point applies to suicide attempts—there are millions every year in the United States, mostly unsuccessful, but when a gun is used, the fatality rate is 80%. In sum, guns *intensify* violence. And because guns can be used to kill quickly, with little effort and from a distance, they give individuals who are so inclined the capacity to terrorize neighborhoods, assassinate even well-guarded public officials, and perpetrate one-man rampages in schools and workplaces and theaters.

To point out that firearms are misused and can do great damage does not deny that they also have value in recreation (hunting, target shooting, collecting) and as tools for self-defense and national defense. Motor vehicle crashes also kill more than 30,000 Americans each year, and a variety of other valuable commodities are misused with deadly effect: For example, 15,000 Americans die each year from overdoses of prescription painkillers, and about 100,000 deaths are associated with infections contracted as a result of hospitalization and medical procedures. For vehicles, drugs, medical care, and many other products, including firearms, it is reasonable to ask, "How can we reduce the problems of misuse while preserving the benefit of normal prudent use?"

For inspiration, we note that the highway-safety "problem" has been greatly reduced over the decades while preserving the value of highway travel. Thanks to better roads, safer vehicles, seatbelt requirements, and DUI enforcement (among other things), the highway fatality rate has been cut in half since 1950 (even though the average person drives more than three times as many miles). For firearms as well we can aspire to reduce misuse while preserving value.

### How Many Americans Own How Many Firearms?

Among the wealthy nations of the world, the United States has the highest prevalence of private gun ownership. Even in the United States, however, only about 35% of households own a gun—which is to say that most households do not own a gun. Actually it is more accurate to say that most *individuals*

do not own a gun, since guns are viewed as personal pos-
sessions, not household appliances with shared ownership. According to national surveys, about 25% of adults in
America own a gun.

How many guns are in private hands altogether? Since guns
are not registered in most jurisdictions, we have to rely on estimates rather than counts. Surveys indicate that 25% of adults
age 18 and over own at least one firearm, which amounts to
about 60 million owners in the United States. Some adolescents
own firearms as well, so the total may be as high as 65 million.
If we knew the average number of guns per gun owner, we'd
be able to estimate the total household firearms inventory. But
it is hard to elicit that information in a survey, and few surveys
have attempted to do so.

Besides surveys, another approach to estimating the total
is to use federal records on firearms commerce. It is possible
to add up all the firearms that have been manufactured in
the United States, add the imports, and subtract the exports.
Applying this approach to data from 1899 to 2011 (excluding
sales to the military), the cumulative total is 328 million. But of
course not all of those firearms still exist today. They do tend to
be durable, especially those of high quality. If we assume that
just 1% of the stock has been scrapped each year since 1945,
and apply that assumption to the federal records, then the current total is reduced to 245 million—about four guns for every
gun owner.

One problem with that estimate (beside the fact that the
true attrition rate is unknown and may be higher or lower
than 1%) is that the official federal records of imports and
exports miss off-the-books transactions. Smuggling guns
from the United States to Mexico, Canada, and the Caribbean
has a long tradition. The flow of guns to Mexican gangs in
recent years has been especially prominent and may amount
to millions of guns during the drug wars there—none of
which are counted in the official export statistics. On the
other side of the ledger, some firearms are smuggled into

the United States, including military weapons brought home by servicemen stationed abroad and never recorded in the import statistics.

The bottom line is that no one knows how many firearms are in private hands in the United States. Based on the calculations presented above, a range of 200 to 300 million seems reasonable.

## Who Owns the Guns?

One in every four adults owns a firearm. It is fair to say that these owners are not a representative sample of the American public. First, most guns are owned by men—a recent poll found 37% of men as compared with just 12% of women said they personally owned a gun. Age and race also differentiate gun owners from nonowners: middle-aged folks are more likely than those under 30 to have a gun, and whites are twice as likely as blacks. Gun ownership is more than twice as common in rural areas than urban, as would be expected given that open spaces are the natural domain of gun sports. Indeed, one survey found that more than 60% of farmers and farmworkers are current gun owners, and almost all of them owned a gun at one time in their lives.

Several other correlates of gun ownership are worth noting. First, adults who grew up with a firearm in the home are far more likely—by a ratio of three to one—to own one now than those who did not. Growing up with guns provides a chance to learn to enjoy gun sports and be comfortable with having guns in the home. Second, firearms, like most pricey commodities, are more common in middle- and upper-class homes than in those with low income. And third, for whatever reason there is some correlation with political outlook—Republicans are almost twice as likely to own as are Democrats.

There are large regional disparities in gun ownership. To paint a very rough picture, the rates in New England, Mid-Atlantic, and Pacific states tend to be relatively low (with certain exceptions, such as Alaska and Vermont), while the rates in the southern,

Midwestern, and old frontier states of the West are considerably higher. This pattern has changed very little over recent decades, although the prevalence of gun ownership has undergone a broad decline. The rural tradition is reflected in the geographic patterns: We can accurately predict the prevalence of gun ownership in a state today by simply knowing what fraction of the state population was living in rural areas in 1950.

Here are the top five states when it comes to household gun ownership: West Virginia, Alabama, Mississippi, Wyoming, and Louisiana.[2]

And here are the five states with the lowest rates: Hawaii, Massachusetts, Rhode Island, New Jersey, and New York (with the District of Columbia as a bonus).

While urban areas generally have lower rates of gun ownership, there are some where gun ownership is the norm. The greatest concentration of urban guns is in the large cities of Texas and Arizona, as well as Tampa–St. Petersburg. At the other end of the spectrum are New York City and Boston. The differences are remarkable. A good proxy for prevalence of guns is the fraction of suicides committed with guns: In Phoenix and Dallas–Fort Worth, more than half the suicides are with guns, whereas in New York City the rate is just 12%.

### Why Do People Choose to Own Guns—or Not?

In a 2013 Pew survey, the leading reason offered by gun owners was protection against crime. In particular, 48% offered protection as their first reason, while another 39% cited hunting or target shooting. As recently as 1999, the same survey found that only 26% of owners mentioned protection as the first reason. You might suppose that the increased concern about self-protection reflects a spike in crime rates, but just the opposite is true—rates have been heading down, and most places are far safer from predatory crime today than in 1999.

So what explains the dramatic increase in self-protection as the stated reason for owning a gun?

We have a theory. Most gun owners grew up with guns in their parents' home and had some experience in hunting or target shooting. Now they typically have several guns, often with different purposes in mind—handguns for self-protection, long guns for target shooting or hunting. In short, they like guns and have several uses for them. The recent tendency to cite self-protection as the lead reason for owning may in part have to do with the public rhetoric over guns, which in recent years has dignified this particular purpose as being at the heart of a constitutional right.

There is some survey information on why most individuals choose not to own a gun. In the 1994 National Survey of Private Ownership of Firearms (NSPOF), 33% of nonowners said that guns were too expensive, while most others mentioned that guns are dangerous, or (relatedly) that they had children at home, or that they were opposed to guns for moral and other reasons.

### How Many Guns Do Gun Owners Own?

One of the great lessons of marketing science is the Law of the Heavy Half (aka the 20/80 Law or the Pareto Law)—namely, that 20% of consumers account for 80% of sales. If that ratio applied to firearms inventories, then the top 20% of firearms owners would account for 80% of all firearms in private hands. The NSPOF did find a high concentration of firearms ownership, but not quite that high. In that survey, the top 20% of firearms owners possessed more than 10 guns apiece on average, and accounted for 55% of all the firearms. At the other end of the spectrum were gun owners who had just one gun—they accounted for one-quarter of all owners. So the norm in 1994, and now as well, is that people who choose to own guns often do not stop at just one, but have several (usually of different types) and in some cases dozens. There is nothing unusual about guns in this respect – the same thing could be said about cameras or computers.

## Is Gun Ownership Rising or Falling?

The answer may be "both."

First, here is the evidence that it is falling. The trend in the household prevalence of firearms ownership is indeed downward over the last generation. In 1980, the best survey evidence indicates half of all households had at least one gun. By 2010 that figure had dropped to about 35%, a remarkable change. The percentage of individuals who own a gun also declined during that period, but not as much. The two trends do not line up perfectly because households are smaller now than they were decades ago, and in particular are less likely to include an adult male. Remember that it is the men who own most of the guns.

So in what sense is gun ownership rising? The federal data on domestic manufactures, imports, and exports, while not perfect (see above), show a dynamic upward trend in recent years. Domestic shipments of new firearms doubled between 2003 and 2011 to an all-time record level of 9.5 million. Even after subtracting reasonable guesses about natural attrition and smuggled exports, this volume of new guns is almost certainly driving an increase in the total private inventory—over and above population growth. Our best guess is that this surge of gun sales is being absorbed primarily (though not entirely) by individuals who already own guns. In short, the average number of guns per owner has been increasing. And while the federal records are not up to date on this matter, media accounts in 2012 and 2013 report a continuing ramp-up in gun sales, so intense that manufacturers and dealers have been unable to meet demand in some cases. One widely reported explanation is that some owners want to stock up on guns before Congress adopts stricter gun regulations, despite the fact that with minor exceptions, the only firearms legislation that Congress has enacted over the last 20 years has had the effect of loosening regulations.

## What Role Do Shooting Sports Play in American Life?

Hunting and other shooting sports have been an important feature of life for centuries. Echoing beliefs of the day, Thomas Jefferson, an avid hunter, advised his teenaged nephew that gun-related pursuits give both "a moderate exercise to the body" and "boldness, enterprise, and independence to the mind. Games played with the ball, and others of that nature, are too violent for the body, and stamp no character on the mind." He advised: "Let your gun, therefore, be the constant companion of your walks."

The shooting sports began to take off in the early nineteenth century, when members of an emerging middle class had both the means to purchase a firearm and aspirations to upward mobility, which meant copying the leisure-time pursuits of the British nobility. In the 1820s and 1830s, sporting magazines appeared, devoting pages to cultivating a culture of gentlemanly bonding. Around the same time, immigrants created target-shooting clubs that became wildly popular among the middling classes, and shooting galleries popped up in many cities. As one historian wrote of the German clubs, "Members wore uniforms, marched in military style with firearms, practiced marksmanship as recreation, ate heartily, drank beer, and caroused with women."[3]

Although rural Americans in the seventeenth through the nineteenth centuries relied heavily on hunting for food and profit, hunting also became a sport—a means of demonstrating skill and manliness. Competitive squirrel hunting was popular in the East, buffalo hunting in the West. Indeed, buffalo were nearly wiped out; some hunters, including Buffalo Bill Cody, vied to see who could shoot the greatest number of bison in the shortest period of time.

Throughout the centuries, hunting in particular has been a family affair, to the point where specialty "youth rifles" began to be actively marketed in the late nineteenth century. Modern studies show that one of the best predictors of whether someone hunts as an adult is whether his father (usually) introduced him to the sport as a child. In some rural areas so many kids hunt with their families that schools traditionally have observed the first day of deer hunting season as an unofficial holiday.

Today, around 13 million adults hunt in any given year, or roughly 6% of the population age sixteen and over. Hunters are mostly white males from rural areas and small towns, and hunting is considerably more popular in the middle of the country than on the coasts.

### Has Participation in Gun Sports Declined?

Broadly speaking, yes. Take hunting, the quintessential American shooting sport. Over the last two decades, the fraction of adults who killed animals for food or sport has declined from 7.4% to 6.0%. The fraction of gun owners who mention hunting as their main reason for having a firearm has dropped to 32%, from 49% in 1999. And hunting licenses declined from the early 1980s through the early 2000s, even though the population increased.

These trends are a product of a combination of factors, including urbanization, expanding leisure-time options, and shifting public attitudes. The decline of America's rural sporting culture is evident in the aging of the hunter population. In 2011, 33% of hunters were 55 or older, up from 14% in 1991. The decline may be self-perpetuating, as hunting often is passed down from father to son. Hunting remains an overwhelmingly white male sport, though there have been slight increases in women and African Americans taking part.

In response to these trends, pro-gun organizations have lobbied for laws permitting children to obtain "apprentice" licenses, allowing them to "give hunting a try" without a hunter education course as long as a licensed adult accompanies them. Similar policies have created short-term licenses for "novice" adults.

About 7% of Americans own a gun for target shooting, unchanged since the late 1990s.

### What Are the Common Types of Modern Firearms?

Every firearm, whether rifle, shotgun, or pistol, has in common that it is designed to shoot projectiles out of a barrel at a high rate of speed, driven by the sudden expansion of gas caused by an explosion. The explosion is contained within the gun's chamber, which surrounds the cartridge case or shell.

Ammunition for rifles and pistols is made up of a cartridge case (typically brass, nickel, aluminum, or steel), primer, gunpowder, and bullet: When the primer, seated in the base of the cartridge case, is struck by the firing pin, it ignites the gunpowder, and the resulting expanding gas drives the bullet (usually made of lead) forward down the barrel. Shotgun shells are somewhat different: They are plastic or cardboard tubes with a brass base, containing a wad on top of the primer and powder—the wad typically consists of a plastic "shot cup" holding a number of pellets, which leave the barrel and spread in a "pattern." Shotguns may also be used to fire solid projectiles called "slugs."

Firearms are classified as either handguns or long guns. The former are relatively small and are designed to be held in one hand when fired. Long guns, including rifles and shotguns, have barrels that are up to 30 inches in length and are designed to be fired from the shoulder using two hands.[4]

Firearms are further differentiated by the mechanism for loading cartridges into firing position, the rapidity with which multiple shots can be fired, and the size of the ammunition.

Single-shot weapons require that a cartridge be loaded by hand after each shot. Early shotguns required hand loading after every shot or two depending on the number of barrels. Modern shotguns may be found in a variety of configurations with ammunition capacity up to 12 shells held in a "drum" magazine.

Modern rifles and handguns are generally repeaters. For handguns, the original repeater was the revolver invented by Samuel Colt in the 1830s. In modern double action versions of a revolver, a built-in cylinder is loaded with a number of rounds (usually six). With each pull of the trigger the cylinder rotates to bring a cartridge into firing position, and the hammer cocks back and then snaps forward. For semiautomatic pistols and long guns, several rounds of ammunition are stored in a magazine, which in most cases is detachable. When inserted, the magazine feeds cartridges into firing position as the trigger is pulled. Magazines differ widely in capacity, typically from 3 rounds up to 30 but even as many as 100.

The firearm's action dictates how fast the rounds in the weapon can be fired. In between each shot a series of actions prepare the gun for the next shot—remove the shell casing, chamber a new round in preparation for firing, and cock the hammer. In a single-shot, bolt-action or lever-action rifle, this work is done manually by manipulating a bolt handle or lever that ejects the old casing and allows a new cartridge to pop into place from the magazine. In a semiautomatic rifle or pistol this sequence is automated, so that the shooter can fire as fast as he can pull the trigger—one round per trigger pull—until the magazine is emptied, at which point it can be removed and replaced with a fresh magazine. Finally, a fully automatic firearm fires continuously with a single pull of the trigger. Weapons of that sort are widely used by armies and rebel militias around the world. Interestingly, some standard infantry rifles of the US armed forces in the M16 family have a selective-fire option including a burst of three rounds for each trigger pull. That setting is designed to save ammunition in comparison with fully automatic fire, and makes the weapon easier to control.

Finally, the diameter of the barrel is an important characteristic of firearms, since it determines the size of the cartridge—which in turn affects the damage done to the target. (The velocity and design of the bullet are also relevant to determining damage.) For rifles and handguns, the diameter of the barrel is denoted as the "caliber." The caliber is measured either in fractions of an inch (.22, .38, .45), or with the metric system in millimeters. Among the most popular sizes are the .38 caliber revolver and 9 mm parabellum pistol, which are close to identical in diameter and ballistic performance.

Once again shotguns are a bit different. The diameter of a shotgun barrel is denoted by its "gauge" rather than caliber. The most common gauge is 12, which is equivalent to .729 caliber. Confusingly, a smaller diameter shotgun has a larger gauge; a 20-gauge shotgun is just .615 caliber and a 410-gauge shotgun equates to .458 caliber. The basic physics of action and reaction explains why larger barrels and the larger ammunition that fits them cause a greater recoil when the gun is fired. A .22 caliber pistol or 20-gauge shotgun is easier to control than their larger counterparts because of less recoil.

### Why Do Gun Owners Usually Have Several Guns?

By and large people say that the main reason they have handguns is for self-defense, while their long guns are primarily for hunting or target shooting. Those who are knowledgeable about guns and enjoy them may be motivated to keep a variety on hand. For self-defense they may want to keep handguns in several locations, with a relatively small pistol to carry concealed when they go out, and larger, more powerful models to keep in the bedside table or next to the front door. For shooting woodchucks and other varmints on the farm a .22 rifle is sufficient (and uses cheap ammunition), but for deer hunting a larger caliber weapon is needed. For bird hunting and skeet shooting they keep one or more shotguns, which may also be deemed good weapons for self-defense.

Different circumstances and purposes call for weapons of differing power, weight, accuracy, rapidity of fire, and so forth. And of course for some gun collectors the utilitarian purposes are less important than the sheer fascination of these intricate machines.

As rural traditions have faded and self-defense uses become more prominent, the mix of guns sold in the United States has changed. Handgun sales have become increasingly prominent, from only 21% of all new guns in the 1950s to 36% in the 1970s to 42% in the 2000s. For 2010–2011 handguns comprised more than half (53%) of total guns sold.

Handguns are also the weapon of choice for criminal use. Between 70% and 80% of murders with firearms are committed with handguns, as are more than 90% of all gun victimizations. The exception may be for gang wars and militia activities, where military-style weapons are more the norm. During Prohibition both gangsters and law enforcement used the Thompson submachine guns (aka "Tommy guns"), the "gun that made the 1920s roar." Today criminal gangs and rebel insurgent groups around the world are using versions of the infamous AK-47 or other assault rifles, which, like the Tommy gun, may have the capacity for fully automatic fire. Congress imposed strict regulations on such guns in 1934 with the National Firearms Act, so that criminal use of fully automatic weapons is uncommon in the United States.

## What Is an Assault Weapon?

An assault weapon is most commonly defined as a semiautomatic firearm with some of the features of a military firearm. (An important difference with a true military assault rifle such as the US Army's M16 is that the latter can be set to fire bursts with a single pull of the trigger.) An assault weapon has a detachable magazine, as well as some other features of certain military weapons such as a pistol grip, a folding stock, a bayonet mount, or a flash suppressor. Most assault weapons are rifles, although some pistols and shotguns qualify under some definitions; the TEC 9 pistol and the Street Sweeper shotgun are particularly infamous. One of the most popular assault weapons is the AR-15, the civilian (semiautomatic) version of the US military's M16.

In 1994 Congress adopted a ban on new assault weapons. The operational definition for this somewhat vague term was written into the law, and included specific models but also any models with specified characteristics that were deemed problematic. Congress allowed that law to sunset in 2004, but several states have adopted bans on assault weapons—each employing its own definition.

A closely related concern for lawmakers has been large-capacity magazines, since they are thought to facilitate rampage shootings. The 1994 federal law limited new magazines to 10 rounds.

### What Devices Are Available to Prevent Misuse?

Even in the hands of a well-intentioned adult, a firearm is a dangerous weapon. There are thousands of accidental shootings each year, including about 600 fatalities. People who have no experience or training with guns may be ignorant of safe practice when it comes to storing, carrying, loading and unloading, cleaning, and lining up a target. (No state requires that a rifle or shotgun buyer have any training or pass a test on gun safety.)

There are a variety of devices designed to prevent guns from being fired accidentally. For example, most rifles and some handguns have an external "safety" that when set prevents discharge. These safeties are usually just manual switches, although some handguns are designed with integral safeties that must be released with a key or combination. (Revolvers and some pistols, including the popular Glock brand, lack a manual safety of this sort.) Most modern firearms, including the Glock, are designed so that they are unlikely to discharge if dropped and in fact will not fire unless the trigger is pulled.

The owner's greatest concern may well be that his or her firearms end up in the wrong hands—a thief, a teenage son, a toddler, an inebriated spouse. In the interests of preventing such unauthorized transfers, owners may invest in a gun safe where some or all of the weapons can be locked up. A trigger lock may be fastened on a gun when it is not in use, although detachable locks of this sort are far from fail-safe and interfere with the quick deployment of a gun for self-defense.

In the near future we expect to see the development of a satisfactory "personalized" or "smart" or "user-authorized" firearm that can only be fired by the rightful owner. Engineers have pursued a number of approaches. The possibilities include fingerprint and other biometric recognition devices, and an RFID mechanism where the lock is released through a radio-frequency signal from a "key" of some sort—essentially the same technology that is built into modern locks on vehicles. As of 2013, there were no user-authorized firearms available in the United States, although a German firm (Armatix GmbH) has sold its RFID Smart System pistol in Europe and Asia.

If guns were designed so that they could not be fired unless the key is nearby, the hundreds of thousands of guns that are stolen each year could be rendered harmless (depending on the difficulty of overcoming the locking mechanism). The possibility of gun accidents within the household would be reduced, and suicidal teenagers could no longer appropriate their parents' guns. Interestingly, much of the R&D effort has been motivated by the goal of finding a way to protect law-enforcement officers from having their own weapons taken away and used against them. The main resistance to buying such guns (aside from the extra cost) appears to be a concern with reliability—the possibility that it might malfunction at a critical moment.

# 2

# THE VALUE OF GUNS FOR SELF-PROTECTION AND COMBATING TYRANNY

### Why Is Self-Defense Central to the Debate over Gun Control?

Personal safety is a vital matter, and self-protection is a more compelling rationale for owning guns than recreation. We can all conjure up the nightmare scenario of being defenseless in a violent confrontation with a burglar, mugger, carjacker, rapist, or gang of youths. For some people, the ready availability of a firearm brings peace of mind. Indeed, the predominant motivation for owning a gun is self-protection.

Self-defense also has a legally privileged status over other uses of firearms. In 2008 the US Supreme Court for the first time recognized a personal right to "keep and bear arms." In *District of Columbia v. Heller*, 554 U.S. 570 (2008), the Court decided that the Second Amendment provided a right to self-defense, and particularly defense of the home. More recently a lower-court decision extended that right to have a gun available for self-defense in public places, thereby overturning Illinois's ban on concealed carrying of guns.

## Is a Gun an Effective Means of Self-Protection against an Assailant?

The answer is a qualified yes. Someone who is able to effectively deploy a firearm when attacked or seriously threatened may emerge from the encounter in better shape than if he or she had been unarmed. Of course it is also true that introducing a firearm into the confrontation may escalate the level of violence and ultimately result in greater harm to the victim than would have been caused by alternative strategies—such as fleeing or reasoning with the assailant or summoning help. And there is always the possibility that the "victim" will misunderstand the other's intentions, in which case the gun can be the mechanism for a tragic mistake.

So while it is surely possible to imagine instances in which having ready access to a firearm would be a lifesaver, it is also possible that it would make a bad situation worse. The data on violent encounters provide some guidance on this matter. The most detailed such study, by Jongyeon Tark and Gary Kleck, used National Crime Victimization Survey (NCVS) data for the decade 1992–2001. More than 27,000 crimes with personal contact were included—assaults, robberies, rapes, and home invasions. In fewer than 1% of these cases (0.9%) did the victim use a gun in self-defense; about twice as many used another type of weapon, while most victims attempted to protect themselves through some other means—they screamed, ran away, reasoned with the assailant, struggled, and so forth. One measure of success for these various self-protective methods is the likelihood of forestalling further injury. Here are the rates of victim injury following self-protective action:

| Self-protective action | Likelihood of subsequent injury |
| --- | --- |
| Used gun | 2.4% |
| Used other weapon | 1.7% |
| Attack or threaten without weapon | 3.6% |
| Any self-protection action | 2.8% |

There is little difference among these injury rates, and surely no obvious advantage to using a gun. (It should be noted that fatal injuries to the victim are not included in this tabulation, as homicide victims cannot respond to surveys.)

The other available evidence on this problem includes anecdotes and common sense. Anecdotes of heroic self-defense cases are published in *The American Rifleman*'s weekly blog, "The Armed Citizen." (That magazine does not publish cases where attempted self-defense with a gun backfired.) Common sense suggests that using a gun in response to a perceived threat could make things better or worse but surely ups the ante in the confrontation.

### How Often Are Guns Used in Self-Defense?

This seemingly simple question has been the subject of intense debate. The answer is important but elusive. Police records are incomplete, since many defensive gun uses (DGUs) are never reported. Surveys seem to have the potential for providing a comprehensive estimate, but it turns out that survey results are hypersensitive to the exact method that is used to elicit this information. Thus the answer is unknown, and in a sense unknowable, although there is no lack of statistics on the subject.

The NCVS is generally considered the most reliable source of information on predatory crime. The survey began in 1973 and incorporates the best thinking of survey methodologists. From this source it appears that the victim uses a gun in about 1 out of every 100 crimes of personal contact. In the particular case of home invasion, about 3% of NCVS respondents who reported a break-in while they were home said that they used a gun to threaten or shoot the intruder. There were 70,000 DGUs in 1995 in violent crimes, and about 50,000 such DGUs in 2010 (when crime rates were far lower overall). About 30,000 additional DGUs against burglars occurred in each of those years.

In contrast, the results of several smaller one-time tele-phone surveys suggest that there are millions of defensive gun uses per year. The most widely circulated estimate from criminologists Gary Kleck and Marc Gertz is 2.5 million, although they and others have provided a range of estimates using this type of survey. Why do these one-time surveys produce estimates that exceed the NCVS estimate by a factor of 25 or more? One explanation is that the NCVS only asks questions about defensive actions to those who report that they were the victim of an assault or other crime with per-sonal contact, while the phone surveys ask such questions of every respondent. As a logical matter it seems that it should make little difference—if the respondent was not the victim of a criminal threat or attack or break-in, how can she say she legitimately used a gun in self-defense? Still, in practice it is quite possible that some NCVS respondents do not have a chance to report a DGU because they forget to report to the interviewer the criminal threat that initiated it. In that case the NCVS will include "false negatives" in its estimate of DGUs. On the other hand, one-shot surveys that ask an open-ended question about self-defense expand the scope for false posi-tives—people who report that they defended themselves in the last year, say, who actually did so 15 months ago, or peo-ple who misremembered an event that occurred when they were drunk, or people who are simply trying to impress the interviewer with their heroics.

More fundamentally, what constitutes a legitimate DGU may be a matter of definition. Someone who picks a fight at a bar and then flashes a gun may consider that he has defended himself with a gun, but it is not clear that the public interest has been served. In many cases people with guns may be respond-ing to vague threats: For example, one respondent reported that he looked out the window and saw several boys stand-ing near his car, which was parked on the street. He pointed his gun at them and ordered them to move. In one study by David Hemenway and his colleagues, a panel of judges was asked to review each self-reported DGU from a one-shot survey; a majority of "self-defense" actions were ruled illegal. The famous case of the Trayvon Martin shooting illustrates the point that the distinction between self-defense and assault can be a matter of interpretation. Martin, an unarmed black youth, was walking home from a store in Sanford, Florida, when George Zimmerman, a member of the community watch, saw him, guessed he was up to no good, followed him, and confronted him, eventually shooting him dead during the ensuing scuffle.

The most compelling challenge to the survey-based claim that there are millions of DGUs per year derives from a comparison with what we know about crime rates. The oft-cited 2.5 million DGU estimate is more than twice the total number of gun crimes estimated at that time in the NCVS, which in turn is far more than the number of gun crimes known to the police. Likewise, the number of shootings reported by those who claimed to be defending themselves vastly exceeds the total number of gunshot cases treated in emergency rooms. The fact is that the estimated number of DGUs from surveys is highly sensitive to the sequence of questions, and to whether the respondent is given some help in placing events in time (so that when asked about the previous 12 months the respondent does not bring in events that happened before that period). When the same respondents in the same sort of one-time survey are asked about both DGUs and about victimization by guns, they report many more victimizations than DGUs.

### What Are the Risks and Benefits of Keeping a Firearm in the Home for Protection?

The risks of keeping a firearm at home include accidental shootings, suicide, and escalation of domestic violence. In a particularly telling analysis, Matthew Miller and several colleagues at the Harvard School of Public Health compared the 16 states with the highest rates of gun ownership with the six states with the lowest rates. The two groups each had a total of about 31 million adults in 2009, but the group of states with high gun ownership had more than four times as times as many gun suicides as the states with low gun ownership. (The nongun suicide rate was virtually identical in the two groups.)

Keeping a firearm at home also has benefits. Most gun owners believe that a gun provides an effective means of fending off intruders, thereby reducing the chance of injury to a household member. In about 3% of such incidents, the occupant used a gun, which means about 30,000 times per year.[1] Hence the annual probability of a gun-owning household's using a gun against a home intruder is less than 1 in 3,500. In other words, there is one defensive gun use per year against an intruder for every 3,500 homes that keep guns.

Keeping a gun at home has other benefits, including recreational hunting, target shooting, and collecting, and practical uses such as shooting hungry woodchucks on the farm. All of those uses are compatible with safe storage practices that reduce the chance of accidental misuse. In the end, the benefits of keeping a firearm in the home must be weighed against the risks. Those who keep a loaded handgun accessible to fend off intruders buy their sense of security at a price, especially if there are children at home, or violence-prone adults, or anyone who abuses drugs or is suicidal.

### Do Burglars Avoid Neighborhoods Where Residents Keep Guns in the Home?

The strongest claim in support of the public virtue of widespread gun possession (and the perversity of regulations that curtail guns) is that guns in private hands generate a general deterrent effect on crime. Early arguments along these lines speculated about the effect on residential burglary, and especially burglaries of occupied homes (known as "hot" burglaries). Philip Cook and Jens Ludwig conducted the first systematic analysis of this issue, demonstrating that the like-lihood of residential burglary or hot burglary is not reduced by living in a county with high gun prevalence. In fact, they found that greater gun prevalence caused an *increase* in the res-idential burglary rate. One reason may be that more prevalent gun ownership increases the profitability of burglary, because stolen guns are readily fenced for good prices. In any event, the fraction of burglaries that are "hot" is not affected by the prevalence of gun ownership.

### How Many People Are Licensed to Carry a Gun?

All but five states require a special permit or license to legally carry a concealed handgun.[2] A total of eight million people currently have obtained a permit of this sort, which works out to 1 out of every 28 adults (3.6%). How many people are actu-ally carrying guns is another question, since some carry with-out benefit of a permit. A 1994 survey found that 7% of adults said they carried a gun at least occasionally.

Some states publish the demographic statistics of permit holders. What we learn from these statistics is that the char-acteristics of permit holders are a lot like those of gun owners. In Florida, which has the highest prevalence of permits in the nation, most are held by men (78%) and people over 50 years old (54%). Similar patterns are found in other states for which there are data. Permits go disproportionately to those from small towns and rural areas, despite the fact that those areas tend to have lower crime rates than big cities.

### What Is It Like to Carry a Concealed Gun?

Polls typically ask why people own guns, not why they carry. But ethnographic studies suggest that the main motivation is the same: protection. In a recent study, a small group of Michigan gun carriers was interviewed on the subject. One theme that emerged from these interviews was that they had decided to go armed because public systems of protection—911, the police—were ineffective or absent. They viewed gun toting as an act of good citizenship in which they serve as defenders not only of themselves but also of loved ones and broader society. In most cases, gun carriers—especially white men—viewed themselves as providing a service to supplement the police. As one journalistic account put it, "Shooters see their guns as emblems of a whole spectrum of virtuous lifestyle choices—rural over urban, self-reliance over dependence on the collective, vigorous outdoorsiness over pallid intellectualism, patriotism over internationalism, action over inaction."[3]

The NRA-sanctioned training that some gun owners undergo to obtain their concealed-carry permit shapes this belief system. Instructors reinforce the notion that gun carriers are good citizens, that taking a life in defense of self or others is a moral act, and that people who don't carry a gun for self-defense deserve whatever comes their way. Instructors refer to concealed gun carriers as "sheepdogs" quietly guarding the flock, while people who refuse to arm themselves are sometimes derided as "sheep." Concealed-carry courses often spend more time preparing people to kill than training them to shoot straight. A gun-owning journalist who took the courses concluded that "it was hard to discern the line between preparing for something awful to happen and praying for something awful to happen." When he asked his instructor if gun carrying didn't "bespeak a needlessly dark view of mankind," the instructor replied, "I'm an optimist, but we live in a world of assholes."

Interestingly, the Michigan study found that African Americans differed from whites in their reasons for carrying, and women differed from men. For many African American permit holders, carrying was not so much an act of supplementing the police as an act of defiance against a law enforcement community that they viewed as racist harassers. For many women, who represent a small fraction of permit holders, guns were tools of psychological empowerment and reassurance that liberated them to go places, including to their jobs, that they might have otherwise avoided. Of course, we must be cautious about drawing sweeping conclusions from a relatively small sample of people in one state; these findings are merely suggestive.

What is it like to carry a gun? Gun carriers report feeling the weight, both physical and moral, of their firearm, and they say that burden imbues them with a sense of civic responsibility. Having a gun puts carriers just one misstep away from breaking the law—for example, by packing heat in a gun-free zone or brandishing the firearm without legitimate cause. As a result, they walk away from unarmed hotheads and avoid misbehaviors, such as speeding, that might catch a police officer's eye.

Here is a journalist's colorful account of what it's like to carry:

Moving through a cocktail party with a gun holstered snug against my ribs makes me feel like James Bond—*I know something you don't know!*—but it's socially and physically unpleasant. I have to remember to keep adjusting the drape of my jacket so as not to expose myself, and make sure to get the arms-inside position when hugging a friend so that the hard lump on my hip or under my arm doesn't give itself away. In some settings my gun feels as big as a toaster oven, and I find myself tense with the expectation of being discovered. What's more, if there's a truly comfortable way to carry a gun, I haven't found it. The revolver's weight and pressure keep me constantly aware of how quickly and utterly my world could change. Gun carriers tell me that's exactly the point: at any moment, violence could change anybody's world. Those who carry guns are the ones prepared to make the change come out in their favor.[4]

Carriers also maintain a heightened state of vigilance, which they call "condition yellow." They might choose a table in the corner of the restaurant, for example, to maximize their view of incoming threats, and they frequently concoct and replay in their minds attack scenarios and the optimal response. "I run sequences in my head," one author and gun carrier says. "If a guy jumps me with a knife, should I throw money to the ground and run? Take two steps back and draw? How about if he has a gun? How will I distract him so I can get the drop? It can be fun. But it can also be exhausting."[5]

### Does Society Benefit If More Civilians Carry Concealed Weapons?

Once again, the strongest claim in support of the public virtue of widespread gun possession is that guns in private hands generate a general deterrent effect on crime. By far the most prominent research findings on the general deterrence issue were based on an evaluation of changes in state laws governing concealed carrying of handguns. Over the 1980s and 1990s a number of states eased restrictions on concealed carry, adopting a regulation that required local authorities to issue permits to all applicants who met minimum conditions. These "shall issue" laws replaced "may issue" laws (which gave the authorities discretion) or outright bans. Economists John Lott and David Mustard published the first evaluation of these shall-issue laws, finding that states that adopted them experienced a reduction in homicide and some other types of crime. Lott went on to publish *More Guns, Less Crime* (1998, 2000), in which he reported these results and several variations on them. He reached differing conclusions about the effect of shall-issue laws on property crime depending on how he did the analysis, but in every version of his statistical model he found that ending restrictive gun-carrying laws reduced homicide rates.

In the finest scientific tradition, a number of analysts have sought to replicate Lott's findings to confirm or disconfirm them. For example, Stanford economist John Donohue concluded that Lott's findings were unsupportable from the data he used, and that there's no reason to believe that lives were saved by the introduction of lax carry laws. Donohue showed that Lott's estimates are sensitive to the correction of several coding errors and to reasonable changes in the statistical method. More importantly, Donohue's reanalysis of the Lott data showed that states that adopted shall-issue laws had systematically different crime trends from the other states even before these law changes went into effect, suggesting that the adoption of these laws may have been the result as well as the cause of homicide and other crime. Donohue and his coauthors have published several additional evaluations of the shall-issue laws, taking advantage of additional years of data and exploring alternative methods and data sets for the period 1977–2006. One robust result from the most recent work is that the introduction of shall-issue laws is associated with an *increase* in aggravated assault rates.

The importance of this academic debate is indicated by the fact that an expert panel of 18 scholars was created by the National Research Council to review the conflicting research. Most of the panelists were chosen because they were experts on the relevant methods and had not been directly involved in research related to gun control. Among other things, this panel reanalyzed Lott's data, and, with just one dissent, judged his findings to be unreliable.

Whether the net effect of relaxing gun-carry laws is to increase or reduce the burden of crime, there is good reason to believe that the effect is not large. One study found that in 12 of the 16 shall-issue concealed-carry states studied, fewer than 2% of adults had obtained permits to carry concealed handguns at the time Lott undertook his analysis. The actual change in gun-carrying prevalence is smaller than the number of permits issued would suggest, because many of those who obtain permits were already carrying guns in public. Moreover, the permits issued were concentrated in rural and suburban areas where crime rates are already relatively low, among people with characteristics associated with a relatively low risk of victimization—white, middle-aged, middle-class. In sum, changes to state laws governing legal gun carrying were unlikely to induce more than negligible change in the incentives facing criminals to go armed themselves or to avoid potentially armed victims.

Lott's remarkable findings received enormous attention because they provide academic support for pro-gun advocates. He has good credentials and utilizes standard social science methods. But his results are too good to be true—how can such a minor change have such a pervasive effect on street crime?— and that is reason to be skeptical. The case for skepticism is stronger yet given that his findings are not "robust"—seemingly minor changes in the data or application of the statistical methods produce different results.

The scientific process has worked well in this case, since replication has challenged dubious findings—just as in the case, say, of the "discovery" of a desktop cold-fusion process in 1989 by Utah chemists. Cold fusion also seemed too good to be true and turned out to be so after many other labs attempted and failed to replicate the results.

### Do Americans Believe That Guns Make Us Safer?

Not surprisingly, the answer depends on whom you ask and what scenario they are asked to consider. Certain subgroups— whites, conservatives, men, and gun owners—are more likely than others to see the protective value of firearms. People across the board are more inclined to see the benefit of a gun if they—as opposed to their fellow citizens—are the ones packing heat. Contrary to America's image as a gun-slinging nation, many Americans are uncomfortable allowing "Joe gun owner" to tote his gun where people go to eat, shop, or govern. But concern abates if the gun carrier is a police officer or otherwise specially trained.

To understand Americans' beliefs about guns and safety, let's start on a personal level. The number one reason for owning a firearm is personal security. Nearly half of gun owners have their gun for protection, up from only a quarter two decades ago. Not surprisingly, having a gun in the home makes the vast majority of gun owners feel safer. Even some nonowners (40% in one recent survey) would be fine having a gun in the home—though women, older people, Democrats, and minority group members were considerably less inclined to feel that way.[6]

So, many Americans are or would be comfortable with guns in their home. That's perhaps not surprising. However, when surveys start asking about the role of guns generally— outside of the intimate personal context—the findings begin to get muddled. For example, polls taken from the mid-1990s through the mid-2000s found Americans roughly split on whether, generally speaking, a gun in the house makes it safer or more dangerous. When survey questions evoke scenarios in which other people are carrying weapons, especially "regular Joes," people get even more skeptical. For example, people are less likely to see the safety benefits of a gun in the home if the weapon belongs to someone else. People are twice as likely to feel less safe, not safer, knowing that many of their fellow citizens own a gun (though, to be fair, most people are indifferent). Most people think allowing citizens to own assault weapons makes the country more dangerous. And people feel less safe, not more safe, knowing gun owners can carry concealed weapons in public—although comfort levels rise if the survey specifies that the gun owner has passed a criminal background check and received training.

People's sentiments on general principles often shift when tested in specific scenarios. And so it is with guns in the public square. Even if a good fraction of Americans are okay with licensed, trained individuals carrying guns, most people are not comfortable having concealed weapons in specific places such as stores, movie theaters, restaurants, college campuses, churches, courts, and government buildings. Indeed, when pollsters tell backers of relaxed gun-carrying rules what their position means in practice—guns in theaters and malls—their support erodes.[7]

But returning to where we started, perceptions of whether guns make "us" safer depend to some extent on whether the person asked or someone else has the weapon. Consider a fun experiment conducted in the mid-1990s. One survey asked whether "ordinary Americans" after "proper training" should be able to carry a gun on their person. In response, 65% said no. The second survey personalized the scenario by asking whether "average Americans, such as yourself" should be allowed to get a concealed-carry license "for self-protection." Here the result flipped: 60% now were in support.[8]

So Americans are more comfortable when they own a gun than when other "random Joes" do. Americans also make broad exceptions for police officers, armed guards, and even civilians who have received special training. The question of armed personnel typically comes up after mass shootings, particularly in schools. After the Sandy Hook massacre, the NRA was mocked in some quarters for suggesting that all schools be equipped with armed guards. But that position enjoys broad support. Polls found that most people thought putting guards in schools was a good idea and would be effective.

### Do Americans Believe That Guns Make Our Democracy Stronger?

Gun rights advocates argue that civilian gun ownership constitutes a bulwark against tyranny. More guns means more freedom. However, as far as we can tell, no publicly available poll has ever asked Americans about whether they agree with these assertions. Nor have pollsters thought to ask whether stricter firearms laws, however defined, would harm or inevitably lead to the downfall of America's democratic system of government. However, several questions have come at the guns-democracy question sideways, and from those questions we know that Americans do equate private firearms ownership with core American values such as liberty, distrust of government, and individual self-reliance.

The National Rifle Association and other gun advocates long have tapped into such values to build a case for unfettered civilian ownership of firearms. The foundation of the NRA's narrative is the so-called slippery-slope argument, that even a mild step in the direction of gun control will put the country on a fast path to the confiscation of guns and the end of constitutional liberties.

The argument has sunk in. By 1993, half of Americans believed that gun control would inevitably lead to "stricter laws which will take guns away from all citizens." By 2013, roughly the same number agreed, but the fear had become especially acute among Republicans (63%) and independents (50%). Nearly half of people who didn't even have a gun in the home thought that there could be truth to the slippery-slope argument.[9] Other polls have found widespread concern among Americans that handgun registration, and even expanded background checks on private sales, could lead to confiscation.

In recent years, the seeds of the slippery-slope narrative have landed in fertile ground. Gallup polls show that more than half of Americans believe that the federal government has too much power, and nearly half believe that "the federal government poses an immediate threat to the rights and freedoms of ordinary citizens." Those numbers are up significantly from the early 2000s, with most of the shift occurring during the Bush administration.

Gun laws speak to these fears, particularly and increasingly among Republicans and independents. In 2013, 57% of Americans believed that gun laws "give too much power to government over average citizens," and that figure is considerably higher among Republicans and independents. Likewise, roughly half of Americans believe that "laws limiting gun ownership" infringe on the right to bear arms—a position that not even the Supreme Court's recent pro-gun rulings embraced.

While the bulk of the evidence points to a fairly widespread concern among Americans about government power, especially when it comes to gun rights, there is one anomalous finding suggesting growing skepticism toward the "slippery-slope" argument. In 2013, 36% of Americans "strongly disagreed" that gun control would eventually lead to laws taking guns away from all citizens, up significantly from the 22% who strongly questioned the slippery slope argument in 1993.

### Do Guns Protect against Tyranny, Even Genocide?

A core tenet of gun rights ideology is that "the people" must deny government a monopoly on the use of force. A well-armed citizenry is necessary to counterbalance the state and, if liberty so requires, to topple it. A corollary to this tenet is that banning private ownership of guns, or even simply regulating them, makes tyranny—even genocide—more likely. Mass armament safeguards democracy by leaving to the people a right of insurrection if they judge that their government has gone astray. As Daniel Polsby and Don B. Kates Jr. argue, "An armed population is simply more difficult to exterminate than one that is defenseless."[10]

Gun rights supporters draw on historical examples. American democracy is indebted to citizens who deployed their muskets to throw off the British Crown So surely the founders intended for future patriots to maintain this right of revolt, and so they enshrined it in state and federal constitutions. A Supreme Court majority embraced this view in 2008, when it agreed that a citizens' militia served as a "safeguard against tyranny." Ardent gun rights supporters go further, citing Thomas Jefferson's admonition that "the tree of liberty must be refreshed from time to time with the blood of patriots and tyrants." And, indeed, a recent poll found that 44% of Republicans (but only 18% of Democrats and 27% of independents) believed that to preserve liberty, America may need an armed revolution in the next few years.[11]

To these gun advocates, the horrors of the twentieth century only strengthen the argument that an armed people are a free people. Hitler, Stalin, and Pol Pot are invoked as evidence for what can happen when the people have no means of mustering private force against madmen. As the NRA's Wayne LaPierre has argued, "If every family on this planet owned a good-quality rifle, genocide would be on the path to extinction." To the argument that, well, "it can't happen here" in the United States or any other advanced industrial democracy, gun rights theorists say that is just blind conceit. Genocides have happened "among civilized, educated, cultured people," and even the United States has its own shameful track record in the form of Indian massacres and Japanese internment.

Gun control advocates see these lessons differently. To them, the best guarantee against tyranny is a strong system of laws and ingrained traditions of tolerance and equality. States tend not to oppress their citizens if they have institutional arrangements that disperse power, safeguard individual rights and political representation, and have mechanisms for peacefully resolving disputes and transferring power. The longer such traditions are locked in, the harder they are to dislodge. The founders vested their faith in a system of ordered liberty—not private citizen gun owners—to frustrate would-be tyrants.

To supporters of this institutional view of democracy, the mass ownership of firearms only increases mayhem. They note that gun violence is higher in societies with more guns and less regulation thereof, so there is a present-day cost of stockpiling weapons. What's more, all those citizen gun owners can easily be mobilized to suppress freedom and threaten democracy—think the Ku Klux Klan in the American South or Hitler's brownshirts. Gun control advocates note that history is littered with examples of revolutionaries who took up arms to throw off tyranny but ended up establishing very undemocratic regimes—China, Russia, and Cuba for starters.

So is it true, as gun rights supporters argue, that "a connection exists between the restrictiveness of a country's civilian weapons policy and its liability to commit genocide against its people"—or even just to impose tyranny upon them? The simplest and perhaps least satisfying answer is that we don't have enough data to judge. To feel comfortable asserting that guns preserve freedom, we would need to be able to point to well-armed democracies that have maintained their liberty and poorly armed (but otherwise similar) democracies that have backslid into tyranny. The problem is that there aren't a lot of countries in either category, certainly not enough to justify sweeping conclusions. Even if we resort to anecdotes, the case isn't all that persuasive. Heavily armed America is a long-standing beacon of democracy, but so is the United Kingdom, even though few in Britain own guns. And, as we discuss later, Germany was actually liberalizing its gun laws when Hitler came to power.

On the question of whether guns or institutions safeguard liberty, advocates of each position, however differing, often invoke the US experience as evidence for their side. But America makes an ambiguous case, for it has both strong democratic institutions and traditions *and* hundreds of millions of firearms in private hands. Which one is holding the nation together after more than two centuries is subject to opinion, not science.[12]

# 3

# THE COSTS OF GUN VIOLENCE

## How Many Americans Are Killed or Injured by Gunfire?

Approximately one million Americans have died from gun-shot wounds in homicides, accidents, and suicides during just the last three decades—more than the sum total of combat deaths in all the wars in US history. In 2010, the most recent year for which the National Center for Health Statistics provides final tabulations on injury deaths, there were 31,672 firearms deaths, including 11,078 homicides, 19,302 suicides, and 606 unintentional killings.[1] As a point of reference, there were almost as many gun deaths as traffic deaths in 2010. Another point of reference is the years of potential life lost before age 65: Gunshot injuries account for 1 of every 15 years lost to early death from all causes.

Of course not all gunshot injuries are fatal. The homicide victims are just the tip of the violence "iceberg." In most cases of gun robbery and assault the victim is not injured—the perpetrator threatens the victim without shooting, or shoots and misses. If the victim is shot, the chances are only about one in six that it will prove fatal—in which case the assault becomes a homicide.

Emergency rooms treated 73,505 nonfatal gunshot injuries in 2010, including 53,738 nonfatal injuries from criminal assaults. In the same year, the police recorded more than 300,000 assaults and robberies in which the perpetrator used a gun to threaten or shoot the victim.

While homicides and suicides are committed with a variety of weapons, firearms predominate. More than two-thirds of homicides, and half of suicides, are committed with a firearm. Other prominent means of committing suicide include suffocation (25%) and poisoning with drugs or other substances (17%). Cutting and stabbing account for just 2% of suicides and 11% of homicides.

### Is Gun Violence Rising or Falling in America?

To note the obvious, gun violence is violence perpetrated with a gun. Gun violence rates are high when and where both guns and violence are plentiful. For the nation as a whole, the trends in gun violence rates follow the trends in overall violence rates. That is particularly true for criminal homicide, where the fraction with firearms remains near two-thirds despite the variation in overall homicide rates. For example, the overall homicide rate in 2011 was just about half of what it was in 1991, and the same is true for the gun homicide rate. In fact, current homicide rates are now at levels that are comparable to those Americans enjoyed in the 1950s— before the national epidemic of violence that began in 1963 and persisted for three decades. These trends are depicted in figure 3.1. The figure indicates the number of homicides each year divided by the US population in millions. The overall rate ranges from about 40 victims per million up to more than 100 victims per million.

One logical reason that homicide rates may be declining in recent years is that medical treatment of trauma victims is improving. Much has been learned from wartime experience with trauma treatment in Vietnam, Iraq, and Afghanistan— and from treating gunshot victims here at home. Both emergency medical response and treatment after hospitalization have become more effective, so that some victims are saved now who would have been lost in previous times. Other things equal (such as the types of firearms in use by criminal

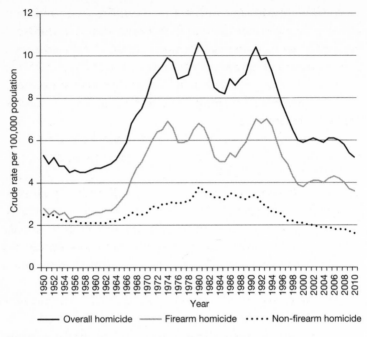

**Figure 3.1** Homicide rates and gun homicide rates fin the United States, 1950–2010

*Source:* A variety of sources were used to construct these time series. For similar data, see http://www.bjs.gov/content/pub/pdf/htius.pdf

assailants), the result is a decline in the "case-fatality rate"—the likelihood that a gunshot victim will die of his or her wounds.

But whether improvements in medical treatment are really an important part of the explanation for declining homicide rates is debatable. There have been sharp declines in all types of criminal violence since the early 1990s. In fact, the (nonfatal) robbery and assault rates recorded in police records, or from the National Crime Victimization Survey, have declined even more than the homicide rates, and those declines have nothing to do with improved medical practice. Our belief is that the homicide decline is closely linked to this larger picture of reduced violence. The main reason that fewer people are dying from homicide is that there is less gun violence.

The one bit of direct evidence pointing to a declining case-fatality rate is the trend in the number of nonfatal gunshot cases treated in emergency rooms. That number is estimated by the National Electronic Injury Surveillance System (NEISS) operated by the US Consumer Product Safety Commission. Estimates based on a national sample of 66 large hospitals are available since 2000. They indicate a sharp increase in the number of gunshot cases being treated in hospitals, and (since the homicide rate was declining) a corresponding decline in the case-fatality rate—from 22% (in 2001) to 17% (in 2010). It is possible that this trend is not a reflection of the quality of medical care, but rather of the likelihood that minor gunshot cases would end up in a large emergency room for treatment. If a larger proportion of victims who were merely grazed by a bullet end up in a large ER in 2010 than in 2001, that would explain the apparent increase in nonfatal gunshot cases.

What about suicide? During the post–World War II era there has been no clear trend in overall suicide rates; the suicide death rate was 114 per million in 1950, and 124 per million in 2010, and has been far less volatile in between than the homicide rate. There was, however, a notable increase in suicides during the decade ending in 2010, prompting speculation that the Great Recession that began in 2007 contributed to this upward trend.

Firearms used to figure even more prominently in suicide than they do today. In 1990, 61% of suicides were committed with firearms. Twenty years later that figure had dropped to 51%. That secular decline in gun use goes hand in hand with the declining prevalence of guns in the home during this period.

### Why Are Attacks with Guns of Any More Concern Than Attacks with Other Weapons?

A popular slogan claims that "guns don't kill people, people kill people." The intent is no doubt to suggest that if "people" were deprived of guns, they would find some other means of killing each other—that what matters is the intent, not the type of weapon. What is missing from this argument is that without a gun, the *capacity* to kill may be greatly diminished. One wag suggested, "Guns don't kill people, they just make it real easy."

Slogans aside, the true causal role of guns in homicide is one of the fundamental issues in gun-violence research and evidence-based policymaking. In some circumstances the claim that the type of weapon matters seems indisputable. There are very few drive-by knifings, or people killed accidentally by stray fists. When well-protected people are murdered, it is almost always with a gun: More than 90% of lethal attacks on law enforcement officers are with firearms, and all assassinations of US presidents have been by firearm. When lone assailants set out to kill as many people as they can in a commuter train, business, or campus, the most readily available weapon that will do the job is a gun. But what about the more mundane attacks that make up the vast bulk of violent crime?

The first piece of evidence is that robberies and assaults committed with guns are more likely to result in the victim's death than are similar violent crimes committed with other weapons. In the public health jargon, the "case-fatality rates" differ by weapon type. Take the case of robbery, a crime that includes holdups, muggings, and other violent confrontations motivated by theft. The case-fatality rate for gun robbery is three times as high as for robberies with knives, and ten times as high as for robberies with other weapons. For aggravated (serious) assault it is more difficult to come up with a meaningful case-fatality estimate, since the crime itself is in part defined by the type of weapon used. (In the FBI's Uniform Crime Reports, a threat delivered at gunpoint is likely to be classified as an "aggravated" assault, while the same threat delivered while shaking a fist would be classified as a "simple" assault.) We do know that for assaults from which the victim sustains an injury, the case-fatality rate is closely linked to the type of weapon. That is particularly true for domestic violence, which is much more likely to result in death (more often of women than of men) if there is a gun handy.

Case-fatality rates do not by themselves prove that the type of weapon has an independent causal effect on the probability of death. It is possible that the type of weapon is simply an indicator of the assailant's intent and that it is the intent, rather than the weapon, that determines whether the victim lives or dies. This view was offered as a reasonable possibility by the revered criminologist Marvin Wolfgang, who in his seminal study of homicide in Philadelphia stated in 1958 that "it is the contention of this observer that few homicides due to shooting could be avoided merely if a firearm were not immediately present, and that the offender would select some other weapon to achieve the same destructive goal."[2] (Wolfgang eventually changed his mind, publishing a retraction in 1995.) The same claim has shown up in the writings of some other criminologists: the gun makes the killing easier and is hence the obvious choice if the assailant's intent is indeed to kill, but if no gun were available, then, it is asserted, most would-be killers would still find a way. In this view, fatal and nonfatal attacks form two distinct sets of events with little overlap, at least in regard to the assailant's intent.

The speculation that the intent is all that matters seems far-fetched. When a tool is available to make a difficult task (such as killing another person) much easier, then we expect that the task will be undertaken with greater frequency and likelihood of success. Perhaps the most telling empirical evidence on this matter is due to Franklin Zimring, who demonstrated that there is actually a good deal of overlap between fatal and nonfatal attacks: Even in the case of earnest and potentially deadly attacks, the victim usually survives. The assailant may be drunk or enraged or scared and unlikely to be acting in a calculating fashion with a clear sustained purpose. Whether the victim lives or dies then depends importantly on the lethality of the weapon with which the assailant strikes the first blow or two.

Zimring's studies of wounds inflicted in gun and knife assaults suggest that the difference between life and death is often just a matter of chance, determined by whether the bullet or blade finds a vital organ. It is relatively rare for assailants to administer the coup de grace that would ensure their victim's demise. For every homicide inflicted with a single bullet wound to the chest, there are two survivors of a bullet wound to the chest who are indistinguishable with respect to the assailant's intent. It is largely because guns are intrinsically more lethal than knives that gunshot injuries are more likely to result in death than sustained attacks with a knife to vital areas of the body. Zimring's second study provided still more compelling evidence by comparing case-fatality rates for gunshot wounds with different calibers—a wound inflicted by a larger caliber gun was more likely to prove lethal than a wound inflicted by a smaller caliber gun. Assuming that the caliber of gun is not correlated with the intent of the assailant, the clear suggestion is that the type of weapon has a causal effect on outcome.

The argument in a nutshell is that robbery-murder is a close relative of robbery, and assaultive homicide is a close relative of armed assault; death is in effect a byproduct of violent crime. Thus while the law determines the seriousness of the crime by whether the victim lives or dies, that outcome is not a reliable guide to the assailant's intent or state of mind.

One logical implication of this perspective is that there should be a close link between the overall volume of violent crimes and the number of murders, moderated by the types of weapons used. Where Zimring provided a detailed description of cases as the basis for his conclusion, tests based on aggregate data are also potentially informative. One study of robbery murder trends in 43 large cities supported the "byproduct" claim: A tight connection was evident between variation in robbery and robbery-murder rates. The bottom line: An increase of

1,000 gun robberies was associated with three times as many additional murders as an increase of 1,000 nongun robberies. The type of weapon matters.

Zimring and Gordon Hawkins (1997) later published *Crime Is Not the Problem*, making the case that violent-crime rates in American cities are not particularly high relative to the rest of the developed world—with the notable exception of homicide. American "exceptionalism" is the result of the fact that in the United States assaults and robberies are much more likely to be committed with guns, and that makes them more lethal. In this view, American perpetrators are not more vicious from those in Canada, western Europe, and Australia—Americans are just better armed.

The type of weapon matters in other respects as well. Consider the role of weapons in the crime of robbery. Use of a gun enhances the robber's power, making it relatively easy for him to control his victim and gain compliance. As a result, other things equal, robbers bearing guns are more likely to succeed than are their knife-wielding counterparts. And when robberies by firearm do succeed, the average value of the offender's "take" nearly doubles. Further, the likelihood of injury to the victim depends on the type of weapon, with gun robberies the least likely to involve injury—the threat is sufficient to gain compliance. Of course when the robber does fire his gun, it is quite likely that the victim will die, making gun robberies (as noted above) by far the most lethal type of robbery. In any event, that gun robberies are so much more lucrative than robberies with other weapons raises an interesting question—why are most robberies committed without a gun? One likely answer is that many robbers lack ready access to one.

In sum, the type of weapon deployed in violent confrontations is not just an incidental detail; it matters in several ways. Because guns provide the power to kill quickly, at a distance, and without much skill or strength, they also provide the power to intimidate other people and gain control of a violent situation without an actual attack. When there is a physical attack, then the type of weapon is an important determinant of whether the victim survives, with guns far more lethal than other commonly used weapons. The idea that the type of weapon affects the outcome is called the instrumentality effect.

The most important implication of the instrumentality effect is that policies that are effective in reducing gun use in violent crime would reduce the murder rate, even if the volume of violent crime were unaffected. As it turns out, about half of the states have incorporated sentencing enhancements for use of a gun in crime. These enhancements, most of which were adopted in the 1970s and 1980s, were intended to reduce gun use in violence; systematic evaluations offer some indication that they have been effective. In any event, the widespread adoption of gun enhancements by state legislatures is a clear indication of the common-sense appeal of the instrumentality effect.

### Does the Availability of a Firearm Increase the Risk of Suicide?

There are literally millions of suicide attempts and gestures every year, but only a relative few involve a self-inflicted gunshot. Yet guns account for fully half of all "successful" suicides. As in the case of assault, guns are simply more lethal than other readily available suicide methods: the case-fatality rate is more than 80%. Of course people who have a sustained determination to kill themselves may eventually find a way. But most suicides are a response to transitory circumstances. One study found that among people who make near-lethal suicide attempts, 24% took less than five minutes between the decision to kill themselves and the actual attempt, and 70% took less than one hour. Teen suicide is particularly impulsive, and if a firearm is readily available, that impulse is likely to result in death. It is no surprise, then, that households that keep firearms on hand have an elevated rate of suicide for all concerned—the owner, spouse, and teen children.

It is really a matter of common sense that in suicide, the means matter. For families and counselors, a high priority for intervening with someone who appears acutely suicidal is to reduce his or her access to firearms.

### Who Is at Risk for Being Shot?

For assault and homicide, young men are vastly overrepresented in the gunshot victimization statistics. Males 15 to 34 are the victims of half of all murders. Within this group lie large differences by race. Homicide victimization rates in 2010 (consistent with earlier years) were 16 times as high for African Americans as for non-Hispanic whites. Indeed, homicide is the leading cause of death for African Americans in this age group, and is the second-leading cause of death for Latino males. For all men in this age range, most (84%) homicides are committed with guns.

Unsurprisingly, the shooters tend to be similar to the victims, with even greater concentration among young men. The violence is engendered by routine altercations or turf contests or other transactions that go wrong. In cities where gangs are prevalent, such as Boston, Chicago, and Los Angeles, the bulk of the deadly violence by youths can be attributed to gang members, since they often have access to guns and may be involved in the underground economy.

About one in five homicides involves women as victims. For women, unlike men, the greatest danger lies within the family, especially spouses or intimate partners. That said, the long-term trend for domestic violence has been highly favorable. The increasing independence of living arrangements gets much of the credit. Compared with, say, the 1950s, women are now far less likely to live with a man, and if they do, they can more easily move out if the relationship becomes violent. Nonetheless, domestic violence remains a very serious problem. When there is a gun in the home, that violence is more likely to escalate to murder—usually of the woman.

Suicide presents a different picture. The most obvious similarity with homicide is with respect to gender. Once again, just one in five victims is female. That male-female difference in suicide rates is surely influenced by the differential access to and familiarity with guns. While females are at least as likely to attempt suicide as males, they are much less likely than men to use a gun—and hence to be successful.

Suicide, unlike homicide, is concentrated among whites. For white men the rates are high and reasonably uniform across the age spectrum from 20 to 80. Other less obvious characteristics actually bring the suicide picture closer to homicide victimization: Suicide victims are disproportionately unmarried, unemployed, low income, and educated at the high school level or less. There is also a high prevalence of mental illness associated with suicide, most commonly depression.

### How Has Gun Violence Touched National Political Life?

Four US presidents have been assassinated—Abraham Lincoln (1865), James A. Garfield (1881), William McKinley (1901), and John F. Kennedy (1963). All of them met their fate at the end of a gun. Lincoln's assassin, John Wilkes Booth, was an actor angry at Lincoln's pursuit of the Civil War and an end to slavery. Garfield's assassin, Charles Guiteau, was angry at not having been given a federal appointment. McKinley's assassin, Leon Czolgosz, was an attention-seeking anarchist. Kennedy's assassin, Lee Harvey Oswald, was a former US marine and temporary defector to the Soviet Union whose motives for killing the president remain widely debated.

Besides the four presidents who died, one—President Ronald Reagan (1981)—was severely wounded in an assassination attempt by a mentally ill man, John Hinckley, seeking to impress the actress Jodie Foster. Former president Theodore Roosevelt was shot in the chest while on the campaign trail in 1912 but finished his speech before seeking medical care. Other presidents have had close calls with gun-wielding assailants but have escaped injury. They include Andrew Jackson (1835), Franklin D. Roosevelt (1933), Harry S Truman (1950), Gerald Ford (1975, twice), and Bill Clinton (1994).

As of this writing, nearly one-quarter of sitting US presidents—10 of 44—have been shot or targeted by gun-wielding assailants. Other prominent figures who have been shot to death in recent decades in the United States include civil rights leaders Medgar Evers (1963) and the Reverend Martin Luther King Jr. (1968); Senator Robert F. Kennedy (1968); and musicians John Lennon (1980), Tupac Shakur (1996), and Biggie Smalls (1997).

### What Is a Mass Shooting?

There is no widely agreed-upon definition of a mass shooting. For example, some accounts omit mass shootings related to gangs or robbery. Others largely exclude cases where domestic violence is involved.

The go-to source for an authoritative definition of "mass shooting" would normally be the Federal Bureau of Investigation (FBI), the government agency in charge of collecting national crime data. However, the closest it has come to such a definition was in a report on a different topic (serial killers), where it differentiated them from "mass murderers," defined as those who kill at least four people in a single location. Criminologists and other researchers have informally adopted that quasi-definition.

Beyond the four-victim minimum, the criteria for what counts as a mass shooting have varied widely such that incidents that are included in one list would be excluded from another. One point of disagreement is whether to consider the shooter's motive—and, if so, which motive should "count" in tallies of mass shootings. Some tallies include all motives. Others exclude shootings rooted in a profit motive (i.e., drug distribution, armed robbery), gang beefs, domestic disputes, or political ideology. Another criterion is where the shooting occurs. Some tallies only consider shootings in places broadly construed as public, such as workplaces, schools, churches, and street corners. Other definitions also include private homes. Some lists are vague about their criteria and perhaps not inclusive or make exceptions (for example, to the assumption that just one shooter be involved). The multitude of criteria means that the same shooting will appear in some lists but not in others.

### Are US Mass Shootings Increasing?

Maybe. It depends.

Mass shootings are traumatic for victims, for their loved ones, and for communities, even nations, whose collective sense of security they shake. These events draw more media attention than most isolated homicides—and in some cases dominate the "news cycle" for days, even weeks. In a 24/7 news cycle, in which shocking events draw prolonged attention, it's easy to assume that they are on the rise.

However, evaluating whether mass shootings are increasing requires (1) attention to the definition of mass shooting and (2) an awareness that, by whatever definition, the number of events may fluctuate naturally, in the absence of any "larger forces" behind those changes. What looks like a trend, in other words, might simply be random variation.

One way of assessing whether mass shootings have increased is to consult the authoritative source for crime statistics, the Federal Bureau of Investigation's Supplementary Homicide Report, a compilation of data reported by local police departments. Although gun homicides have declined over the past two decades, mass murders as defined by the FBI have shown no clear trend, generally between 11 and 27 per year between 1980 and 2010. Likewise, there has been no clear trend in the number of victims, which typically has fluctuated from 45 to 122 annually. Mass shootings claimed less than 1% of all gun homicide victims in 2010.

However, one study suggests that the types of shootings that attract media attention—those that don't involve gang or domestic disputes and that are conducted in public spaces such as schools and workplaces—may have begun to rise slightly in the mid-2000s, from around one per year to three or four per year, and then reached an unusually high level in 2012—six shootings, including two in 2012—at an Aurora, Colorado, movie theater and at the Sandy Hook Elementary School in Newtown, Connecticut.

### What Are the Worst Mass Shootings in History?

The most lethal mass shooting in modern history, outside of war zones, took place in otherwise peaceful Norway in 2011. In that attack a 32-year-old anti-Islamic extremist with paranoid schizophrenia exploded a bomb outside the government headquarters in downtown Oslo, killing 8, then moved to a labor party summer camp on an island 25 miles away and mowed down 69 people, mostly teenagers. Mass shootings are rare in advanced nations outside the United States,, but not unheard of, as table 3.1 shows.

In the United States, the most lethal mass shooting occurred at Virginia Polytechnic and State University, better known as Virginia Tech, on April 16, 2007. In two closely timed sprees, senior Seung Hui Cho killed 32 students and teachers and wounded 17 others, before killing himself. Cho, a South Korean national who had moved with his family to Virginia when he was in third grade, had a history of depression, severe social anxiety, and withdrawal and had exhibited bizarre, angry behavior shortly before the shooting.

While Virginia Tech had the most fatalities, the mass shooting with the most victims occurred five years later, at the Century movie theater in Aurora, Colorado, during the midnight showing of the Batman movie *The Dark Knight Rises*. There a neuroscience PhD dropout, James Holmes, unleashed a fusillade that struck 70 patrons, killing 12. He pled not guilty by reason of insanity.

The first mass public shooting in the modern era occurred at the University of Texas in 1966, when an engineering student and former marine, Charles Whitman, opened fire from the campus tower, killing 14 people and an unborn child. Before the rampage, the gunman had murdered his wife and his mother. Another 32 were wounded that day.

As gripping as they are, mass shootings rarely change policy. The ones that do typically involve schoolchildren. On April 20, 1999, in suburban Denver, two Columbine High School students shot to death 12 of their classmates and a teacher and wounded 12 other students before killing themselves. The Columbine massacre was the fifth—and by far the most deadly—multiple-fatality shooting that had unfolded in American public schools over roughly a two-year period. Columbine, along with a shooting in Springfield, Oregon, one year earlier, led voters in those states to approve popular referenda requiring all firearms buyers at gun shows to undergo a background check.

The worst firearms massacre at a K-12 institution occurred on December 14, 2012, at Sandy Hook Elementary School in Newtown, Connecticut. Nearly twice as many children were killed there as at Columbine. After Adam Lanza, a mentally ill 20-year-old who had attended the school briefly years earlier, completed his rampage, 20 first-graders and six educators were dead. He also killed his mother and himself that day. Like Columbine, the Sandy Hook massacre was the culmination of a string of especially high-profile mass shootings, including that of Congresswoman Gabrielle Giffords (D-AZ) and 19 others in 2011 and that of 70 Aurora theater patrons, 10 Sikh worshippers, and 8 signage-company employees just in the prior five months of 2012.

As of this writing, the Sandy Hook massacre had contributed to passage of stricter firearms laws in seven states

(California, Colorado, Connecticut, Delaware, Maryland, New Jersey, and New York). It also had galvanized the first serious push in Congress to strengthen federal gun laws since 2007, when the Virginia Tech massacre led to a new law incentivizing states to enter mental health records into the national instant background check system.

A historical footnote: America's worst school massacre did not involve firearms, but rather dynamite. In 1927, a farmer and school board treasurer in tiny Bath, Michigan, blew up the local consolidated school and killed 38 children. Six adults, including the farmer and his wife, also died in his killing spree, while 58 were injured. As a news account reported at the time, "Hardly a family in the village did not have at least one child enrolled among the school's normal attendance of about 200."[3]

Mass shootings are more common in the United States than in other advanced industrialized democracies. However, a handful of especially gruesome mass shootings have occurred outside the United States. Table 3.1 lists some of the

**Table 3.1** Notable Mass Shootings outside the United States

| 1989 | Montreal | École Polytechnique (college) | 14 female students dead, plus the gunman |
|------|----------|-------------------------------|------------------------------------------|
| 1996 | Dunblane, Scotland | Dunblane Primary School | 16 children and 1 teacher dead, plus the gunman |
| 1996 | Tasmania, Australia | Port Arthur Historic Site | 35 dead, shooter imprisoned |
| 2001 | Zug, Switzerland | Parliament Building | 14 politicians dead, plus the shooter |
| 2002 | Erfurt, Germany | Gutenberg-Gymnasium | 13 teachers and 3 others dead, plus the shooter |
| 2008 | Kauhajoki, Finland | Seinäjoki University of Applied Sciences | 10 dead, plus the shooter |
| 2009 | Baku, Azerbaijan | Azerbaijan State Oil Academy | 12 dead, plus the shooter |
| 2011 | Utøya, Norway | Workers' Youth League summer camp | 69 dead, shooter arrested |

more notorious shootings outside of war zones in the modern period.

Canada, Great Britain, Australia, and Finland each tightened its gun laws after its respective massacre.

### Are There Common Elements in Mass Shootings?

Identifying common elements has proved difficult, in part because different studies define mass shootings differently and in part because, even with highly publicized incidents, there are many unknowns.

However, some trends are apparent. First, shooters are almost exclusively male, and they tend to operate alone. Second, random shootings are often not as random as they seem. For example, 33% of mass public shootings between 1983 and 2012 occurred at the shooter's current or former workplace.[4] In 57% of mass shootings between 2009 and 2012 the shooter killed a current or former intimate partner, along with others. In a tally of particularly media-worthy mass shootings, at least two-thirds of the time the shooter had an immediate connection to the location—he had worked, studied, done business, or prayed there, or he was targeting a family member on the job. Finally, roughly half the time, mass shooters take their own life at the scene.

In some of the most deadly shootings—at Virginia Tech, the Aurora movie theater, and the Sandy Hook school, for example—the perpetrator turned out to have had either documented mental illness or clear warning signs.

A particular concern during the 1990s was the epidemic of mass shootings in secondary schools, culminating in the April 1999 incident at Colorado's Columbine High School, where two seniors shot more than three dozen people, killing a dozen of their classmates and a teacher and then themselves. In response to that and other such events, the US Secret Service and US Department of Education conducted an analysis using the "threat assessment" approach developed for protecting public figures. Among their findings:[5]

- "Incidents of targeted violence at school rarely were sudden, impulsive acts."
- Before most incidents other people—usually classmates—knew about the attacker's plans.
- "Most attackers had difficulty coping with significant losses or personal failures. Moreover, many had considered or attempted suicide."
- "Many attackers felt bullied, persecuted or injured by others prior to the attack."
- "Most attackers had access to and had used weapons prior to the attack."

The report encouraged school officials to develop better sources of information, as most of the serious rampages could have been stopped if one of the students who was in the know had thought to tell an adult.

Beyond that good advice, policymakers have struggled with how to prevent mass shootings. Predicting violent behavior is difficult, even when mental illness is present, and the difficulty is compounded for rare events such as mass shootings (one leading violence researcher likened predicting massacres to "trying to find a very small needle in a very large haystack").[6] Federal gun laws allow all but a small fraction of the most severely mentally ill to possess a firearm, and the system that is supposed to flag those prohibited purchasers is subject to uneven reporting and missing records. Medical privacy and civil liberties protections often prevent preemptive action by family members or authorities, however well meaning. And, of course, guns are plentiful.

### Does the United States Have More Crime Than Other Countries?

It depends on the comparison. When the US violence rates are compared with those of other high-income countries, America ends up near the high end of the spectrum. But where the US rates are really off the charts is with respect to homicide, and that is due almost entirely to the difference in gun-homicide rates—which in turn reflect the high rates of gun assault and robbery in the United States. For example, although the US nongun homicide rate is only slightly higher than Canada's, the US rate of homicide with guns is about seven times as high. The same is true for robberies—nongun robbery rates are similar, but the United States has five times Canada's rate per capita of gun robberies. Similar comparisons can be made with Europe, Australia, and other wealthy nations.

But it should be said that a number of middle-income nations, particularly in Latin America and the Caribbean, have still higher rates of gun violence and murder than the United States. Much of that violence comes from conflict around the illicit drug trade, which also provides the means to arm the combatants with deadly weapons.

### How Much Does Gun Violence Cost America?

Generating a comprehensive measure of the societal impact of gun violence requires imagining all the ways in which it affects the quality of life. The elevated rate of homicide, as important as it is, provides just the beginning in this calculation.

The traditional approach for valuing disease and injury is the "cost of illness" method, a method that unfortunately misses most of what is important about gun violence. In essence, the cost-of-illness approach values people the way a farmer would value livestock, based on their productivity and the market value of their "output." The alternative approach, generally favored by economists, also values the subjective quality of life. In short, the difference in the two approaches is between whether we value safety on the basis of how the lives saved contribute to GDP (the cost-of-illness approach), or rather by the value that people place on living in a safer environment.

In the latter perspective, violence, particularly gun violence, is like pollution, traffic, and poor schools. Anyone living in a neighborhood where gunshots are commonly heard is likely to be negatively affected. The possibility of being shot, or of a loved one's being shot, engenders fear and costly efforts at avoidance and self-protection—as when mothers keep their children from playing outside for fear of stray bullets. Property values suffer as people with sufficient means move to safer neighborhoods, and business suffers as customers gravitate to shopping areas where they feel comfortable. Tax revenues are diverted to cover the financial costs of medically treating gunshot victims (usually at public expense) and of law enforcement needs.

The costs of fear, suffering, and avoidance are largely subjective. The challenge is to place a monetary value on these subjective effects, and in particular to estimate how much households would be willing to pay to reduce the perceived risks. One approach is to analyze property values, comparing neighborhoods that are differentially affected by gun violence while controlling for other factors that may be relevant in the realestate market. That approach is bound to be incomplete (since at best it only can capture the local place-related effects of gun violence) and poses an almost insurmountable statistical challenge (since other neighborhood problems are highly correlated with gun violence). Given the difficulty of extracting estimates from property values, a preferred approach is to survey the public about people's willingness to pay for increased safety. This "contingent valuation" method is widely used by economists in valuing different aspects of the environment.

The first contingent valuation of the cost of gun violence asked respondents to a national survey whether they would be willing to vote for a measure that would reduce gun violence in their community by 30% if it were going to cost them a specified amount (which was randomly varied across respondents). The pattern of answers was interesting and quite reasonable:

for example, respondents with children at home had a greater willingness to pay than those without. The overall estimate was that such a reduction would be worth $24 billion.[7] Multiplying up to a hypothetical 100% reduction suggests that interpersonal gun violence was at the time an $80 billion problem, and that the subjective costs were by no means confined to the people and communities that were at highest risk of injury—indeed, the willingness to pay for this reduction actually increased with income.

In sum, the threat of gun violence degrades the quality of life in affected communities. Reducing gun violence would have tangible societal value.

# 4

# CAUSES OF GUN VIOLENCE

## *Who Can Be Trusted with a Gun?*

A simplistic but common understanding of crime is that the population can be divided neatly into two groups, good guys and bad guys. In this view, the bad guys commit crime unless they are locked up, and the good guys are reliably law-abiding. This is a familiar storyline of the old movie westerns, with the actors handily identified by whether they wore a white hat or a black hat. The "white hat, black hat" myth continues to permeate the discussion of gun violence and gun regulation.

Consider this quote from a speech by NRA executive vice president Wayne LaPierre: "The truth is that our society is populated by an unknown number of genuine monsters—people so deranged, so evil, so possessed by voices and driven by demons that no sane person can possibly ever comprehend them. They walk among us every day." He goes on to say: "The only thing that stops a bad guy with a gun is a good guy with a gun."

Like most myths, this one has some element of truth. Serious criminal activity tends to be quite concentrated. If we could keep guns out of the hands of gang members, predatory criminals, and violence-prone people (including domestic batterers), then the number of murders would be substantially reduced. But how are these dangerous people to be identified in advance?

The federal Gun Control Act of 1968 attempts to accomplish just that. It specifies 10 categories of people who are banned

from buying or possessing a firearm. That list includes anyone who has been convicted of a felony (e.g., a crime with the
possible sentence exceeding one year), is under indictment
for a felony, is a fugitive from justice, has been convicted of a
crime of domestic violence or is subject to a restraining order,
is an illegal alien, has been adjudicated "mental defective" (the
unfortunate term in the law for those with severe mental dis-
ability or illness), is a drug abuser, or has been dishonorably
discharged from the military. There are also age restrictions on
purchase and possession.

The problem is that this list misses many of the most dangerous people. For example, a study of adult murder defendants in Chicago found that while most of them had extensive
records of arrests and convictions for minor crimes, only 40%
of them had actually been convicted of a felony. Most of the
others were not disqualified by federal law from buying a gun
legally. So in practice it is not so easy to tell the white hats from
the black hats based on official records.

The list of prohibited categories could be extended to
include, say, conviction of any violent misdemeanor or drug
violation, or conviction for one or more DUIs. Perhaps we
could think of those as the "gray hats." A broader list of disqualification would ensure fewer dangerous people could
legally possess a gun, but at the cost of depriving some people
who are relatively reliable.

It is also imaginable to reverse the presumption about gun
rights. Federal law is guided by the premise that owning a
gun is a right granted to all adults who are legal residents of
the United States, *unless* they are disqualified. A quite different approach would be to treat gun ownership as a privilege
to be reserved for those who can demonstrate that they are
trustworthy. That approach has been incorporated in state law
for handgun permits. For example, in North Carolina a law
dating back to 1921 required that anyone buying a handgun
would have to get a permit from the sheriff and that the permit
would be issued only to those who could produce two character witnesses and demonstrate a home-defense need for the

gun. Similarly stringent rules have been applied in some states to those seeking a license to carry a concealed gun. While the last 20 years have seen a broad retreat from this kind of regulation, it is still found in a handful of states.

The question of who can be trusted with a gun tends to play out differently in the regulation of hunting. States often require that hunters pass both written tests and field tests demonstrating their knowledge of the rules and of weapons handling. Such requirements are nonexistent for buying a gun—and in most states for carrying it away from home. It is ironic that in most states a person who knows nothing about how to handle a gun safely can legally carry a firearm in the city but is not allowed to carry it for the purpose of hunting deer.

Incidentally, the question of who can be trusted with a gun is not just a matter for state and federal law. It is also an issue for family and friends. Should you let your child visit a home where you know guns are stored? Should Granddad be encouraged to give up his gun now that he is becoming senile or depressed? Can a wife whose husband often threatens her with his gun persuade him to give it up? Will old friends continue to go hunting together when one of them has started to drink too much in the duck blind?

### Do More Guns Cause More Crime—or Less?

Criminals rarely buy their guns from a licensed dealer—most obtain them by buying or borrowing from family members or friends, or stealing, or making a connection in the underground market. (Fewer than 20% of prisoners in national surveys who admit to having a firearm indicate that they purchased it from a store.) Where firearms ownership is widespread, it will be easier for delinquents and gang members and predatory criminals to obtain one. A teen looking to appropriate a gun in Mississippi, where 60% of the households have one (or many), probably need look no farther than his parents' closet or dresser drawer; the search may take a lot longer for a teen in

Massachusetts, where just 13% of households are armed. The same differences show up in other informal channels by which guns find their way into the hands of youths or felons or others who are disqualified from buying them from a gun store.

So we expect that dangerous people will find it easier to obtain a firearm in a gun-rich environment than in one in which gun ownership is relatively unusual. This "availability" hypothesis finds support in a variety of scientific studies. Among the findings: a positive statistical association across counties between the prevalence of gun ownership and (1) the theft of firearms in burglary; (2) the likelihood that teenage males carry guns; and (3) the percentage of robberies committed with guns.

However, the interpretation of such results is in some doubt. Gun-rich jurisdictions, such as Mississippi, are systematically different in various ways from jurisdictions with relatively few guns, such as Massachusetts. These differences make it difficult to demonstrate that it is gun density per se that accounts for the differences in criminal use of guns. The usual approach for addressing this problem has been to statistically control for other state characteristics, such as population density, poverty, and the age and racial composition of the population. But these variables never explain very much of the cross-sectional variation in crime rates, suggesting that the list of available control variables is inadequate to the task. Also unclear is whether widespread gun ownership is the cause or effect of an area's crime problem, since high crime rates may induce residents to buy guns for self-protection.

Some of the problems with cross-sectional studies can be overcome by using panel data—measurements at multiple points in time—to compare *changes* in gun ownership with *changes* in crime across jurisdictions. Compared with Massachusetts, the state of Mississippi may have much higher homicide rates year after year for reasons that cannot be fully explained from existing data sources. But by comparing changes rather than levels, we implicitly control for any unmeasured differences across states that are relatively fixed over time, such as a "southern culture of violence." The best available evidence suggests that a change in gun prevalence has a direct effect on weapon choice in robbery and assault, and most importantly, that more guns leads to more gun homicides (and more homicides overall).[1]

Finally, it is worth emphasizing that the conclusion is not "More guns, more crime." Research findings have been quite consistent in demonstrating that gun prevalence is unrelated to the rates of assault and robbery. The strong finding that emerges from this research is that gun use *intensifies* violence, making it more likely that the victim of an assault or robbery will die. The positive effect is on the murder rate, not on the overall violent-crime rate. In other words: More guns, more deaths.

### Is Gun Violence Closely Linked to Other Types of Violence?

Yes. And it follows that if we could curtail the underlying causes of criminal violence, then guns would do less damage. In fact, that is precisely the American experience with violent crime during the last two decades. A sharp drop in overall rates of violence has been coupled with an equally sharp drop in gun violence. Robberies, rapes, and aggravated assaults declined by 75% between 1993 and 2011, from 29.1 per 1,000 persons age 12 or older to 7.2 per 1,000. Throughout this period, the fraction of these crimes committed with firearms remained steady at about one-quarter. The "gun violence" problem declined lockstep with the overall violence problem.

The same point could be made by comparing different neighborhoods. Gun crime is a devastating problem in Chicago's high-poverty inner-city neighborhoods and a relatively minor problem in its wealthier neighborhoods. The difference is not so much in the availability of guns, but rather in the overall amount of violence. It is the combination of violence and guns that produces a high murder rate.

Without a doubt, then, one strategy for reducing gun violence is to reduce criminal violence generally. If we would take steps to reduce alcohol and drug abuse, offer better treatment for mental illness, reduce school dropout rates, and deploy police resources more strategically, crime rates would fall further and guns would be of correspondingly less concern. But when and where violent crime is a problem, we cannot afford to ignore the role that guns play in intensifying that violence.

Suicide is also an important concern closely associated with guns. And as in the case of criminal violence, it is true in principle that we could reduce the gun-suicide problem by addressing the conditions that lead people to give serious consideration to ending their lives—or bring into counseling those who do consider suicide. The US military has given increasingly high priority to suicide prevention (with uncertain results) as rates have climbed during the many years of war in Iraq and Afghanistan. The stresses of serving in war zones lead to post-traumatic stress disorder, drug abuse, and other risk factors for suicide—and the ready availability of firearms translates those risks into high death rates.

### What Do Israel and Switzerland Teach Us about the Importance of Gun Ownership as a Cause of Gun Violence?

Switzerland and Israel are often used by pro-gun advocates as evidence of the effectiveness of a heavily armed public in combating crime and terrorism. A variety of claims are made about these countries to the effect that firearms possession is prevalent and largely unregulated or (in the case of Israel) actively promoted. But the reality is quite different. In fact, firearms are more closely regulated and scarcer in these countries than in the United States. Gun policy in both countries recognizes that civilian firearms possession and carrying pose a threat to public safety.

It is true that both countries have a large military presence. In Israel most citizens are obligated to serve in the military—three years for men, 21 months for women—and the men continue to serve in the reserves for several years thereafter. But this high level of mobilization has little effect on gun availability away from military bases. Since 2006, the Israeli Defense Forces changed their policy so that personnel no longer carry their weapons while on weekend leave. The intended result, apparently achieved, was to reduce the rate of suicide. Otherwise Israel has a low rate of firearms ownership and possession, as indicated by the fact that only about 20% of suicides nationwide are committed with firearms, as compared with 50% in the United States. The government requires all civilian gun owners to be licensed and keeps a registry of licenses, which must be renewed every three years. All gun transfers are to be registered with the government. Gun carrying, either concealed or in the open, requires a permit.

In Switzerland, gun ownership is more common than in Israel, but still comprehensively regulated. All able-bodied Swiss men are required to perform military service until age 34 (up to age 50 for general officers), which for the most part consists of reserve duties. The commitment to national preparedness is reflected in the fact that target shooting is a national sport. (The celebrated purpose of good marksmanship is national defense, not self-defense.) While in the reserve, men are issued a personal weapon, in most cases an assault rifle, to be stored at home or (if they choose) in the local armory. They are entitled to keep their military weapon after leaving service, but only after it is converted to semiautomatic firing mode and registered with the federal government. The army stopped issuing ammunition for home storage in 2008.

Civilian weaponry is regulated by the Swiss federal government and the cantons. Automatic weapons are banned, a government-issued acquisition permit is required to purchase a handgun from a dealer, and private transfers require that the seller determine the identity of the buyer and keep detailed records about the transaction. Those seeking a permit to carry for self-defense purposes must pass a series of tests demonstrating their knowledge of gun safety and use, and make an argument that the firearm is needed in response to a specific risk.

The relative scarcity of available firearms in Switzerland is indicated by the fact that only 20% of suicides are committed with firearms, as compared with half in the United States.

Switzerland and Israel have lower rates of violence than the United States, but it is not because they have more guns or more gun carrying. Just the reverse is true. These countries illustrate the general point made previously: Gun violence requires both guns and violence. Violence rates in these countries are much lower than in the United States, regardless of weapon type.

### Do Cultural Differences Help Account for Differences in Levels of Gun Violence?

For more than a century, "culture" has been invoked to explain different levels of violence within the United States and between the United States and other nations. But what does it mean to blame "culture" for differing levels of violence in general and gun violence in particular? And how might we evaluate cultural explanations against other types of explanations?

In the present context the term "culture" is akin to widely shared belief systems—or in the words of the historian David Hackett Fischer, "folkways"—governing the appropriate response to threats to one's person and to the social order generally. As we discuss in chapter 8, there is a strong American tradition of associating guns with protection, and these ideas took root early. In Appalachia, historians argue, eighteenth-century Scotch-Irish settlers brought with them a belief that violence was necessary to "conquer their own peace." In the Deep South, violent folkways emerged from a plantation system in which individual status depended on the often violent domination of others. Westward expansion brought lawlessness among cattlemen, frontiersmen, and miners and violence among Anglos,

Native Americans, and Hispanics. Even after slavery was abolished, the frontier was settled, and southerners moved north and vice versa, these folkways persisted.

Cultural explanations tend to be deployed not to explain crime in general (rape, robbery, domestic violence, etc.), but rather to account for particular *types* of crime, namely assaults and homicides arising from personal disputes between unrelated people. These encounters are said to stem from a "culture of honor" that originated in the South and is rooted in age-old status grievances exacerbated by a "siege mentality." How else to explain why, historically, suicide and property crimes have been lower in the South, but homicide higher? "It is the 'personal difficulties' with deadly weapons, street-fights, and affrays in the Southern States that swell the number of homicides out of all proportion," wrote the journalist H. V. Redfield in his classic 1880 study, *Homicide: North and South*.[2]

Culture-based theories have great intuitive appeal, but they are tricky to prove empirically. One problem is that belief systems are hard to quantify and often seem to go hand in hand with other factors that facilitate violence, such as disadvantage and the breakdown of order. Thus, while early studies blamed high rates of violence on Southern culture, later scholars found that effect was just a product of the South's unusually large rates of poverty, illiteracy, lack of education, and other afflictions. (More recent work has insisted that, even after accounting for these problems, the "southern effect" persists.) Even at the individual level, it is hard to sort out cultural folkways from other drivers of violent encounters. Take the paradigmatic nineteenth-century southern ruffians squabbling over an insult or the modern gang member who pulls his weapon in response to a sideways glance. If shots are fired, what was the underlying cause? A widely accepted cultural understanding of how men are to resolve disputes? An instinctive psychological reaction? A quick cost-benefit calculation about how best to survive the encounter? A subconscious adaptation to ineffective systems of law and order? It's hard to know.

Muddling things further, violence rates can be very different across regions that look pretty similar. Take the filmmaker Michael Moore's examination of the United States and Canada, neighboring nations that share a British heritage and frontier traditions, high levels of economic development, open democratic governance, even popular culture—but have very different levels of gun violence. In *Bowling for Columbine*, Moore suggests that Canadians have less gun violence because they are less volatile and more deferential to collective, consensus approaches to problem solving, a common characterization. But it's also true that Canada has much stricter gun laws than does the United States and much lower rates of handgun ownership. So is Canadian cultural "niceness" keeping the gun homicide rate low? Or are Canada's gun laws keeping matters in check? Or is it both—the culture gave rise to the laws, which reinforce the culture?

No one can say for sure, at least as of now. But circumstantial evidence leads us to question "culture" as the overriding explanation for violence (though we believe it may matter in certain circumstances). Our general skepticism stems from the fact that, although the United States has a *gun* homicide rate roughly seven times that of Canada, the two countries actually have comparable rates of *nongun* homicides.[3] Likewise, within the United States, the exceptional rate of southern violence is really a problem of gun violence, not violence by other means. If cultural predispositions were to blame for violence, we would expect to see disparities between the United States and peer nations, and between the American South and other regions, in *nongun* assaults and homicides. But where these differences exist, they tend to be small.

Another challenge to culture-based theories is that, while folkways are supposed to stick around from generation to generation, homicide rates have fluctuated greatly *within* geographic areas, and *between* them, over time. For example, within the United States, homicide rates were comparatively high in the years around the American Revolution, hit an all-time low in the decades after the War of 1812 (at least outside the slave South), rose again in the Civil War era, then declined, then rose again. Just in the last two decades, the gun-homicide rate has declined by half, even though American culture has changed little. Making matters more complicated, these broad trends mask large, often divergent, patterns between regions and racial groups that are inconsistent with "sticky" cultural explanations. Looking across nations, the role of culture becomes even more puzzling. The United States now has a homicide rate roughly five to seven times that of other wealthy nations, but in the first half of the nineteenth century, US rates, at least in the North, were on a par with, or even lower than, Canada's and western Europe's.

So using culture to explain different levels of violence in general, or gun violence in particular, poses some challenges. But we are persuaded that there is something to these theories, in part because of creative recent work on the long-standing puzzle of southern homicide and gang violence. Most straightforwardly, while white southern men (the honor culture's standard-bearers) don't differ much from their nonsouthern brethren in general attitudes toward force and violence, these southerners are comparatively supportive of using violence in particular situations where honor is at stake—for example, in defense of the home and in response to an affront. Southern males attending college in the North are more likely than their classmates to get measurably angry when provoked. And cities and rural areas with large numbers of southern white transplants have unusually high rates of argument-based homicides, all else being equal. Careful studies of northern urban gangs make a persuasive argument that cultural codes of preemptive aggression can spread quickly within these tightly knit groups.

So where does this leave us? Culture—understood in this context to signify beliefs about, and ways of handling, personal threats—probably does account for some of the "excess" lethal violence that we see in the American South and in urban areas. Cultural folkways may also account for differences in lethal violence across nations, though other factors—such as economic development, governance structures, and access to guns—no doubt play a much stronger role. We are inclined to see cultural beliefs as one of an interlocking and mutually supportive constellation of factors that influence how violent or peaceful a community, state, or nation is.

### Do the Media Contribute to Gun Violence in America?

A week after the Sandy Hook school shooting, the National Rifle Association's chief executive, Wayne LaPierre, excoriated the mass media for their coverage of the tragedy: "How many more copycats are waiting in the wings," he asked, "for their moment of fame from a national media machine that rewards them with wall-to-wall attention and a sense of identity that they crave, while provoking others to try to make their mark?" At the time, many people (not just in the media) brushed off LaPierre's question as a diversion. But it turns out that his core claim, that mass media and entertainment can encourage violent behavior, has a long history and some scholarly support.

As early as the 1920s, scholars debated whether movies—then called "talkies" because audio had just been introduced—were "lowering the moral consciousness of youth" and contributing to delinquency, homicide, and crime waves generally. Presaging LaPierre's complaint, early twentieth-century commentators and scholars also fingered the sensationalist "yellow journalism" of the day, saying that it bred "an unwholesome curiosity about criminals" and thereby contributed to "the growth of criminality." Scholars undertook large-scale studies and concluded that movies probably had little if any effect on misbehavior. These researchers surmised that delinquents by their nature simply liked violent movies. Surveys of law enforcement officers found mixed opinions about whether sensationalist reporting encouraged copycat crime. In short, there were plenty of commentators sounding dire warnings but only "scanty and inconclusive" evidence for their case. Almost a century and thousands of sophisticated studies later, the basic conclusions are much the same.

## What about Violent TV and Movies?

Scholars have produced a rich body of research on whether exposure to violence in mass entertainment, especially on television, increases aggressive or criminal activity. Using high-tech methods of analysis not available to scholars in the 1920s, these studies offer a broadly similar takeaway: Media effects are really hard to measure, the relationships between media consumption and misbehavior are conflicting, and it's difficult to sort out whether violent images cause kids to be aggressive or simply attract those already prone to misbehavior. At least one study suggested that watching violent television might insulate kids from criminal activity—since they're home watching TV instead of carousing with the local street gang.

Most scholars, however, believe that watching violent television has a modest effect on aggression, more so in children than in adults and more so in the short term than in the long term. Watching dramatic violence on TV may encourage actual violence by teaching kids that aggression is an acceptable means of solving problems and providing examples for them to follow. Televised violence may also numb viewers to the effects of real-life violence on others, making such violence easier to commit.

One study looked at the home lives, peer interactions, and TV viewing habits of 550 elementary school children who came of age in the 1970s and 1980s, then tracked them down in the early 1990s to see how their lives had turned out. The scholars were interested in whether childhood TV viewing would predict later abusive or even criminal behavior. They found that the amount of violent TV the study subjects had watched as a child—and the degree to which they identified with violent characters and viewed TV as reflective of real life—significantly predicted violent behavior in adulthood. These relationships held up even after the authors statistically "controlled for" the effects of some other influences, such as violence and poor parenting in the childhood home, childhood poverty, and adult viewing of violent TV.

The evidence is suggestive. Nonexperimental studies such as these must be viewed with skepticism, as they aren't equipped to capture the full range of individual character-istics that might drive both media consumption and violent behavior. What's more, even scholars whose work demon-strates a statistically significant effect of TV violence on actual violence note that it is one of many factors that interact in complex ways. These factors include mental illness, bad parenting, poverty, lack of constructive friendships, sub-stance abuse, life frustrations, opportunities to misbehave, and so forth. Another caveat is that these studies examine a wide range of aggressive behaviors but almost never include firearms-related assaults or murders. Most American gun violence involves suicides, gang and drug beefs in disad-vantaged neighborhoods, and attacks on intimate partners. We are hard-pressed to blame childhood viewing of, say, *Gunsmoke* for these shootings.

That said, we take seriously the findings that TV adds a bit of fuel to a fire that, as any comparison with America's peer countries makes clear, needs no additional stoking. Policymakers have acted accordingly by introducing a TV rating system that guides parents away from shows inap-propriate for kids. In chapter 7 we address policy interven-tions that are arguably more consequential for reducing gun violence.

## What about Copycat Crimes?

Thankfully, Wayne LaPierre's post–Sandy Hook warning that nonstop media coverage encourages copycat shootings proved wrong: Nothing approximating the Newtown event occurred in the rest of the 2012–2013 school year. But threats were made against schools in California, Indiana, Maryland, and Tennessee. Authorities responded aggressively, with good reason. For decades, scholars have demonstrated that "copycat crime" is a real phenomenon, precipitated by the dangerous combination of unstable attention-seekers and a voracious media eager to cover their misdeeds. How much the media are to blame in a larger moral sense is a matter of debate—they are, after all, *supposed* to cover newsworthy events. But no matter. There is strong evidence for the copycatting phenomenon.

In pioneering work in the 1890s, the French sociologist Gustave Le Bon argued that misbehavior is contagious. Like a bad cold, it spreads from person to person. Modern social scientists applied this intuition to the study of phenomena such as airline hijackings, teen suicides, fire setting, product-tampering hoaxes, and crime generally. The most-studied copycat phenomenon, however, is suicide.

Here, the evidence is strong and consistent, both within the United States and internationally: Reports of suicide in the media lead to spikes in suicide rates in patterns hard to explain by random chance. In an analysis of more than 50 studies, one scholar found that the factors most likely to set off copycats include media coverage of celebrity suicides and suicides by women. Tellingly, suicides tend to decline during newspaper strikes. In Austria, after a spike in suicides committed by jumping in front of subway trains, the media tempered their coverage, and these incidents dropped and remained low.

In response to consistent research findings, US public health agencies, along with public health–oriented nonprofits, have endorsed guidelines that discourage using "suicide" in the headline, reporting on suicide "epidemics," or showcasing grieving relatives or suicide survivors—all types of coverage that could encourage suicidal behavior. Instead, the guidelines suggest that the media avoid glamorizing the victim and focus on how treatment can be effective.

### What about Violent Video Games?

When teenaged boys shoot up schools, the question invariably arises: Are violent video games partly to blame? The claim is plausible enough, in part because the timing works. Highly graphic games, including the "first-person shooter" genre, became popular in the mid- to late 1990s, around the time of the first wave of mass shootings in otherwise quiet schools. And the connection between video and real-life violence is easy to imagine. First-person shooter games absorb youngsters in a fantasy world where guns mean power, and violence has neither costs nor consequences. Indeed, press accounts of mass shootings often report that the killers were preoccupied with gaming. In a 2000 poll, nearly 75% of Americans thought video games contributed somewhat or a great deal to real-life violence.

On the other hand, skeptics look at larger trends and wonder how bad video games really could be for society. As gaming has taken hold in America over the last two decades, they note, rates of violent crime—including crime against youths—have been plunging. And gaming is wildly popular in countries such as the Netherlands and South Korea, which have very little violence. Indeed, a *Washington Post* analysis found no relationship between per capita gaming expenditures and violent crime rates across 10 advanced industrialized nations. And then there's the obvious fact that millions of kids play violent games and manage to lead peaceful lives. Young people who shoot up schools, it is reasonable to believe, have problems far more serious than their unsavory choice in recreation.

What does the research say? Evidence is growing that video games may have some effect on antisocial behavior, though the effects are small and sometimes conflicting, and tell us little about the implications for major crimes, such as assault and murder. In general, researchers whose studies measure low-level aggression—having hostile thoughts or shoving a classmate, for example—have tended to find stronger video-game effects than have researchers interested in criminal violence. What's more, most of the research is conducted in controlled laboratory settings: A kid plays a video game, then undergoes some sort of testing or observation to look for aggression. Scholars have long cautioned about generalizing any laboratory findings to predictions about the effects of video games on real-world violence over the long term.

Since 1994, video games have been subject to a rating system similar to the one used for movies to help guide parents toward age-appropriate products. In 2005 California went further, passing a law banning sales or rentals of violent video games to minors. The Supreme Court overturned the law in 2011 on the grounds that it violated the First Amendment. In the majority opinion, Justice Antonin Scalia noted that the wicked queen tries to poison Cinderella, and Hansel and Gretel "off" their captor by baking her in an oven, but we don't ban *Grimm's Fairy Tales*.

As with the discussion of media effects above, we suspect that violent video game usage may exacerbate violent tendencies in at-risk kids. No doubt studies will continue to look for linkages between gaming and violence. As we discuss in chapter 6, however, policies aimed at other aspects of America's gun violence problem are likely to have a greater impact.

### What Do We Know about the Connection between Mental Health and Gun Violence?

The nexus between violence and mental illness is one of the most complicated and sensitive issues when it comes to gun violence—one that is receiving long-overdue attention from the White House and violence prevention groups.

Studies suggest that people with serious mental illness, including schizophrenia, bipolar disorder, and depression, are at increased risk of committing violence against others, particularly if the perpetrator is not undergoing medical treatment or is abusing drugs or alcohol. A review of more than 20 studies estimated that seriously mentally ill people are three to five times more likely to commit violence than are people without such a diagnosis. However, people with mental illness commit only a small fraction of violent crime—5% by one Swedish estimate—and the vast majority of people with such disorders will never run afoul of the law. When they do commit violence, it tends to be directed at those they know and in private spaces.

Indeed, mentally ill people are disproportionately likely to be victims of violent death. A recent Swedish study, for example, found they had a fivefold risk of death by homicide relative to the general population. Likewise, suicides in the United States outnumber homicides by more than two to one, with depression, substance abuse, or other psychiatric disorders estimated to be a factor in some 80% to 90% of self-inflicted death.

# 5

# MANUFACTURE AND MARKETING OF GUNS

### How Large Is the Gun Industry in America?

Much larger in some years than others.

In 2012, the value of firearms shipments from domestic manufactures was $3.3 billion, while manufacturers shipped $3.7 billion worth of ammunition (most of which—$3.0 billion—was exported). The combined $7.0 billion in shipments of guns and ammo makes this a relatively small industry, comparable in value to shipments of potato chips or ice cream.

Imports play an important role in both the market for firearms ($1.9 billion) and ammunition ($1.1 billion). Netting out exports from imports, the domestic market was $4.5 billion for firearms, and $1.8 billion for ammo. Note that these figures refer to the value of shipments by producers and importers, not to retail expenditures.

The firearms market has been quite volatile, and even more so for handguns than for rifles and shotguns. Recent peak years with respect to domestic sales (manufactures plus imports minus exports) are 1968, 1974, 1993, and (it would appear at the time of this writing) 2013; troughs occurred in 1986 and 2001. Figure 5.1 tells the story.

These data document the large swings in sales, and also an important trend: Handguns have assumed an increasingly important share of the total, moving from one-quarter (in

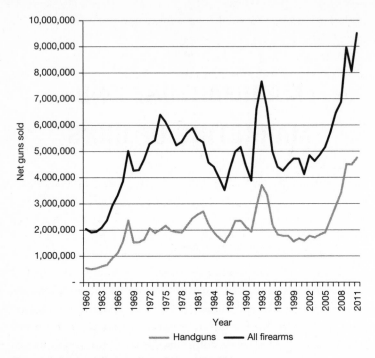

**Figure 5.1** Firearms sales in the United States, 1960–2011

1960) to one-half (in 2011). The mix of handguns has changed over this time as well: As recently as 1980 the handgun market was dominated by revolver sales but now is primarily pistols. An increasing share of handguns has come from abroad, with imports rising from about 300,000 in the early 1980s to 2.6 million by 2012.

### How Is Firearms Production Organized?

A recent study for the Small Arms Survey counted 2,282 US-based firearms manufacturers supplying the civilian market. The great bulk of these are very small, with fewer than 10 guns produced per year. At the upper end of the spectrum are three firms that each have produced more than 10 million units since 1986, and together account for more than 40% of all domestic manufactures: Smith and Wesson, Remington, and Sturm Ruger.

Most revolvers are produced by Ruger or by Smith and Wesson, and almost all shotguns by either Remington Arms or by OF Mossberg/Maverick. The production of pistols is more competitive, with foreign-held companies like Sig Sauer and Glock making inroads into the territory traditionally held by Ruger, Smith & Wesson, Beretta, and others.

Several of the leading firms in handgun manufacturing in the 1980s and 1990s were Southern California's "Ring of Fire" companies. These companies (Lorcin Engineering, Bryco Arms, Davis Industries, Phoenix Arms, AMT, and Sundance Industries) produced low-quality weapons selling in some cases for $50 or less, often known by the pejorative term "Saturday night special." By the early 1990s, Ring of Fire companies accounted for one-third of all US handgun sales and were heavily overrepresented in criminal use. Under regulatory pressure and other problems, five of the six original Ring of Fire companies ended up declaring bankruptcy.

The manufacturers serving the high end of the market also have had their problems over the years, including running afoul of the politics of the market. In March 2000 Smith & Wesson was the only major gun manufacturer to sign an agreement with the Clinton administration to voluntarily adopt various safety and design standards. In response, gun rights groups and gun clubs organized a boycott, leading to a steep drop in sales. The owners of S&W sold it at a fire-sale price to the Saf-T-Hammer Corporation; the new company canceled the agreement to make safe guns and was able to restore its reputation and sales position in the market. A similar story involves Colt (the famous revolver maker), which in 1998 took a hit following remarks by its CEO to the effect that he favored a federal permit system with training and testing for gun ownership. A grassroots boycott of Colt products was successful in pushing down sales, and Colt is now a relatively minor player in the civilian market.

The industry has had more than its share of mergers and acquisitions in recent years. The largest firearms maker in the United States was created very recently through a series of acquisitions by Cerberus Capital Management LP, a private-equity firm. In 2007, the year that Cerberus bought a controlling interest in Chrysler, it also began buying up a number of firearms manufacturing firms, including Remington, Marlin, and Bushmaster—and assembled them in a private entity called the Freedom Group. (Well-known brand names are typically preserved in these private acquisitions.) The result is that the industry is less competitive than it may appear.

The most prominent industry trade group is the National Shooting Sports Foundation. According to its Internet site, "Members include manufacturers of sporting firearms and ammunition, a wide array of accessory and equipment manufacturers as well as distributors, retailers, shooting ranges and many other companies and organizations in the hunting and shooting sports community. Today, membership includes more than 8,000 companies and organizations." NSSF runs the annual SHOT Show (Shooting, Hunting, Outdoor Trade Show), the largest of its kind in the world with 630,000 square feet of exhibition space. NSSF is active in representing members with respect to legal, regulatory, and legislative issues.

### How Does the Industry Market Its Products?

The volatile sales cycles are self-evidently driven by politics. Peak sales in 1968 and 1993 coincided respectively with enactment of the Gun Control Act and the Brady Handgun Violence Prevention Act, both of which substantially tightened federal regulation of firearms commerce. More recently, firearms sales increased sharply beginning in 2006, when a Democratic majority was elected to both houses of Congress, and continued sharply upward through President Obama's two terms.

Gun owners were encouraged by pro-gun propaganda to believe that the Democrats, and especially Obama, would take away their guns or at least make it more difficult to obtain the kind of gun they wanted. The irony is that nothing actually happened at the federal level; during Obama's first term the only change in gun policy was to remove the ban on carrying loaded guns in national parks and transporting checked firearms on Amtrak.

The fundamentals of the gun market have much to do with the decline of hunting. The traditional market for rifles and shotguns suitable for this activity has dwindled accordingly. The recent growth in unit sales to unparalleled heights reflects the success of the industry and pro-gun groups in reorienting from sports to self-defense and something more sinister—fear of social chaos and government tyranny. Self-defense has been extended from the home to public places by the sea change in state laws; most states have either deregulated concealed carrying in public, or placed only modest requirements on those wanting a permit. About half the states have adopted so-called stand-your-ground laws that further encourage a self-help mind-set. These laws have increased the demand for readily concealable pistols and suitable accessories.

Another important trend that has helped the gun makers is the growing subculture that rests on doomsday narratives of social disorder, invasion by the United Nations forces (to confiscate guns), and other beliefs that strike many people as far-fetched. The industry's marketing efforts have exploited the image of well-armed private citizens serving as the bulwark of freedom. The slogan of the NRA Business Alliance is "The Business of Freedom," and the largest gun company in the United States calls itself the Freedom Group. Indeed, the themes of patriotism, heroism, and fighting for freedom have become prominent in gun marketing. The message is complemented by the product mix, which increasingly consists of rifles that mimic the assault rifles used in military services in the US and abroad, high-capacity, high-powered pistols, sniper rifles, and so forth. (The industry has sought to rebrand knockoffs of military assault rifles as "modern sporting rifles" or "tactical rifles.") Beretta has been explicit about its marketing strategy for what became the M-9 pistol adopted by the US military in 1990—win the military contract and then advertise it to the public as a military weapon. Glock had earlier succeeded with a similar strategy with the Austrian army.

### What Is Required to Become a Licensed Dealer?

Anyone in the business of manufacturing, importing, and retailing firearms must obtain the appropriate federal license. Licenses are issued by the Bureau of Alcohol, Tobacco, Firearms, and Explosives (ATF) in the US Department of Justice. For dealing in ordinary firearms, the license fee is $200 for the first three years, with a $90 renewal fee thereafter. In addition to paying the fee, applicants must have a place of business with secure storage, and not be disqualified from firearms possession because of, say, a serious criminal record. Only those with a federal license may legally receive shipments of firearms from distributors. Unlicensed individuals may sell firearms privately from their personal collection, but not as a regular business. (The legal line here is murky at best.)

With the privilege of being a firearms dealer comes a number of responsibilities: storing inventory safely, initiating background checks on would-be buyers, keeping records on all sales, providing information on specific sales when queried by ATF's National Tracing Center, and generally obeying not only federal regulations but also applicable state and local regulations.

There are currently (May 2013) about 55,000 dealers with a Type 1 or Type 2 (pawnbrokers) license. That is a considerable reduction from the early 1990s, when there were more than 200,000 licensees; at that time ATF was issuing them to most anyone who chose to pay the trivial fee ($30), whether or not they had a place of business. A study by the Violence Policy Center pointed out at the time that there were more gun dealers than gas stations. In 1994 new legislation raised the fee to its current level, and the "place of business" requirement began to receive greater attention from ATF.

### How Many Guns Does an Average Dealer Sell in a Year? A Successful Dealer?

Licensed dealers sell both new and used firearms. As noted above, federal records indicate that in 2011 there were 9.5 million firearms manufactured for domestic use or imported. There are no readily available records of the number of used firearms sold by dealers, but a recent estimate by the Small Arms Survey provides a ballpark estimate—25% of the total. So for that year the total may have been 12.7 million, which works out to 226 per licensed dealer.

If an average of 226 sounds low (less than one per business day), that is because most licensees, like most licensed manufacturers, are more hobby than business. The relative handful of dealers who are seriously in the retail business account for the bulk of all sales. For example, an analysis of California handgun sales by dealers found that those that sold more than 100 per year constituted only 12% of all dealers, but 81% of all sales. (This study was made possible by the fact that California requires handgun sales to be reported to a state agency.)

### How Are Dealers Regulated?

Lightly, if at all.

The federal agency responsible for regulating licensed dealers does not have the resources to do much enforcement. ATF's rather modest goal is to inspect all licensees at least once every five years, but it has fallen far short of that in practice. In fact, the most recent internal review found that only 42% of licensees had been inspected for regulatory compliance between 2007 and 2012. The reason is simple—Congress refuses to provide ATF with the necessary resources to do its job well.

In 2012, ATF reported that about 50% of the 13,000 licensees inspected were in full compliance with the regulations and no violations were cited. Just 0.5% (67 in all) were found to be so greatly in violation of regulations that the license was revoked or denied renewal, but more minor violations were common: inadequate record keeping, failure to verify purchaser eligibility, and failure to report multiple sales of handguns.

It should be noted that federal licensees are required to follow state regulations, and that 17 states in fact have their own licensing program for dealers. In several of those states there is an active program of regulatory enforcement that supplements ATF efforts.

### What Fraction of Gun Transactions Go through Licensed Dealers?

In the national debate over gun control following the massacre of schoolchildren in Newtown, Connecticut (December 2012), one of the oft-repeated claims was that 40% of all gun sales did not involve a licensed dealer and hence were exempt from the federal requirement for a background check. The point of citing that statistic was to demonstrate that the "private sale loophole" was very large and should be closed.

As it turns out, the 40% statistic is loosely based on the results of a national survey conducted 20 years earlier. Respondents in that survey who reported acquiring a gun in the previous two years were asked about their source: 60% mentioned a store or pawnshop, which ordinarily would be licensed. Most of the other respondents (30%) said the source was a member of the family or an acquaintance—presumably unlicensed. (Those transactions were more likely to be gifts than purchases.) Some of the other sources named (gun show, flea market) could be either licensed or not.

In any event, the more relevant statistic is the percentage of firearms used in crime that were obtained directly from licensed dealers. One important source here is a national survey of prisoners conducted in 2004. Of the prisoners who said that they had used a firearm in their most recent crime, just one of every nine indicated that they had obtained it from a gun store or pawnbroker.

### What Are Gun Shows, and Why Are They Problematic?

Gun shows are weekend gatherings in public buildings organized by promoters to bring together buyers and sellers of firearms, ammunition, accessories, and related items. Exhibition space is rented to licensed dealers and private sellers. There are more than 4,000 gun shows per year, and the largest have as many as 2,000 tables.

Gun shows are controversial in part because they facilitate sales by unlicensed individuals. Federal law requires anyone in the business of selling guns to have a federal license, conduct background checks on buyers, and keep records. But no license is required to sell guns out of one's private collection, and no federal rules regulate such sales except to ban transfers to an individual who the seller knows is disqualified (as a felon, fugitive, undocumented immigrant, etc.). The seller can avoid legal liability by simply being careful not to ask any questions. Unlicensed sellers are reported to make up 25% to 50% of all gun vendors at gun shows.

Gun shows are one source of firearms to criminals and traffickers. What is not clear is how important they are relative to other sources. Surveys of prison inmates suggest that very few of them acquired their guns at gun shows. But that only tells us something about the final transaction in what is typically a chain of transactions. It is possible that gun shows figure more prominently in the supply chain by which guns move from the legitimate market to the underground market and ultimately into criminal use.

### Can Guns Be Sold on the Internet? Ammunition?

The Internet helps connect buyers and sellers of all kinds of merchandise, including firearms and ammunition. Furthermore, shipments of ammunition are essentially unregulated. That fact came to the fore when it was discovered that the man who shot up a movie theater in Aurora, Colorado, in 2012 had legally obtained more than 6,000 rounds of ammunition by mail order.

The situation is a bit more complicated for shipping firearms. Unlicensed sellers can ship a firearm by a parcel service to a resident of the same state. (Ironically, such shipments are not allowed for licensed dealers, who must transact in person.) For both dealers and nondealers, interstate shipments must be channeled through a licensed dealer.

### What Is the Supply Chain for Guns Used in Crime?

Almost all firearms that end up being used in crime originate with a sale by a licensed dealer. (The relatively rare exceptions are homemade guns, off-the-books imports, and thefts from manufacturers and shippers.) After that first sale by a dealer the firearm may be transacted several more times before being used in a robbery or assault. Once in the possession of an active criminal or a gang the firearm may continue to circulate until confiscated or discarded.

We can imagine a variety of paths from that first retail sale to the illegal use against another person. At one end of the spectrum are the cases of "direct sale": Perhaps a pistol is purchased from a gun store, kept a few years for self-defense purposes, and then used in a domestic violence incident. Or an 18-year-old purchases a shotgun from a pawnshop, saws off the barrel to make it concealable, and then uses it to rob a filling station.

More typical are cases in which that first sale by the dealer is just the beginning of a series of transactions. One possibility is that the gun is purchased from the dealer on behalf of another individual (who either cannot pass the background check because of age or criminal record or does not want to have his name on file in connection with a gun. That transaction, known as a straw purchase, is technically illegal but not uncommon. Such transactions seem likely to go directly into criminal use.

The most common pattern is that the firearm is in circulation for years before ending up as evidence in a crime. During that time it may be given as a gift, loaned to a family member or friend, stolen, sold to an acquaintance or at a gun show, or kept in a gang's inventory to be doled out to youthful members when they need protection. In some cases there are unlicensed middlemen involved in this supply chain, those who seek to make a profit by acquiring a number of guns with the intent of reselling them off the books—an activity known as "trafficking."

Available sources of information on the supply chain are incomplete and require a good deal of interpretation. One source has been surveys of prisoners or arrestees, which tell us something about the immediate transactions by which criminals obtain guns. A variation on this approach has been ethnographic research on "the street"—interviews with gang members or others operating in the underground economy about their experience with guns.

Also useful are data generated from attempts to trace firearms confiscated (or otherwise obtained) by law enforcement agencies as part of a criminal investigation. These traces are conducted by the ATF's National Tracing Center, which uses the make, model, and serial number of the firearm to identify it and then trace it through the chain that begins with manufacturer or importer, then distributors, and then retail dealer. That dealer—if the chain of paperwork is not broken—should have a record of sale (the 4473 form) that identifies the original buyer. ATF is also the source of other useful information pertaining to hundreds of firearms-trafficking investigations the agency initiates each year.

One important finding from ATF's trace data is that a large percentage of firearms eventually travel across state lines after first being retailed. The interstate flow is far from random—guns tend to move from states where they are plentiful and easily accessed (because of lack of state and local regulations) to states where they are tightly regulated and scarce. While nationwide about 30% of traced guns were first retailed out of state, that percentage tends to be far higher in states like New York and Massachusetts that have stringent regulations. The so-called Iron Pipeline along the Eastern Seaboard illustrates the point—guns flow from Georgia and South Carolina up to the more tightly regulated states of the Northeast. Similarly, a large percentage of the guns confiscated in Chicago originate in the Deep South.

Systematic trafficking is one part of this story. Evidence from ATF investigation files suggests that traffickers are typically small operators who are not making a living off of moving guns. Instead of a "gun kingpin," the right image is of some guy in Boston with a cousin from South Carolina who occasionally drives north with 5 or 10 guns in his trunk, making both of them a small profit. Larger operations typically involve licensed dealers who exploit their ability to obtain shipments of guns wholesale. It should also be noted that not all the guns that move in from out of state are trafficked—much of this movement may be entirely legal, as when someone moves his household, including his gun collection, from one state to another.

The extent to which dealers are regulated can make a considerable difference in interstate trafficking. For example, when the federal Brady Act was implemented in 1994, it required that dealers conduct a background check before selling a handgun. Some states, including Illinois, already had a requirement of this sort, but for the states of the Deep South the new federal requirements made an immediate difference. One result was to shut down much of the pipeline from those unregulated states into Chicago. Before Brady, one-third of the handguns confiscated in Chicago originated in Mississippi, Alabama, and other loosely regulated states—starting in 1994, that fraction was cut in half, to just 16%.

Regulation also affects local movements of firearms. One example comes from state *de*regulation. Missouri required all handgun buyers to obtain a purchase permit from the local sheriff until 2007. Then the permit requirement was repealed, with the result that private sales were unregulated and sales by dealers subject only to the federal requirement of a background check. There is an abrupt change visible in the trace data—the percentage of traced handguns that had moved directly (within three months) from dealer to criminal use in Missouri jumped from 3% to 9%.

These and other examples suggest that there is a rather direct connection between regulations on legitimate transactions and the supply chain for guns used in crime. That fact does not in itself prove that the dealers are complicit. But ATF investigations demonstrate that some dealers are in fact running criminal enterprises, supplying thousands of guns to gangs and other illicit customers. Others may simply be careless or clueless.

## How Are Illicit Gun Markets Different from Illicit Drug Markets?

The underground market in firearms is much smaller than the market for illicit drugs. One analysis of a neighborhood in Chicago compared illicit drug and gun sales. There were no more than 1,400 gun sales per year, or about one sale per year for every 30 people living in this very high-crime neighborhood. By comparison there were at least 200,000 and perhaps more than 500,000 cocaine sales in this community every year. Thus there were more than 100 cocaine sales for every gun sale. Total revenue in this community for gun sales would be on the order of $500,000, compared to perhaps $10 or $20 million in the market for cocaine. The drug-dealing gangs in this neighborhood did not sell guns because the extra heat from the police was not worth the meager profit to be made.

## How Do American Dealers Supply Gangs in Mexico and Canada?

Regulations in both Mexico and Canada are more stringent than in the United States, and the numbers of firearms in circulation per capita are far lower in those countries. The result is that the United States is a relatively low-cost source of illegal firearms for the rest of North America. Many of the firearms used by criminal gangs in Canada, and by the drug cartels in Mexico, can be traced to US sources, as is also true for crime guns in Jamaica and elsewhere in the Caribbean.

In particular, licensed dealers and gun shows near the US–Mexico border are thought to be an important source of the assault guns that are the weapons of choice in the devastating drug-cartel wars. Overland smugglers for these weapons typically follow the same routes heading south as the illicit drugs that are heading north. As a US ambassador to Mexico said, "Mexico would not be the center of cartel activity or be experiencing this level of violence were the United States not the largest consumer of illicit drugs and the main suppliers of weapons to the cartels."[1]

Actually there is considerable debate about just what fraction of the weapons used in the Mexican drug wars originate in the United States. The north-south smuggling operations are by no means the only source. The pool of weapons used to fight old insurgencies in Central America find their way north through Guatemala, and a surprising number of military-style weapons are diverted from the inventories of the Mexican army and police. Still, if it were possible to close down US sources, the black market prices would increase, which might place some check on the epidemic of Mexican gang violence.

### How Many Guns Are Stolen Each Year?

A good guess is a quarter million. During the six-year period from 2005 to 2010, an annual average of 232,000 firearms were stolen in noncommercial property crimes, primarily residential burglaries. As large as that number is, it has been much larger in the past. Burglary rates have greatly declined in recent decades, and the rate of firearms theft has declined in proportion: The percentage of burglaries in which at least one gun was stolen has remained steady at around 4%.

Most (63%) stolen firearms are handguns, even though the majority of firearms in private hands are long guns. It is interesting to speculate about the difference. Perhaps handguns have greater value when fenced or are stored in more accessible locations.

It should be noted that some gun thefts are not included in these figures, which are based on the National Crime Victimization Survey. The NCVS does not include thefts from commercial outlets or factories.

### How Do Criminals Obtain Their Guns?

Most guns used in crime were obtained from family members or friends or from the informal "secondary" market. It is relatively unusual for an individual to buy a firearm directly from a dealer and use it in crime.

The best source of national data on this topic is the Survey of Inmates in State and Federal Correctional Facilities, conducted from time to time by the US Department of Justice. One might ask why we should trust convicts to tell the truth about their crimes. The reason is that the respondents have nothing to gain by misrepresentation, since they are guaranteed anonymity and because the crime in question has already been adjudicated. (They lost!) Furthermore, the statistical patterns from one survey to the next are quite consistent.

Here are the sources of guns listed in 2004 by inmates who said they used a gun in the crime that put them in prison this time.[2]

41% from friend/family member
32% off the street, from a drug dealer, or from a fence or black market source
12% from gun shop or pawnshop (presumably licensed)

Those are the major sources. The rest are minor: 2% from a gun show or flea market, 2% from the victim, and just 1% in a burglary, as well as 9% from some other source.

Only about half of these inmates indicated that they purchased the gun with cash. A quarter of them said the gun was a gift or that they had "borrowed" it. Just 4% admitted that they had stolen it.

The national inmate surveys are limited to adults age 18 and older. Knowing how and when juvenile delinquents obtain their guns is also of importance. One interesting survey documented the sources of juvenile inmates' first guns. A surprising number mentioned simply finding a gun in a local alley or park. Others mentioned family or friends, who typically wanted them to have a gun for self-protection. The sense from this and other surveys is of youths living in dangerous neighborhoods where guns are in active circulation.

Still, it is easy to exaggerate the ease of obtaining a gun. Most assaults and robberies are not committed with guns, and most people who are arrested for violent crimes do not own a gun. When asked, a high percentage of people say that they would have difficulty in obtaining a gun or could not afford it. In an ethnographic study of the underground market for guns in a high-crime area of Chicago, it was found that some individuals, unable to find a gun on their own, hire informal "brokers" for a fee of $30 to $50; even they sometimes have trouble locating a suitable weapon for sale.

# 6

# HOW AMERICA REGULATES FIREARMS

## Generally Speaking, How Does America Regulate Guns?

Gun regulations have a long history, stretching back to the colonial era. By and large, the laws have been enacted to secure the common defense, to protect individuals from harm, to assist law enforcement officers in maintaining order, and to assert the collective values of the time.

For good or ill, American gun laws reflect the country's system of federalism, which limits the role of the national government in matters of law and order and leaves broad policymaking discretion to the states. A patchwork of laws determines who can own or carry a gun, what kinds of guns and ammunition can be bought and sold, and under what circumstances guns may (or may not) be deployed. Other laws set out the procedures that gun sellers must follow.

Table 6.1 shows the broad categories of firearms laws, together with illustrative examples that exist in one or more states and localities. We provide a more complete summary of federal and state laws later in this chapter.

Federal gun regulations, enacted in earnest beginning in the 1930s, provide a sort of legal "floor," establishing a basic set of public safety measures by which all Americans must abide. Generally speaking, the federal government's role is to license and oversee firearms dealers, regulate sales and transfers

**Table 6.1** Categories of gun regulations

| Target of law | Jurisdiction | | |
|---|---|---|---|
| | *Federal* | *State* | *Local* |
| *Ownership* | Bans on purchases, possession by felons, "mental defectives," youths, other presumably high-risk groups | Handgun owner licensing, concealed weapons training, waiting periods to buy guns, safe-storage requirements | Permit to purchase a rifle or shotgun, requirement to notify police of stolen gun |
| *Firearms* | Ban on machine guns (except those owned pre-1986), ban on armor-piercing ammunition | Bans on assault weapons, high-capacity magazines, "unsafe" handguns | Assault weapons bans |
| *Use* | Ban on carrying guns on airplanes or in federal buildings | Licenses to carry concealed gun, "stand your ground" laws on self-defense, hunting laws, criminal penalties for firearms misuse | Bans on openly carrying firearms, ordinances against publicly firing a gun |
| *Sales* | Licensing and inspections of dealers, record-keeping requirements, required background checks on sales by licensed dealers, reporting of multiple sales, bans on interstate handgun sales to private individuals | Required background checks on private sales, dealer licensing, one-handgun-per-month laws | Zoning ordinances barring gun shows on public property |

across international and state lines, and keep certain categories of people from owning weapons.

States, and sometimes cities, complement and often strengthen the federal laws with measures of their own. State criminal laws make it illegal to use firearms to threaten or harm another person, except in self-defense, and often establish stricter penalties for crimes when the perpetrator uses a gun. State laws also lay out the parameters for the lawful use of weapons, such as carrying a concealed weapon for self-defense. Some states have chosen to augment federal laws by imposing tighter restrictions on the transfer and possession of weapons. Some cities and counties have passed their own firearms ordinances—though states have increasingly denied localities such lawmaking powers.

When passing laws, legislators must take care that they don't run afoul of state and federal constitutional provisions protecting the right to bear arms. Historically, courts have interpreted such provisions in a way that leaves legislatures broad discretion to regulate firearms. While that is still true, federal courts have begun to set limits in recent years. However, it is politics—not the courts—that serve as the greatest brake on gun control.

### What Is the Second Amendment?

The Second Amendment to the Constitution was ratified, along with nine other amendments in the Bill of Rights, in 1791. The Second Amendment reads: "A well regulated Militia, being necessary to the security of a free State, the right of the people to keep and bear Arms, shall not be infringed."

To modern readers the sentence seems awkwardly constructed, helping fuel a vigorous debate among historians, legal scholars, and judges—to say nothing of activists on both sides of the gun control question—about what the amendment was intended to cover. Answering that question has required contemporary legal sleuths to draw inferences from

the evidence at hand, including eighteenth-century state constitutions and other documents known to have influenced the
framers' thinking, the social context and political debates of
the founding period, the meaning of pivotal words, such as
"militia" and "people," and even historical norms of sentence
construction.

Two dominant interpretations—and a third, hybrid interpretation—have vied for dominance. The first holds that the
amendment was designed to protect the right of states to
maintain militias—armed citizens mobilized for common
defense (the militia theory). Another interpretation holds that
the amendment was designed to protect the individual right to
possess a firearm, regardless of militia service (the individual
rights theory). A third, hybrid theory, holds that the Second
Amendment protected an individual (civic) right that was
inextricably bound to a collective (civic) responsibility of bearing arms for the common defense.

In the American system, however, the Supreme Court gets
to decide what the Constitution means, even though as Justice
John Paul Stevens pointed out, the justices were not empan-
eled to be "amateur historians." The Court has considered the
Second Amendment very rarely. The court's first three rulings
(all in the latter decades of the nineteenth century) did not
consider the question of whose rights the Second Amendment
protected—just whether it applied to entities other than
Congress. In 1939, after Congress passed a gangster-era law
barring sawed-off shotguns, the Court was forced to wade
into the thorny question of whether the Second Amendment
protected individual or collective rights. In *U.S. v. Miller*, the
Court found that two suspected bank robbers had no right to
their sawed-off shotgun because such weapons did not bear
"some reasonable relationship to the preservation or efficiency
of a well regulated militia." By inference, the ruling gave rise
to the view that the Second Amendment protected a collective
right rooted in militia service and "gave individuals no protection from ordinary gun control."

For nearly 60 years that understanding prevailed, and no federal appeals court overturned a gun control law on Second Amendment grounds. That changed in 2008, when the Court in *District of Columbia v. Heller* invalidated the capital city's 1976 law that generally banned civilian handgun possession and required lawful firearms in the home to be trigger-locked or disassembled. The case was brought by a young, little-known libertarian lawyer, against the wishes of the mighty National Rifle Association, which feared that pushing the issue would be a lose-lose. If the Court found no individual right to a gun, the ruling would constitute an authoritative repudiation of the NRA's core beliefs, but if the Court sided with gun rights advocates, it would sap the NRA's ability to use the threat of gun confiscation to scare up money and members. The lawyer's gambit paid off. Writing for a five-to-four majority, Justice Antonin Scalia wrote that the Second Amendment indeed protected an individual right to possess a firearm for defensive purposes.

Drawing on early state constitutions, legal commentaries, and ratification debates—as well as the contemporary writings of an ideologically diverse group of law professors and pro-gun lawyer-advocates—Justice Scalia argued that the founders had understood the Second Amendment to enshrine a preexisting right of the people to keep and bear arms for their own personal protection. The District's sweeping ban on functional guns in the home, Justice Scalia ruled, went too far. "The inherent right of self-defense has been central to the Second Amendment right," he argued. "The handgun ban amounts to a prohibition of an entire class of 'arms' that is overwhelmingly chosen by American society for that lawful purpose. The prohibition extends, moreover, to the home, where the need for defense of self, family, and property is most acute." Although he understood that some people thought gun bans would reduce violence, Justice Scalia nevertheless argued that "the enshrinement of constitutional rights necessarily takes certain policy choices off the table."

Two years later, in *McDonald v. City of Chicago*, the Court ruled that in-home handgun bans outside the federal city are similarly unconstitutional. Whereas the Court's nineteenth-century rulings had suggested that the Second Amendment was intended to constrain Congress only, the Court now said that, under the Fourteenth Amendment's due process clause, states and cities likewise must respect the constitutional right to keep and bear arms as understood by the courts. In legal lingo, the protections in the Second Amendment were now "incorporated" via the Fourteenth Amendment, as most of the other amendments had been over the past century.

The *Heller* and *McDonald* rulings were controversial, even among members of the Court. Writing on behalf of the four-justice minority, Justice John Paul Stevens accused the *Heller* majority of relying on a "strained and unpersuasive reading" of the Second Amendment to justify an interpretation of history rejected by most professional historians and, for more than a century, by the Court itself. Embracing the traditional collective-rights perspective, Stevens argued that the Second Amendment had been motivated by "an overriding concern about the potential threat to state sovereignty that a federal standing army would pose, and a desire to protect the States' militias as the means by which to guard against that danger." He took the Court majority to task for having failed to produce any new evidence contradicting this long-settled view.

In his *McDonald* dissent, Justice Stevens took on modern gun rights ideology, which the majority had embraced. Far from guaranteeing liberty, he said, guns have a "fundamentally ambivalent relationship" to it. Indeed, he argued, the experience of other advanced democracies, which have stricter gun laws than the United States, "undercuts the notion that an expansive right to keep and bear arms is intrinsic to ordered liberty." He rejected the notion that owning a handgun "is critical to leading a life of autonomy, dignity, or political equality." Given the toll that firearms take, and the federalist tradition of deferring to state policy experimentation, the Court had no business "meddling" in local elected officials' efforts to safe-guard their communities.

The Court's back-to-back rulings affirming the individual rights view have foreclosed banning handguns in America. In practice, however, even the most fervent gun control proponents had long ago abandoned such aspirations in order to pursue more moderate, mainstream measures.

### What Gun Controls Are Unconstitutional under the Second Amendment—and What Laws Are Presumed to Be Lawful?

Although groundbreaking and precedent setting, the *Heller* and *McDonald* decisions were narrow in scope: They invalidated a tiny handful of unusually strict laws and appeared to leave plenty of room for lawmakers to regulate guns. Yes, the Court said, governments cannot pass blanket bans on handguns in the home, but the right to keep and bear arms is "not unlimited." An indeterminate number of gun laws are "presumptively lawful." Justice Scalia warned that the *Heller* ruling should not "cast doubt on" laws that, for example, bar felons and the mentally ill from possessing guns, ban firearms in "sensitive spaces" such as schools and government buildings, or mandate "conditions and qualifications" on commercial firearm sales. He also suggested that lawmakers might restrict weapons not in "common use" or regulate the carrying of "dangerous or unusual" weapons.

These suggestions notwithstanding, the Court unleashed what Justice Stevens called a "tsunami of legal uncertainty and thus litigation." In the first five years after Heller, state and federal courts issued more than 700 rulings concerning the Second Amendment. These cases involved criminal defendants seeking to challenge the charges against them and law-abiding citizens who believed that long-standing local, state, and federal gun regulations were unconstitutional. While many cases are still making their way through the courts, judges so far have been inclined to defer to existing laws. So, for example, courts have upheld laws barring felons and minors from owning a gun, restrictions on who may carry a concealed weapon, bans on particularly dangerous weapons, and laws requiring licensing of gun owners and registration of firearms.

In the wake of *Heller* and *McDonald*, the most significant victory for gun rights advocates came in late 2012, when a federal appeals court struck down Illinois's ban on the carrying of concealed weapons outside the home. In *Heller* the Supreme Court had left open the possibility that the Second Amendment protected the right to "carry weapons in case of confrontation." The appeals court agreed. But by that time, the finding was almost beside the point—after a decades-long campaign orchestrated by the National Rifle Association, most states had liberalized their concealed-carry laws anyway. Along with the District of Columbia, Illinois was the last holdout.[1] Even if states can't go so far as to *ban* concealed carrying—and the Supreme Court has yet to take up that question—federal courts have consistently ruled that states can regulate the practice by, for example, requiring people to be of a certain age or to show good cause before obtaining a license.

With both *Heller* and *McDonald*, the Supreme Court left lower courts to figure out which gun laws are constitutional. Generally speaking, courts use a two-step process. First they decide whether the challenged law poses a burden on conduct (e.g., gun ownership) covered by the Second Amendment. If so, they next evaluate whether the government had an adequate justification for imposing that burden. That is, do the collective interests protected by the law (for example, public safety) justify the costs to individual interests (e.g., in being free from regulation).[2] As legal scholars Lawrence Rosenthal and Adam Winkler note, "Not all regulations restricting guns burden the right to keep and bear arms, and not all regulations that do burden the right are unconstitutional."

However, neither in *Heller* nor in *McDonald* did the Supreme Court spell out for the lower courts what legal standard to use when evaluating a law's constitutionality. What counts as an adequate justification for the law? In legal parlance the Court did not spell out the "level of scrutiny" that judges should bring to bear in deciding whether the collective interests outweigh those of the individuals burdened by the law. Most courts have settled on a middle-ground strategy, finding that gun laws must be "reasonably related to an important or significant governmental interest." This standard lies between what gun control supporters would like and what gun rights advocates would favor.

As of May 2013, the Supreme Court had turned down requests to hear more than 60 firearms cases, meaning that the lower courts will continue to grapple without higher court guidance for the foreseeable future.

### How Many Gun Laws Are There?

At least since the mid-1960s, the National Rifle Association and other pro-gun advocates routinely claim that there are 20,000 gun laws on the books. In the wake of Sandy Hook, NRA chief Wayne LaPierre claimed that there were 9,000 *federal* gun laws alone. These figures, especially the 20,000 number, are widely repeated in the press.

The earliest known sighting of the 20,000 statistic was at a 1965 US Senate hearing, when US Rep. John Dingell, a long time gun rights advocate and erstwhile NRA board member, offered it as evidence that the United States did not need more gun control. Other gun rights advocates offered the same statistic in another hearing the same year. Nobody knows where the number came from, but it stuck. In 2013, the *Washington Post* found nearly 500 references in media reports—surely a low-ball figure.

In the early 2000s, scholars sought to assess the actual number of gun laws in the United States. After an exhaustive search, they counted perhaps 400—only one-fiftieth the number enshrined in the conventional wisdom. To be fair, however, by then the number of gun laws had been falling as gun rights supporters persuaded state legislatures to ban localities from enacting firearms regulations. The authors estimated that there were perhaps 300 major state laws, and an additional 100 or so left in major cities. (They admitted that they could not count laws in every hamlet, but the NRA's "preemption" campaign was quickly making such research obsolete.)

Of course, how many gun laws America has depends on how we define "a law." Many state laws have multiple sub-parts—do we count each subpart separately? And what do we do with statutes that place marginal limits on generally permissive laws? For example, most states say it's fine to carry a gun openly, just so long as you don't brandish it. Are laws against brandishing weapons to threaten others "gun control laws"?

Incorporating the NRA's own skepticism about the 20,000 figure, the *Washington Post* concluded in 2013 that the number "appears to be an ancient guesstimate that has hardened over the decades into a constantly repeated, never-questioned talking point" that has "been used for almost five decades, without much research or diligence to back it up."

Regardless of the precise figure, America's gun laws do vary greatly from place to place, as described below. Depending on your perspective, this system represents either a triumph of federalism, allowing for America's geographically diverse constituencies to decide the laws that govern them, or a nightmarish landscape dotted with legal snares ready to trap law-abiding gun owners.

### What Are the Key Gun Control Laws?

Federal, state, and in some cases local laws govern the transfer, possession, carrying, and use of firearms. A handful of federal laws going back to 1927 created the legal foundation by which all Americans must abide, but states and sometimes localities remain free to impose stricter regulations so long as they do so within the bounds of the federal constitutions.

As with most laws, gun regulations can change quickly as advocates win over legislatures, courts, and administrative bodies. High-profile shootings and electoral swings especially—both of which have happened frequently in the last decade—can have a dramatic impact on gun laws. As a result, the discussion below is necessarily general, providing a view from 30,000 feet of how America regulates firearms. The NRA's admonition is worth heeding: "This summary is not intended as legal advice or restatement of law....For any particular situation, a licensed local attorney must be consulted for an accurate interpretation. YOU MUST ABIDE [BY] ALL LAWS: STATE, FEDERAL AND LOCAL."

The federal government has been in the gun policy business since 1919, when it enacted a tax on gun sales to help pay for World War I. But the major federal gun laws were passed in three spurts, each driven by an uptick in firearms violence.

The first wave of federal lawmaking came in the era of Prohibition and gangster violence. In 1927, Congress banned shipments of handguns via the US Postal Service. In 1934, the National Firearms Act required registration of machine guns and sawed-off shotguns and taxed their transfer; a proposal to register handguns nationally was dropped before passage. Four years later, the Federal Firearms Act created a national licensing system for gun dealers, manufacturers, and importers and imposed (largely unenforceable) restrictions on interstate transfers. The act barred dealer sales to (and purchases by) individuals known to be felons, fugitives, under indictment, or prohibited by state law from buying guns. This early wave of lawmaking foreshadowed now-familiar dynamics: The battles pitted law enforcement and citizen groups concerned with crime against a focused set of gun owner and manufacturer interests, with legislation coming after the crisis had passed and in watered-down form.

The second wave of federal lawmaking came in 1968, a year so chaotic and painful for the nation that numerous books have been devoted to it. Urban crime had been on the rise, and national gun control proposals had been debated in Congress for five years. But with the back-to-back assassinations of the Reverend Martin Luther King Jr. in April and Senator (and presidential candidate) Robert F. Kennedy in June, Congress acted. The first bill, the Omnibus Crime Control and Safe Streets Act—which the House approved the day after Bobby Kennedy was shot—banned the shipment of handguns to individuals across state lines as well as prohibiting people from buying handguns outside their state of residency.

Three months later, after intensive grassroots campaigning, inside maneuvering, and rhetorical bomb throwing on all sides, Congress passed the Gun Control Act of 1968 (GCA). The foundation for today's most prominent national gun laws, the GCA essentially protects strong-law states from states that prefer to see guns only lightly regulated. Specifically, the law extended the ban on interstate shipments of handguns to include rifles and shotguns and ammunition, created penalties for using a gun while committing a federal crime, and imposed new rules on federally licensed gun dealers. Perhaps most importantly, the Gun Control Act expanded the categories of people to whom sales of guns would be banned (so-called prohibited purchasers, as described below). Fugitives and most felons had been covered under the 1938 law. The 1968 law barred transfers to, and possession by, people who have been "adjudicated as a mental defective" or "committed to a mental institution," as well as people who are unlawful users of, or addicts to, certain drugs. In addition, the law barred licensed dealers from transfering firearms to minors (under 21 for handguns and under 18 for long guns). Although popular accounts often portray the National Rifle Association's fierce opposition to gun laws as a relatively new phenomenon, the group's president at the time called the Gun Control Act an attempt to "foist upon an unsuspecting and aroused public" a law that would "eventually disarm the American public." Meanwhile, the bill's chief sponsor, Senator Thomas Dodd

(D-CT), charged that the NRA's attack on the bill amounted to "blackmail, intimidation and unscrupulous propaganda."

In 1986, under NRA pressure and a conservative resurgence, Congress passed and President Reagan signed the Firearm Owners' Protection Act, which eased some federal laws but also imposed new, stricter regulations. Gun owners were happy with provisions clarifying the definition of what constitutes a dealer "engaged in the business" of firearms sales, allowing dealers to sell at gun shows, limiting inspections of gun dealers to no more than once per year, facilitating purchases across state lines, providing protections to gun owners traveling with their weapons through strict-control states, and prohibiting the federal government from establishing a system of registration for firearms, firearm owners, or firearm transfers. Gun control advocates got a ban on private possession of machine guns, except for those weapons already registered a requirement that federally licensed dealers report multiple firearms sales; and prohibitions on *all* gun sales to illegal immigrants, dishonorably discharged service members, and those who have renounced their US citizenship.[3]

The third wave of lawmaking came in the early 1990s, on the heels of a dramatic increase in gun-related crimes over a seven-year period. As was the case in the 1960s, the laws had been in the hopper for years, awaiting the right political conditions to ease their passage. In 1993, under newly elected Democratic President Bill Clinton, Congress passed the Brady Handgun Violence Prevention Act, named after former presidential spokesman James Brady, who had been gravely wounded in the 1981 assassination attempt on his boss, Ronald Reagan. The former President delivered a critical endorsement of the bill. The Brady law created a way to enforce the prior restrictions on "prohibited purchasers" by requiring federally licensed gun dealers—but not private sellers—to conduct a background check on would-be buyers of handguns. The law originally required a waiting period, but that ended with the implementation of an instant "phone in" background check system in 1998. The background check system was also extended to would-be buyers of rifles and shotguns that year. Also in the 1990s, people with a conviction for misdemeanor domestic violence, or under a restraining order, were added to the list of federally "prohibited purchasers."

With gang violence in urban areas seemingly unremitting, Congress followed the Brady bill with a ban on the future production of so-called assault weapons, as well as feeding devices (magazines) that held more than 10 bullets. The 1994 law banned production of 19 specific guns and their knockoffs, as well as firearms with two or more military-style design characteristics and the capacity to accept a detachable magazine (with the last criterion not applying to shotguns). People who already owned such weapons were allowed to keep them and to transfer them to other legal buyers. Gun rights advocates have argued that the assault-weapons ban failed to reduce gun violence and that its only effect was to flip the House of Representatives to the more gun-friendly Republican Party in that year's elections. We assess these assertions in chapters 7 and 9. Congress declined to renew the ban when it expired in 2004.

Over the past decade, Congress has not fundamentally altered federal gun policy, but there have been several noteworthy changes in the law. After more than a dozen cities sued gun manufacturers and dealers to recover the costs of what they saw as preventable gun violence, Congress in 2005 passed the Protection of Lawful Commerce in Arms Act and the Child Safety Lock Act, which effectively doomed the litigation strategy. The new law gave the industry and its trade associations new protections from liability for harm caused by guns. The law also required that secure-storage or safety devices be distributed with new handguns sold to private individuals. In 2007, after the shooting at Virginia Tech, Congress passed a law, the NICS Improvement Amendments Act of 2007, to incentivize states to enter mental-health and other records into the federal database of people barred from purchasing a gun. (NICS is the commonly used acronym for the National Instant

Criminal Background Check System.) More recently Congress relaxed restrictions on carrying loaded guns in national parks and unloaded weapons in the luggage compartment of Amtrak trains.

Normally, questions of domestic law and order fall to states. The federal government has based its prerogative to control guns on Article 1, Section 8, of the US Constitution, which grants Congress the authority to regulate foreign and interstate commerce. The legal theory is that, because guns are distributed or otherwise flow easily across state lines, firearms sales constitute a national marketplace.

However, in two modern cases, the Supreme Court has invalidated gun control laws on the grounds that Congress exceeded its constitutional authority. In *U.S. v. Lopez* (1995), the Court struck down the Gun Free School Zones Act of 1990, which generally had barred guns within 1,000 feet of school grounds. The case involved a Texas twelfth grader who had been arrested for bringing a handgun to his high school. The Court ruled that Congress had no business meddling in such local matters. As Chief Justice William Rehnquist noted, "There is no indication that [the student] had recently moved in interstate commerce, and there is no requirement that his possession of the firearm have any concrete tie to interstate commerce." In 1996, Congress amended the law to clarify it applied only to guns that had moved in, or affected, interstate or foreign commerce; presumably most firearms fall into one of those categories. Congress left states and school districts the authority to license people, such as guards, to carry guns on school property.

In the second case, *Printz v. United States* (1997), the Court ruled that Congress could not require state or local law enforcement officials to conduct the background checks mandated under the Brady Act. Writing for the five-to-four majority, Justice Scalia argued that the federal mandate to state and local officials violated the principles embedded in the Tenth Amendment to the Constitution giving the states "dual sovereignty" with the federal government. In the end, the ruling had little effect. Most local law enforcement officers were happy to comply voluntarily with the background check system. And the issue became moot in 1998, when the National Instant Background Check System came on line, allowing gun dealers to run the background checks directly through the FBI, rather than having to rely on a state or local law enforcement agency.

Table 6.2 summarizes the major federal actions, as well as the context in which the laws were enacted.

## State Laws

Although the federal government has used its power under the commerce clause to regulate firearms, state and local governments retain primary authority for maintaining law and order, and therefore most gun regulations are state laws and local ordinances. There is no definitive count of such regulations, though one estimate put it at approximately 400 significant laws. The federal Bureau of Alcohol, Tobacco, Firearms, and Explosives, the National Rifle Association, and the Law Center to Prevent Gun Violence do a good job keeping a record of laws in specific states, and we urge you to consult those sources for details.

Below, we briefly review the major categories of state gun laws that apply to the law-abiding population. (We exclude laws governing criminal use of firearms.)

### State Right-to-Bear-Arms Provisions

Nearly all states—44—protect the right to bear arms in their constitutions. Early provisions, such as North Carolina's, linked the exercise of the right to the common defense. In the modern era some states, such as Alaska, have added an explicit protection of individual rights. Other states strike a balance between state power and private rights. For example, the Illinois provision holds, "Subject only to the police power, the right of the individual citizen to keep and bear arms shall not be infringed."

**Table 6.2** Timeline of federal gun policy

| Era | Crime patterns | Federal crime policy innovations |
|---|---|---|
| 1920s | Prohibition-related gang violence Tommy-gun era | 1919 Federal excise tax on handguns (10%) and long guns (11%) 1927 Handgun shipments banned from the US mail |
| 1930s | End of Prohibition in 1933 Declining violence rates | 1934 **National Firearms Act** Requires registration and high transfer tax on fully automatic weapons and other gangster weapons 1938 **Federal Firearms Act** Requires anyone in the business of shipping and selling guns to obtain a federal license and record names of purchasers |
| 1960s | Crime begins steep climb in 1963 with Vietnam era & heroin epidemic Assassinations Urban riots | 1968 **Gun Control Act** Bans mail-order shipments except between federally licensed dealers (FFLs); strengthens licensing and record-keeping requirements Limits purchases to in-state or neighboring-state residents Defines categories of people (felons, adjudicated "mentally defective," etc.) who are banned from possession Bans import of "Saturday night specials" |
| 1970s | Violence rates peak in 1975 (heroin) and again in 1980 (powder cocaine era) | 1972 Bureau of Alcohol, Tobacco & Firearms (ATF) created and located in the US Department of Treasury |
| 1980s | Epidemic of youth violence begins in 1984 with introduction of crack | 1986 **Firearm Owners' Protection Act** Eases restrictions on in-person purchases of firearms by people from out of state Bars private sales to illegal immigrants, dishonorably discharged service members, citizenship renouncers Limits FFL inspections by ATF, and bans the maintenance of some databases on gun transfers Ends manufacture of National Firearms Act–regulated weapons for civilian use |

*(Continued)*

**Table 6.2** (Continued)

| Era | Crime patterns | Federal crime policy innovations |
| --- | --- | --- |
| 1990s | Violence rates peak in early 1990s, begin to subside<br>School rampage shootings | 1993 **Brady Handgun Violence Prevention Act** Requires licensed dealers to perform a background check on each customer before transferring a firearm<br>1994 **Violent Crime Control and Law Enforcement Act.** Ban on manufacture of certain "assault" weapons and large magazines for civilian use<br>1996 **Lautenberg Amendment to the Gun Control Act of 1968** bans possession by those convicted of misdemeanor domestic violence |
| 2000s | Crime and violence continue to decline<br>Virginia Tech shooting | 2004 Assault weapons ban is allowed to expire<br>2005 Congress immunizes firearms industry against civil suits in cases where a gun was used in crime<br>2007 Congress passes the NICS Improvement Amendments Act providing incentives to states to submit records of prohibited purchasers to national background check system |

Only rarely have courts struck down state or local gun control laws based on state constitutional provisions. For example, a federal appeals court held that an Illinois village's 1981 ban on handgun possession did not violate the state (or federal) constitution. The US Supreme Court later invalidated such bans, but on Second Amendment grounds.

## Licensing and Registration of Firearms

Gun control advocates have long argued that we should treat guns like cars: require owners to be licensed and trained, and require the equipment to be registered with a government authority. In opinion polls most Americans agree, but the argument has proved unpersuasive in the political realm.

Only about a dozen states—and a few cities, including the District of Columbia—require a license to own or permit to purchase a handgun. A handful of additional states also require a permit to purchase an assault weapon or other long guns. Only four states and a few cities require handguns to be registered, and several other states require registration of long guns, usually assault weapons as opposed to "old-fashioned" hunting rifles and shotguns.

Gun rights advocates view registration laws as a particular threat on the grounds that governments might use these lists to confiscate guns from law-abiding owners. As a result, Congress and at least nine state legislatures have explicitly prohibited government authorities from assembling or maintaining a registry of privately held guns. In addition, records of successful background checks run through the federal NICS system must be destroyed within 24 hours. As a result of these precautions, the most complete registry of gun owners may be a list that the National Rifle Association has reportedly compiled of millions of current, former, and potential members.

## Laws Regulating Carrying of Guns in Public

People may *openly* carry a firearm in all but a handful of states, and in the majority of states no permit is required to do so. However, the practice is rare, certainly in cities and suburbs. In recent years, open carry has become a form of political protest for gun owners unhappy with national healthcare reform and state and federal proposals to expand background checks for gun sales.

States regulate the carrying of *concealed* guns a bit more tightly, though the trend has been to make it easier for people to pack heat. A very conservative estimate is that 8 million people, or roughly 3% of the adult population, are licensed by a state to carry a gun concealed on their person.[4] As of this writing, every state permits private individuals to carry a concealed weapon (CCW), though the conditions that an individual must meet vary widely. In some states, no firearms training, criminal, or mental health background check or government permit is required to carry a weapon, while in other states, applicants must submit to a background screening, undergo firearms training, and demonstrate a need to carry a gun.

### Assault Weapon Bans

Even after the federal assault weapons ban ended in 2004, five states maintained their own bans. In the wake of the Sandy Hook school shooting in 2012—in which a Bushmaster assault rifle was used to kill 20 first graders and six educators—three of these states (Connecticut, Maryland, and New York) expanded their bans to include more types of assault weapons. Colorado, the site of two of the most infamous mass shootings in American history, did not ban assault rifles but did ban the high-capacity magazines that feed bullets to them.

As chapter 5 notes, gun manufacturers are finding a market for military-style weapons adapted for civilian use—what the gun makers call "modern sporting rifles." As Congress considered reinstituting the federal assault weapons ban, gun rights supporters suggested that such bans would be unconstitutional under the Supreme Court's implied protection of firearms "in common use." Gun rights advocates have challenged Maryland's ban on assault weapons and high-capacity magazines on these grounds.

### Preemption of Local Ordinances

In 1981, the suburban Chicago hamlet of Morton Grove wanted to prohibit a gun store from opening near a school. Unable to find the authority to do so under local zoning laws, the village trustees enacted a ban on the sale and possession of handguns. That move, coming on the heels of the assassination attempt on President Reagan and Chicago's freeze on handguns, sent the National Rifle Association and other gun rights advocates into a fury. When the Seventh Circuit Court of Appeals upheld the ban the following year, the NRA's top lobbyist invoked Pearl Harbor, calling the ruling one that "will live in infamy."

Gun control advocates were uninterested in using, or unable to pursue, a local-ordinance strategy as a springboard for more encompassing gun control laws nationwide. But gun rights advocates saw Morton Grove as a potential threat and fought back immediately with a state-by-state campaign to secure "preemption" laws barring localities from regulating guns.

Around the time of Morton Grove, cities and counties in most states had some freedom to regulate guns. Only two states had comprehensive preemption laws, and five states preempted certain types of gun laws. Today, the situation is reversed: All but two states have some form of preemption, either by law or court ruling. The vast majority of these states prohibit localities from passing what we commonly think of as "gun control" policies—regulations on firearm sales and ownership. In many cases, states have refused to carve out any exceptions, even for traditionally municipal responsibilities like zoning laws.

### Which States Have the Strongest Laws, and Which Have the Weakest?

Relatively strict gun laws are concentrated in a small handful of states, mostly on the east and west coasts. These states include California, New Jersey, Massachusetts, New York, Connecticut, Hawaii, Maryland, and Rhode Island, plus a couple of urbanized Midwestern states, Illinois and Michigan. The states with the least stringent gun laws tend to be in the South and Southwest (Arizona, Kentucky, Louisiana, Oklahoma, and Mississippi) and in the West (Alaska, Idaho, the Dakotas,

Kansas, Montana, Utah, and Wyoming). One "outlier" is Vermont, a northeastern generally liberal state with some of the most gun-friendly laws in the country.

### If I Want to Buy a Gun, What Is the Process?

We assume that you're asking about the process for buying a gun legally. The answer is, it depends on who is selling the gun—a private seller or an official gun dealer—and what state you live in.

If you are buying your gun from a private seller—your brother, or a local guy selling off his private collection at a gun show—in the majority of states the process will mainly involve negotiating a good price. The seller is free to conduct the transaction so long as he doesn't have reason to believe that the law bars you from buying the gun. However, in a minority of states—about one-third—buyers going through private sellers are subject to a background check, which you may already have satisfied. Of the states that regulate private sales, a few require that the buyer first obtain a gun permit, which requires a background check. The rest of the states regulating private sales require a background check at the time the sale is made, at least for handguns. In a couple of states, this requirement applies only to private sales at gun shows.

If you are buying a firearm from a federally licensed dealer—your local gun store or Walmart, for example—you and the dealer are subject to federal law, and the process is more tightly regulated. In these cases, the dealer is required to perform a background check, either through the federal NICS system, operated by the FBI, or in some cases through a state "point of contact" agency.

To start the process—which is typically completed within a few minutes—you will fill out a Form 4473, though in roughly 20 states people who hold a valid state permit to own or carry firearms are exempted from the background check requirement. Those who need to fill out the one-page form will provide their name, address, place of birth, height, weight, gender, birthdate, race and ethnicity, state of residence, country of citizenship, and (if not a citizen) alien/admission number. Each applicant also must answer 13 yes/no questions aimed at determining that he or she is legally allowed to buy a gun. Some of the questions include the following: Are you a felon? Under indictment? A fugitive? Under a restraining order? In the United States illegally? Addicted to drugs? Have you been convicted of misdemeanor domestic violence? How about "adjudicated mentally defective" or committed to a mental institution?

Once you fill out the form, the dealer fills out his part—including information on the type of firearm being sold, the location of the sale, and the number and expiration date of your driver's license or other government-issued identification. The dealer then accesses online or by phone the FBI's National Instant Background Check System (or "point of contact" partner in the state) and provides your basic information. The agent on the other end runs it through the system and usually on the spot returns a verdict: The sale can proceed, must be denied, or needs to be delayed for further checking. In "proceed" cases, the record of the check is destroyed within 24 hours. In cases of denial, the dealer can't sell you the gun (though the NICS agent does not tell him the reason). In cases of delay, the government authority has three business days to render a final decision, after which the sale can go through at the seller's discretion.

Between 1998 and 2013, there were 180 million background checks (most of them for gun sales), leading to more than 2 million denials. The denial rate has been approximately 1.5% in recent years. In chapter 7, we discuss the impact of the national background check system on violent crime, as well as suicide.

### Who Is Barred from Owning a Firearm?

Federal law governs most of the rules on who may own a gun. The feds began lawmaking in this realm in 1938, when the Federal Firearms Act barred federal dealers from knowingly shipping a gun across state lines to a felon, fugitive, anyone under indictment, or anyone barred by state law from possessing the weapon. The classes of "prohibited purchasers" have expanded since then, and the law applies to all gun sales—not merely those involving interstate shipments from dealer to buyer. Under federal law, it is illegal "for any person to sell or otherwise dispose of any firearm or ammunition to any person knowing or having reasonable cause to believe that such person" falls into one of the categories in table 6.3.

Under federal law, licensed dealers are required to subject the would-be buyer to a background check to verify that he is eligible to buy the gun, and private sellers must not sell a gun to anyone who they have reason to believe is a prohibited purchaser.

### Felons

Anyone convicted of a serious crime (punishable by more than a year in prison) is by default barred from buying a gun, even after he has "paid his debt to society." But with the cooperation of Congress—and at the urging of the National Rifle Association—several states have developed procedures that allow felons to have their gun rights restored. A 2011 exposé by the *New York Times* found that in at least 11 states, restoration of gun rights was automatic for nonviolent felons who had served their time, and violent felons could petition for restoration in several states. Examining records from Washington State, the newspaper found that over a six-year period, more than 3,300 felons and domestic-violence convicts had regained their right to own firearms, and about 13% of them had gone on to commit crimes—including murder, assault, and child rape.

Reflecting on the common-sense belief that the law surely bars criminals from buying guns, the *Times* concluded: "This gradual pulling back of what many Americans have unquestioningly assumed was a blanket prohibition has drawn relatively little public notice. Indeed, state law enforcement

**Table 6.3** Prohibited purchasers under federal

| Shorthand | Formal definition |
| --- | --- |
| Felons/suspects | "is under indictment for, or has been convicted in any court of, a crime punishable by imprisonment for a term exceeding one year" |
| Fugitives | "is a fugitive from justice" |
| Drug users | "is an unlawful user of or addicted to any controlled substance" as defined in section 102 of the Controlled Substances Act |
| Mentally ill | "has been adjudicated as a mental defective or has been committed to any mental institution" |
| Undocumented | "is illegally or unlawfully in the United States" |
| Foreigners | "has been admitted to the United States under a nonimmigrant visa," with exceptions for those holding American hunting licenses, foreign representatives, and certain others. |
| Dishonorably discharged | "has been discharged from the Armed Forces under dishonorable conditions" |
| Former citizens | "having been a citizen of the United States, has renounced his citizenship" |
| Batterers | "is subject to a court order that restrains such person from harassing, stalking, or threatening an intimate partner of such person or child of such intimate partner or person, or engaging in other conduct that would place an intimate partner in reasonable fear of bodily injury to the partner or child" (with procedural conditions); or "has been convicted in any court of a misdemeanor crime of domestic violence" |

*Note*: See 18 USC § 922 (d), at http://www.law.cornell.edu/uscode/text/18/922.

agencies have scant information, if any, on which felons are getting their gun rights back, let alone how many have gone on to commit new crimes."

## Age Restrictions

Federal law generally controls gun possession by adults, but when it comes to minors, both the feds and the states weigh in.

Federal law bars licensed dealers from transferring handguns to anyone they believe to be under 21, and it bars private sellers from selling handguns to those under 18. In other words, youths 18 to 20 can buy handguns, but just not from the local Walmart and other licensed dealers. (This distinction becomes important below.) Federal law also bars licensed dealers from selling long guns to those under 18, but the law does not apply to private sellers.

Within those constraints, states are free to make the laws around kids and guns. With respect to handguns, a dozen states bar anyone under 21 from possessing such weapons. With respect to long guns, about half of the states have chosen to fill the federal gap by defining a minimum age (usually 18) for purchasing or possessing these weapons. However, states often make exceptions for kids who are hunting or sport shooting with their parents. As of this writing, the NRA had petitioned the Supreme Court to overturn the long-standing ban on federally licensed dealers' sales of handguns to those under 21.

### Who Enforces Gun Control Laws?

Local police, county sheriffs, and state law enforcement authorities do most of the work, though federal authorities play certain designated roles.

The principal federal agency enforcing gun laws is the Bureau of Alcohol, Tobacco, Firearms, and Explosives (known by its old acronym, ATF). ATF traces its roots to America's earliest years as the agency charged with collecting alcohol taxes. It got jurisdiction over firearms in 1942, an expanded portfolio after enactment of the Gun Control Act in 1968, and independent bureau status within the Treasury Department in 1972. In 2003, the ATF moved to the Justice Department as part of Congress's reorganization of the federal security apparatus following the 9/11 terrorist attacks. With respect to guns, ATF is charged with assisting local and state law enforcement with criminal investigations, including by tracing firearms used in crime to their original seller, licensing and inspecting federal firearms dealers, and making technical judgments about weapons banned from importation.

The other key federal law enforcement agency is the Federal Bureau of Investigation (FBI), which runs the National Instant Background Check System (NICS) and processes mandated background checks on firearms sales going through licensed dealers and in some states through private sellers, as well. The FBI also investigates, and US attorney offices prosecute, federal crimes involving guns.

You will also see federal agencies involved in special joint operations, including Project Safe Neighborhoods, through which the federal government provides resources to local and state law enforcement agencies to combat gang violence. In high-visibility or especially complicated cases—for example, the DC-area sniper shootings in 2002 or the Boston Marathon shooting and bombing in 2013—federal authorities will play a prominent role alongside their state and local counterparts.

### What Are the Challenges of Enforcing Gun Laws?

While gun control advocates seek stricter gun laws, gun rights supporters typically implore the authorities to just "enforce the laws we already have." On occasion the two groups have found common ground and supported programs to do just that, but mostly the two sides talk past each other. Historically, law enforcement agencies have quietly complained that they needed gun control groups to show up and fight for them when they have come under political attack by pro-gun forces. Meanwhile, gun rights advocates have talked out of both sides of their mouths—saying all the right things about the value of enforcement while at the same time actively undermining it.

As the federal agency primarily responsible for enforcing federal gun laws, ATF operates, in the words of gun control advocates, "blindfolded, and with one hand tied behind the back." These constraints come in many forms: Legal restrictions placed on its ability to fulfill its mission efficiently, vulnerability to uneven political support from the White House, the absence of pressure groups willing to offer support, and a lack of money to perform its tasks.

Behind these problems lie the National Rifle Association and other pro-gun interests, which have devoted decades to vilifying and attempting to handicap the ATF. Most accounts trace the animosity to 1971, shortly after ATF had acquired expanded responsibilities under the Gun Control Act. That year, ATF agents raided the home of a suburban Washington NRA member and gun collector, but when the man rushed out in response to his wife's screams, an agent shot him in the head. The event became a cause célèbre and helped to transform the NRA into the hard-line organization that we recognize today.

In the late 1970s and early 1980s, gun rights groups stepped up their attacks. Pressure from gun rights groups prevented ATF from collecting firearms turned in through a private gun buy-back program, hastened the retirement of the agency's director, produced withering congressional oversight hearings purporting to show widespread malfeasance within ATF, and persuaded Congress to hit the agency with a budget cut.

In a famous incident in 1995, the NRA sent a mass fundraising mailing that called federal agents "jack-booted government thugs" and accused federal agents of wearing "Nazi bucket helmets and black storm trooper uniforms." The letter drew a firestorm of criticism several weeks later, when antigovernment militia sympathizers blew up the Oklahoma City federal building, killing 168 people. The NRA's letter led lifetime member and former president George H. W. Bush to publicly resign from the group.

Distrust of federal firearms enforcement agencies has led to enactment of several important laws limiting these agencies' ability to use data to investigate gun trafficking and other crimes. As noted above, Congress has barred the federal government from saving records of successful background checks, leading critics to charge that it's virtually impossible to detect patterns in "straw purchasing," in which a legal buyer goes from store to store buying up weapons for confederates who are barred from owning them.

Congress also has placed restrictions on the use of data gathered by ATF when it traces guns used in crime. Often when local, state, or federal authorities recover a firearm at a crime scene, they ask the ATF to run a trace, which consists of the agent's calling the manufacturer with the serial number and asking for the name of the dealer to whom the gun was first shipped. If that dealer is still in business, ATF then calls the dealer and requests that he search through sales records to identify the initial buyer. If the dealer is out of business, however, the ATF has the records—millions of them arrive each year—and must search them manually. Since 1979, Congress has barred ATF from computerizing these records.

In 2004 Congress passed the so-called Tiahrt Amendments, sponsored by then-representative Todd Tiahrt, Republican of Kansas. These amendments barred ATF from disclosing to the public any data, either detailed or aggregated, on its traces of crime guns. The amendments also restricted law enforcement officers' access only to trace data pertaining to a specific investigation or prosecution within their own jurisdiction. Under pressure from mayors and police chiefs Congress has since loosened these restrictions, for example by allowing ATF to issue aggregate gun-trace reports and allowing local and state police broader access to the data.

Also in 2004, Congress barred the ATF from requiring federally licensed firearms dealers to keep an inventory of their weapons—standard practice in virtually every business. Such inventories would help agents identify "missing" guns that may have been sold illegally. Congress also barred trace data from being used as evidence in civil proceedings.

In congressional hearings after the Sandy Hook school shootings, gun rights advocates—including senators—were openly critical of the US Department of Justice for not vigorously prosecuting felons who had attempted to illegally purchase a weapon. Federal authorities argued that they had to focus their limited resources on the bad guys who had already committed a crime with their gun, not those whom the system had stopped from obtaining one.

### How Do US Laws Compare to Those in Other Countries?

Most nations—certainly advanced industrialized democracies—have gun laws considerably stricter than those in the United States. The US system starts with the premise that citizens should be allowed to own guns unless there is a compelling reason to bar them from doing so, while other nations begin with the opposite premise—severely restrict or ban ownership unless there is good reason to allow it.

A comprehensive comparative analysis of gun laws in the world's nearly 200 nations is well beyond what we have room for here. But table 6.4 offers a broad overview of national gun laws in other Anglo nations, in nations often discussed in gun policy debates, and in a sample of the world's economic powerhouses. Note that the laws are complicated, and the table provides a simplified view.

Of course, the table merely provides a snapshot of the laws. Enforcement of national gun laws inevitably will vary, as will the degree to which citizens obey them. While the United States has a far higher gun violence rate than many peer nations that regulate firearms more strictly, the rate in the United States is lower, often significantly, than in developing countries with tougher gun laws, such as the Central American nations.

### Why Aren't Guns Treated Like Other Consumer Products—Cars, Toys, Even Cigarettes?

Politics mostly.

Gun control advocates have argued for close to 40 years that the government should treat firearms like any other

**Table 6.4** Gun regulation around the globe: A sampler

| | Firearms banned for civilian ownership? | Owner license required for nonprohibited guns? | Requirements for gun owner license? | Must demonstrate need to own? |
|---|---|---|---|---|
| Australia | Automatic, semiautomatic firearms, certain shotguns, short-barreled handguns | Yes | Background check; character reference in some circumstances; training course | Yes; hunting, sports, collecting, occupational needs constitute valid reasons; personal protection does not. |
| Brazil | Automatic firearms | Yes | Background check; training course | Yes; protection is valid reason. |
| Canada | Automatic firearms (pre 1978), short-barreled handguns, certain modified firearms | Yes | Background check, character reference, training course, notification of spouse/partner or next of kin | No, except in case of restricted weapons |
| China | All firearms, with very limited exceptions | Private ownership banned | Private ownership banned | Private ownership banned |
| Germany | Automatic weapons | Yes | Background check, training course | Yes; hunting, sports, collecting, protection are valid reasons. |
| Israel | n/a | Yes | Background check; must reapply and requalify every three years | Yes; hunting, sports, self-protection are valid reasons. |

(*Continued*)

**Table 6.4** (Continued)

| | Firearms banned for civilian ownership? | Owner license required for nonprohibited guns? | Requirements for gun owner license? | Must demonstrate need to own? |
|---|---|---|---|---|
| Japan | Automatic and semiautomatic weapons, handguns except for accomplished sports shooters | Yes | Background check, training | Yes; hunting, sports (with permission) constitute valid reasons. |
| New Zealand | No | Yes, with special licenses required for automatic and assault weapons | Background check; character reference; training course, notification of spouse/partner or next of kin | Yes, for handguns; self-defense not a valid reason. |
| Switzerland | Automatic weapons | Yes, dealer sales only; primarily for handguns | Background check; license limits number of purchases; training for concealed-carry license only. | Yes; hunting, sports, collecting, self-defense constitute valid reasons. |
| United Kingdom | Handguns, semiautomatic assault weapons, automatic weapons | Yes | Background check, character reference | Yes; hunting, sports, collecting constitute valid reasons. |
| United States | Machine guns, sawed-off long guns | No, except in a few states | No national license, but background check required for sales by dealers and by private sellers in some states | No |

*Source:* GunPolicy.org; http://www.loc.gov/law/help/firearms-control/switzerland.php.

potentially dangerous consumer product. If we require drivers to get training and a government-issued license, and to register their cars with a government agency, why not impose similar rules on gun owners? If we regulate toy guns, why not real guns? If we can heavily tax cigarettes and hold tobacco companies responsible for the harm their products cause, why can't we do the same for guns and gun manufacturers? In some cases advocates made headway with these arguments, only to be stopped in their tracks by lawmakers and the gun lobby.

## Cars

Let's start with the automobile analogy. It is apt as far as it goes: Both cars and guns are commonplace and have productive uses, but both can cause harm in untrained, reckless, or criminal hands. Extending registration and licensing to firearms and their users was a top priority of gun control advocates in the 1970s through the 1990s but met with furious resistance from gun rights groups. They argued, successfully, that if the government had a central record of gun owners and firearms, it would provide a road map for confiscation and hasten the demise of a free American society.

Gun control advocates never came close to seeing national licensing of gun owners or registration of everyday firearms. (In 1934, the National Firearms Act required owners to register their existing stocks of machine guns.) Indeed, since 1979 ATF's appropriations legislation has barred the agency from maintaining or centralizing gun purchase records, and the 1986 Firearm Owners' Protection Act specifically prohibits a national gun registry. Licensing and registration, particularly of assault weapons, exists in a handful of states. However, not even the most "antigun" jurisdictions, including New York City, have used these registries to confiscate firearms.[5] The one narrow exception is California, where authorities have begun a new program to retrieve guns from owners who committed a felony or otherwise became disqualified from owning their gun after they bought it.

As licensing and registration have proved politically radioactive, gun control advocates have sought to translate other lessons from the experience of automobile safety, considered a major success story in using public health methods to solve public problems. The public health perspective—developed by physician-researchers, epidemiologists, and some economists—maintains that people will inevitably behave carelessly, so we might be better off finding ways to prevent or mitigate the harm they cause by altering their environment and "idiot-proofing" (our words) the products they use.

Consider product design. Until the 1950s, society treated deaths and injuries in car crashes as the inevitable result of reckless driving—"Cars don't kill people, people kill people." However, in that decade physician-researchers began making the case that many lives could be saved if cars were better designed, an argument developed famously a decade later by the consumer advocate Ralph Nader in his groundbreaking exposé *Unsafe at Any Speed* (1965). In the 1980s, physicians and public health experts adopted those lessons to guns. If seat belts could save lives, what about safety mechanisms that prevent a gun from firing if a bullet is unknowingly left in the chamber? If we have child-safety seats, why not childproof guns? Similar analogies extend to the driving (or gun-owning) environment. If speed limits could reduce deaths, what about laws mandating safe storage of guns in the home?

Advocates have made some headway with such proposals. For example, at least eight states regulate handgun design to keep cheaply made and unreliable "junk guns" out of the marketplace; nearly a dozen states and the federal government require dealers to sell locking devices on handguns intended for private use; and more than half of states have laws imposing criminal liability on gun owners who leave their firearms accessible to children. And companies are working on "smart gun" technology that would prevent anyone other than an authorized user from firing the weapon.

After the Sandy Hook school shooting, media commentators, and even some lawyers, began to discuss whether gun owners, like car owners, should have to buy liability insurance. Although the proposal sounds intriguing to many, there are problems with the gun-car parallel. Drivers only need insurance if they drive their car off their property; many guns remain in the home—and accidental misuse may be covered by some homeowner policies in any event. Insurance also doesn't cover criminal activity, and it's unclear whether insurers would want to provide coverage for noncriminal incidents outside the home. That said, the proposal remains to be fully explored.

## Toys

A recent dispatch from the liberal advocacy group the Children's Defense Fund asked a question along these lines: If your kindergartner visits a friend's house, which of these do you want to be sure has been regulated for safety: the teddy bear, the plastic gun, or the real handgun in the father's nightstand? The question is intended to be rhetorical, dramatizing a little-known law that prohibits the nation's product safety watchdog from regulating firearms and ammunition.

The story line by now is familiar. In the 1970s, gun control advocates sought stricter controls on handguns, which were wreaking havoc in big cities. Getting nowhere in Congress, these advocates turned to the newly formed Consumer Product Safety Commission, which is charged with devising and enforcing safety standards for thousands of commonly used items, such as paint, lawnmowers, pajamas, household chemicals, and, yes, teddy bears and toy guns. When Congress created the commission in 1972, Rep. John Dingell (D-MI), an NRA board member, slipped into the legislation a provision barring the new agency from regulating guns; the commission interpreted that prohibition to extend to ammunition.

However, in 1974 a group of Chicago gun control advocates found a loophole—the commission was also charged with enforcing a separate law, the Hazardous Substances Act, and that legislation made no mention of bullets. Thus began the group's "Ban the Bullets" campaign. After the commission balked at the petition, a federal court ordered it to hold hearings, and gun rights supporters mobilized en masse. When the commission indicated that it intended to promulgate rules on ammunition, more than 37,000 letters poured in—all but about 100 of which opposed the move. Congress quickly ended the matter by excluding ammunition from the commission's jurisdiction.

In 2000, the Massachusetts attorney general made headlines by using the commonwealth's consumer protection law to promulgate regulations, still in effect, barring sales of cheaply made handguns (so-called Saturday night specials) and requiring new handguns sold in the state to include tamperproof serial numbers, childproof triggers, and safety devices.

Today advocates are trying another consumer protection approach. Legislation is pending in Congress to spur the development of personalized handguns (those that only an authorized user can fire) and to authorize the Consumer Product Safety Commission to develop a deadline by which all new handguns must have this technology.

## Cigarettes

Seeing strong parallels between harm caused by cigarettes and harm caused by firearms, gun control advocates have long looked to the antismoking movement for strategies. While efforts by state regulators and private advocacy groups have dramatically changed laws and social norms around smoking in just a few decades, gun control advocates have enjoyed far less success.

Consider some of the parallel strategies.

*Taxation.* A principle long enshrined in both law and economic theory holds that it's socially desirable to tax products and practices that impose costs on society, what economists call "negative externalities." Lawmakers also impose "sin taxes" to discourage private behavior that society deems morally objectionable.

The individual dangers and social costs of smoking having been long established, antitobacco advocates have secured significant increases in cigarette excise taxes imposed by many cities and states, as well as by the federal government. The federal government has taxed firearms since 1919, at a level that currently stands at 10% of the manufacturer's price for handguns and 11% for long guns. But lawmakers and gun control advocates have not until very recently embraced taxation as a strategy.[6] Chicago imposed a new $25 gun tax in 2013, and lawmakers in several states have introduced measures to tax guns, ammunition, or both. The intent is to use the new revenue to cover the costs of gun violence prevention programs.

*Place-based restrictions.* Thirty years ago, it was common to find people smoking in offices, restaurants, even on airplanes. Today, smoking is banned in virtually every enclosed public space. With respect to firearms, the trend has gone in the other direction, as concealed-carry laws have been liberalized in many states. Gun control advocates have had to play defense as gun rights groups have secured laws and court rulings allowing guns in bars (four states and counting) and limiting or removing the discretion of public colleges and universities to ban weapons on their grounds (six states and counting).[7] In 2010, President Obama signed legislation permitting loaded guns in national parks.

*Litigation.* Antismoking advocates, including state attorneys general, have enjoyed some of their biggest successes in the courtroom. In the 1990s, states sued Big Tobacco for deceptive and fraudulent marketing, targeting children in their campaigns, and hiding the harm caused by their products; these lawsuits resulted in a series of settlements totaling nearly $250 billion and the release of voluminous evidence documenting underhanded industry practices. The federal government also successfully sued the tobacco companies for conspiracy to conceal the health risks of smoking and to market to kids.

In the 1990s and early 2000s, cities, advocacy groups, and gun violence victims pursued a similar litigation strategy against gun manufacturers and dealers. In some of these cases, the plaintiffs sued firearms manufacturers for negligently marketing their products in a way that they knew, or should have known, would be especially attractive to criminals. Gun manufacturers were also sued for failing to design guns with features to prevent accidental shootings. In yet other cases, gun dealers were sued for flooding the market with firearms in violation of "public nuisance" laws and for selling their wares to suspicious buyers in violation of laws against negligent distribution. New York City famously sued out-of-state gun dealers for providing guns that ended up in the "Iron Pipeline," the colloquial name for the I-95 highway corridor along which guns are trafficked from dealers in the South to criminal enterprises in the North. (Laying the groundwork for these cases, police sting operations had caught dealers selling to "customers" who were sending strong signals that they were buying the gun illegally.)

In all these lawsuits, the claim was *not* that gun makers and dealers should be held to account because their products were designed to kill—and often do. Rather, the legal theory was that manufacturers and dealers should be held liable (and thus forced to pay up) when they could have foreseen the misuse of their products *and* taken reasonable care to prevent it. The goal was to compensate those bearing the costs of gun violence—either individuals or governments—and to change corporate conduct so as to reduce future harm.

Gun industry representatives and pro-gun groups vigorously fought these lawsuits, both in court and through the legislative process. They argued that whatever happens down the line with a gun, the industry is "remote" from the crime, and its hands therefore are clean. They also argued that cities are not entitled to recover the costs of gun violence from private entities. Legalese aside, gun industry representatives saw the lawsuits as nothing but an abuse of the legal system— a sneaky way of securing public policy goals that served no purpose except to bankrupt lawful businesses.

Whatever the particulars of the legal claim, these cases did not deliver the victories for which cities, victims, and gun control advocates had hoped. Courts dismissed most cases outright, and those that succeeded initially were almost universally overturned on appeal.

In cases brought against out-of-state sellers, New York City was able to secure settlement agreements aimed at curbing gun trafficking. But at the national level, the big breakthrough settlement—the proverbial "game changer"—fell apart. The story will sound familiar by now. Manufacturer Smith & Wesson reached an agreement with the Clinton administration and various cities to take steps to curb careless distribution and sales, but the company had to abandon the pact after a crippling boycott and the departure of the company's CEO.

By 2005, 33 states had enacted laws barring antigun litigation, and that year the federal government sealed the deal nationally by enacting the Protection of Lawful Commerce in Arms Act, which barred future lawsuits against dealers and manufacturers except when they had negligently or knowingly violated firearms laws. The law allowed suits over firearm defects, but only when the gun had been "used as intended or in a reasonably foreseeable manner" and not in crime. The so-called immunity law also required the dismissal of pending cases. In anticipation of signing the bill, President George W. Bush said it would "further our efforts to stem frivolous lawsuits, which cause a logjam in America's courts, harm America's small businesses, and benefit a handful of lawyers at the expense of victims and consumers." With passage of the

NRA-backed law, individuals and localities especially affected by gun violence largely stopped turning to the courts for help.

To answer the question we posed—why aren't guns treated like any other consumer product?—the answer is mostly rooted in politics. No other consumer product has been championed by a lobby as politically powerful *at the grassroots* as the gun rights lobby. To be sure, business is powerful: Automakers, tobacco companies, and other manufacturing interests are often able to get their way in Washington and state capitals. But these interests don't have the same passionate voter base that the gun lobby does, a base that keeps lawmakers in a state of electoral vigilance. What's more, many Americans associate guns with deeply personal and democratic values to a degree not enjoyed by cars, toys, and cigarettes. When values and their attendant emotions are at stake, policy change based on dry cost-benefit calculations or technocratic approaches becomes difficult for lawmakers to entertain. Finally, of course, there is the Constitution. Since 2008, the Second Amendment has been interpreted to protect ownership of a gun for self-protection; there is no right to cars, cigarettes, or toys.

### Do Stand-Your-Ground Laws Reduce Violence—or Increase It?

Self-defense is a time-honored protection against legal liability, but its boundaries are constantly changing. Either through statute or case law, some US states have imposed a duty to retreat before using deadly force in self-defense. The Castle Doctrine (a set of principles incorporated in the law in most states) has provided an exception to this duty for people attacked in their homes. (The term refers to the seventeenth-century English legal precept that "a man's home is his castle.") And since 2005, 23 states have adopted stand-your-ground laws that formally extend the Castle Doctrine to public places, conferring the right to use deadly force when someone reasonably fears serious injury at the hands of another. Such a person may be entitled to immunity from criminal prosecution and civil liability. In effect, these laws confer police powers on private citizens, without requiring the kind of training and account-ability that police have.

Florida was the first state to pass a stand-your-ground law, and a national controversy erupted after teenager Trayvon Martin was shot dead by George Zimmerman on the night of February 26, 2012, in Sanford, a small city in central Florida. Martin, an unarmed 17-year-old high school student, was walking home from the store in a gated community when he was tracked down and, after an altercation, shot to death by Zimmerman, who was acting as a volunteer neighborhood watchman. The local police initially released Zimmerman, but after a broad public outcry, he was charged and tried for Martin's death. On July 13, 2013, a six-person jury acquitted Zimmerman of second-degree murder and of manslaugh-ter. Though he did not invoke the stand-your-ground law in response to the criminal charges, the trial focused on possible interactions between Zimmerman and Martin on the night of the events, and the judge's instructions to the jury echoed the statute's language: "If George Zimmerman was not engaged in an unlawful activity, and was attacked in any place where he had a right to be, he had no duty to retreat and had the right to stand his ground and meet force with force, including deadly force if he reasonably believed that it was necessary to do so to prevent death or great bodily harm to himself or another."

It is interesting to speculate about what would have trans-pired if Trayvon Martin had killed Zimmerman. In that sce-nario, Martin might well have invoked the stand-your-ground law on the basis that he was not engaged in an unlawful activ-ity, was attacked by Zimmerman in a place where he had a right to be, and reasonably believed that deadly force was necessary to defend himself. That counterfactual illustrates an important point, that stand-your-ground laws—dubbed "Shoot First" by critics—make it easier to get away with what would heretofore have been considered criminal homicide. Because legal presumptions favor defendants, the prosecution has the burden of disproving the survivor's story, a hard thing to do if the defendant has killed the only witness.

The National Rifle Association promotes and defends concealed-carry and stand-your-ground laws, using arguments that resonate with many Americans worried that police cannot defend them. Proponents argue that stand your ground coupled with laws allowing people to carry concealed guns make criminals think twice about attempting a carjacking or a rape—or even a bar fight—because they know that intended victims enjoy the legal right to shoot them. However, the best empirical work suggests otherwise. Two recent studies by economists at Texas A&M and at Georgia State University conclude that stand-your-ground laws do not result in a reduction in rates of assault, robbery, or rape—and have the costly effect of increasing homicide rates.

In evaluating these costs, it is impossible to ignore the interaction between stand-your-ground laws and the prevalence of guns. Florida, for example, has issued more than one million concealed-carry permits, with issuances tripling since stand your ground passed. Proponents might celebrate this as akin to a well-armed civilian police force. But police are required to have training in handling weapons and dealing with threats, and they are subject to internal rules as well as legal restraints whenever they discharge a weapon. As Miami's former chief of police explains: "Trying to control shootings by members of a well-trained and disciplined police department is a daunting enough task. Laws like 'stand your ground' give citizens unfettered power and discretion with no accountability. It is a recipe for disaster."

The *Tampa Bay Times* documented nearly 200 cases in which defendants asserted stand–your-ground claims. That defense worked to get cases dismissed 70% of the time and is now used in hundreds of cases per year. In nearly a third of the cases, explains the *Times*, "defendants initiated the fight, shot an unarmed person or pursued their victim—and still went free." Judges appear uncertain about the boundaries of the doctrine, and outcomes in courts are highly inconsistent. This gives defense attorneys a strong incentive to invoke stand-your-ground claims in most violent crime cases. The extra procedural protections are a burden on the prosecution.

In short, stand-your-ground laws encourage the use of deadly force. These laws open the door to a more dangerous world where everyone feels pressure to carry a gun—and if he feels threatened, shoot first and tell his story later.

# 7

# EFFECTIVENESS OF
# FIREARMS POLICY

*With 200 to 300 Million Guns in Civilian Hands, Is There Any Point in Regulating Firearms?*

Yes. The evidence suggests that certain regulations have been effective in reducing gun use in crime. And even in the United States, guns are not so readily available as some commentators have claimed.

While there are enough firearms in circulation for every adult to have one, only 25% of adults actually do own firearms. Most violent crime is committed not with guns, but rather with knives, clubs, and bare fists; even for robbery, a crime where a gun is a very useful tool, the perpetrators are more likely to use a less intimidating weapon. One explanation: Most criminals are not in possession of a firearm.

Those who argue that offenders will do whatever is necessary to obtain their guns may have in mind some hard-core group of violent gang members or "professionals." But even if such people are successful in obtaining the firearms they want, that does not necessarily extend to the "amateurs"—the much larger group of people who get into fights, abuse their intimate partners, steal autos, sell drugs, or otherwise are involved in the underground economy.

As we have seen, most criminals who do become armed obtain their guns from friends, family members, or street sources, rather than from gun dealers. These informal trans-actions are likely easier to arrange in Mississippi, where 60% of households have at least one gun, than in Massachusetts, where just 13% are owners. Various studies have found a close statistical link between the prevalence of gun ownership and illegal use of guns. For example, across the 200 largest urban counties, gun carrying by teenage males is highly correlated with the prevalence of gun ownership, as is the percentage of robberies committed with a gun. The old bumper sticker says, "When guns are outlawed, only outlaws will have guns." Perhaps a more accurate statement is "When guns are scarce, outlaws will use less lethal weapons."

Other evidence indicates a close link between the preva-lence of gun ownership and the use of firearms in attempted suicides. In fact, the percentage of suicides committed with a gun is highly correlated with the percentage of gun-owning households—so highly that the weapon mix in suicide serves as an accurate proxy for the prevalence of guns in the popula-tion. Thus the weapon selected to attempt suicide appears to be greatly influenced by what is readily at hand. A firearm in the home becomes a risk to residents who may (at least occa-sionally) consider suicide. And when a firearm is used rather than razor blades or pills, the chance of "success" is greatly elevated. (Chapter 3 develops this point more fully.)

Given that availability influences weapon choice in crime and suicide, regulations that make it more difficult for violence-prone people to obtain firearms will curtail misuse and save lives. But what sorts of regulations are effective in reducing availability to dangerous people? Availability is closely linked to the local prevalence of gun ownership, sug-gesting that regulations that reduce the overall prevalence of gun ownership will reduce gun violence. In the United States that approach has been used selectively, usually for particular types of guns (machine guns, assault weapons, and in a few jurisdictions, handguns). But other regulatory strategies that do not attempt to reduce the number of guns in circulation have promise as well and have been widely applied in federal law and local practice.

One strategy is to deter gun use in crime by increasing the likelihood or severity of punishment. The list of possibilities here includes criminalizing gun possession by ex-cons, patrolling against illegal carrying, imposing enhanced sentences for gun use in crime, and using ballistic evidence to solve gun crimes. The goal in all these cases is to make guns a liability to the criminal so that he will choose to desist from crime, or at least use some other type of weapon. Note that in this approach the firearms regulations are a complement to effective law enforcement. For example, legal restrictions on carrying concealed weapons facilitate police efforts to prevent gang members from carrying guns in public. And solving gun crimes through ballistics investigations is greatly facilitated if regulations require that records be kept of firearm transactions and owners be licensed.

A second broad strategy is what might be called "partial prohibition"—banning gun possession by people who are identified as high risk (teenagers, ex-cons, those with severe mental illness). For the most part, partial prohibitions have been enforced by regulating transactions, rather than by attempting to confiscate firearms. Much of what is generally known as "gun control" focuses on transactions, including dealer licensing, restrictions on gun shipments, a background check requirement for firearms transactions, and so forth.

Regulations and laws are never 100% effective. The question is whether they are effective enough to justify the cost. It seems that in the gun control arena everyone has an opinion about what works, but scientific evidence is often lacking. This chapter summarizes some of the relevant research. What we would like ideally is direct evidence that the adoption of a new law or regulation caused a change in the rate of homicide or suicide—or not. Unfortunately that sort of direct evidence is not always available or is hotly contested.

## *Did the Federal Assault Weapons Ban Reduce Gun Violence? What about the 1934 Law on Machine Guns?*

The federal assault weapons ban was implemented in 1994 and ended in 2004, when Congress allowed it to expire. There is no compelling evidence that it saved lives. A more stringent or longer-lasting ban might well have been more effective.

The law banned the introduction of new assault weapons into commerce, and also banned new large-capacity magazines that could accommodate more than 10 rounds of ammunition. The assault weapons ban was directed at semiautomatic firearms that adopt design features from infantry weapons that are useless in traditional civilian environments. Such firearms are in fact rarely used in routine criminal violence. The ban on large-capacity magazines (LCMs) had greater potential to make a real difference; such magazines, which hold 30, 50, or even 100 rounds of ammunition, can be used with a wide variety of semiautomatic firearms (not just "assault" weapons) and allow the shooter to fire many times without pausing to reload. That is a real advantage to rampage shooters bent on killing as many people as possible. There were 12 incidents between 2007 and 2012 with eight or more casualties where the shooter used a large-capacity magazine—including the infamous massacres at Virginia Tech, Tucson, Aurora, and Newtown.

The details of the 1994 ban undercut its effectiveness. Assault weapons and LCMs already manufactured were "grandfathered," so they could continue to be bought and sold. There were something like 25 million LCMs and additional millions available for legal import from Europe. Eventually the ban on newly produced LCMs would have reduced their availability, but 10 years was not enough to dry up the available supply. We can hope to learn more in the future from the experience of the handful of states that currently ban assault weapons and LCMs.

It is interesting to compare the 1994 assault weapons ban with another federal initiative from 60 years earlier, the

National Firearms Act. As explained in the previous chapter, the NFA was intended to end the use of the gangster weapons that became notorious during the Roaring Twenties. But rather than an outright ban on Thompson submachine guns and the like, it required that owners register them with the federal government. The NFA also intended to shut down the secondhand market in these weapons by imposing a $200 tax on any transaction, an amount that was confiscatory at the time of the sale. Unfortunately there are no good statistics on the use of fully automatic weapons prior to the NFA, and hence it's impossible to determine whether the NFA suppressed criminal use. Currently there are about 500,000 fully automatic weapons registered under the NFA, so they are definitely available to collectors and shooting ranges and the like. But they are very rarely used in crime these days. Of the crime guns submitted for tracing by law-enforcement agencies, only 3 in 1,000 were machine guns. Thus a type of weapon that would likely appeal to modern-day gangsters, as it did to Al Capone, has been for the most part kept out of criminal hands by federal regulation.

### What Do the Handgun Bans in Chicago and Washington, DC, Teach Us about the Effectiveness of Gun Control?

These cities play a distinctive role in the history of gun control. They were the only large cities to attempt to ban handgun acquisition in modern times—Washington, DC, in 1976, and Chicago in 1982. And their bans became the basis for the two recent rulings of the US Supreme Court on the Second Amendment, having the effect of establishing a right of the public to keep a handgun in the home for self-defense (*District of Columbia v. Heller* in 2008) and extending that ruling to prohibit state and local handgun bans (*McDonald v. City of Chicago* in 2010). But the fact that the bans in both cities were ultimately ruled unconstitutional does not answer the interesting question of whether they were effective when in force.

Evaluating these bans requires a comparison between observed gun violence while they were in effect with an estimate of the volume of gun violence that *would have* occurred in the counterfactual condition of no ban. What we actually observe in Washington is an initial drop in gun violence in the late 1970s followed by a devastating increase during the late 1980s, when the city was dubbed the nation's "murder capital." Thankfully that violent epidemic, associated with the introduction of crack cocaine to the city, has long since passed by, and murder rates are relatively low now. A similar epidemic occurred in Chicago, and for that matter in every large city in the nation. Estimating the counterfactual is very difficult in such volatile circumstances. Could lethal violence rates during the crack epidemic have climbed still higher in Chicago and Washington in the absence of the handgun bans? Perhaps, but it is impossible to say with any confidence. All too evident is that dangerous gang members and drug dealers have been able to arm themselves despite the bans.

Further doubts about the bans' efficacy are raised by the fact that the general prevalence of gun ownership in these cities appears to have been little affected by the bans. Tracking our preferred proxy for gun ownership rates (the percentage of suicides with guns), we see no evidence of an unusual decline following the implementation of either ban. Our tentative conclusion is that the bans were largely ineffective, not only in reducing gun use by criminals, but also in reducing handgun ownership by ordinary people.

One reasonable explanation is that these cities are not islands. Chicago residents could purchase handguns legally at any number of gun shops located just outside the city limit, and while it was technically illegal for them to then bring the guns back to their homes, that restriction was tough to enforce. DC residents also live close to gun shops and gun shows located in the Virginia and Maryland suburbs.

The apparent failures of these local bans tells us very little about what would happen in a jurisdiction that could better enforce an imposed ban. For evidence on that score we might turn to the experience of Great Britain, which had stringent regulations of handguns in place and then banned them outright in 1998 following the massacre of schoolchildren in Dunblane, Scotland. Needless to say, Great Britain *is* an island. Since the ban went into effect, the prevalence of gun ownership has declined from a very low level (by American standards) to a still lower level. As usual, weapon choice in suicide provides a guide to the prevalence of gun ownership: In the UK, gun suicides declined from 2.1% of the total in 1998 down to 1.5% in 2011—compared with around 50% in the United States. And the UK suffers only about three dozen gun homicides each year.

This experience suggests yet another version of the old bumper sticker that asserts, "When guns are outlawed, only outlaws will have guns." The experience with Great Britain tells us that "when guns are *effectively* outlawed, then almost no one will have guns."

### Do Gun Buy-Backs Reduce Gun Violence?

Government agencies, churches, and nonprofit groups sponsor occasional gun buy-back programs in an attempt to dry up local availability. Typically these programs offer cash or goods in exchange for guns for a few days. The evidence suggests that these approaches are not effective at reducing gun violence. Unsurprisingly people are inclined to turn in guns that are no longer useful—they are broken or have become redundant, given all the other guns owned by the individual. And these programs can even have perverse effects: If the reward is in the form of cash, there is always a possibility that the cash will be used to buy a new gun.

The one apparent exception to this conclusion is Australia's 1997 buy-back of semiautomatic rifles, a program inspired by the rampage shooting in Port Arthur. Not only was Australia's buy-back vastly larger than anything tried in the United States, but it was also mandatory as part of a new law outlawing most private ownership of these weapons. Thus, Australian owners could not exploit the buy-back to exchange their old gun for a new one, nor was the buy-back limited to owners who had no further use for the weapon. Ultimately, more than one million firearms were sent to the smelter—something like one-third of the entire stock of firearms in Australia. There is strong evidence that the great Australian buy-back reduced gun homicide and ended rampage shootings. But such a program would not be even remotely politically possible in the United States.

## What Measures Are Effective in Reducing Gun Trafficking?

The Gun Control Act of 1968 (GCA) was designed to regulate gun commerce so as to prevent states with weak laws from the stronger laws in other states. Only federally licensed dealers could receive interstate firearms shipments, and they are barred from selling handguns to anyone from out of state. (Private sales have the same restriction.) The intended effect is to protect states with relatively stringent state laws (Massachusetts, New York, California, and others) from states with essentially no regulations on firearms commerce except the bare minimum imposed by federal law (Mississippi, West Virginia, Vermont, and many others).

The GCA has provided the more regulated states some protection from the laxer states, but needless to say it does not achieve 100% compliance. There is a well-established pattern whereby firearms sold in unregulated states flow to those with stringent regulations. New York City mayor Michael Bloomberg was particularly outspoken about the illicit flow of guns, and justifiably so since some 90% of all crime guns in the city came from out of state. While New York City has been highly successful in reducing gun violence over the last two decades, the mayor believed it could do still more if its efforts were not undercut by the Iron Pipeline of illicit shipments from Virginia, the Carolinas, Georgia, and Florida.

A couple of specific case studies help document the economics of interstate gun flows—and establish the importance of regulation in influencing these flows. First is the federal Brady Act, which since 1994 has required licensed dealers to conduct background checks on would-be buyers. The background check requirement makes it more difficult for felons and other disqualified people to "lie and buy" from dealers. Some states had their own background check requirements in place before the federal requirement went into effect. One of those states was Illinois, and prior to 1994, its background check requirement was undermined by lax practices in other states. In fact a large percentage of the guns that ended up in the hands of Chicago criminals were first sold by dealers in the Deep South. Those states became less attractive as sources to gun traffickers with the advent of the federal background check requirement. Overnight the percentage of new Chicago crime guns that originated in the states that were required by the Brady Act to adopt background checks dropped from around 35% to just 10%. Thus the Midwestern version of the Iron Pipeline was reined in by this modest federal requirement. (It should be said that Mississippi remains a major illicit "exporter" of guns to other states, the most prolific source on a per capita basis in the nation, but still is more restrained than in the pre-Brady era.)

A second case study is of a state that relaxed its regulations. In August 2007 Missouri rescinded its long-standing requirement that all handgun buyers obtain a pistol permit from the local sheriff. Without that requirement private sales became unregulated, and sales by dealers no longer required the sheriff's approval. One result was an abrupt reduction in the percentage of crime guns originating out of state; the repeal of the pistol-permit law made it easier for felons to buy guns from local souces. Similarly there was a sharp increase in the percentage of crime guns that flowed quickly from a licensed dealer into crime. In 2006, 3.2% of guns recovered by the police had been sold by a dealer within the prior three months. By 2008, just after the regulation was rescinded, that figure had tripled to 9.4%. It appears that some scofflaw dealers in Missouri took advantage of deregulation to sell directly to criminals or their straw purchasers—still illegal transactions, but with the sheriff out of the picture, harder to regulate.

The clear conclusion is that laws matter. State and federal regulations influence how quickly or easily firearms flow from legitimate sales to criminal use.

### Do Federal Prosecutions of "Felon in Possession" Cases Deter Gun Crime?

One noteworthy approach to deterring illicit carrying and use has been to threaten convicted felons with federal prosecution if they are arrested in possession of a gun. Since federal law specifies longer prison sentences for "felons in possession" than do state laws, federalizing such cases might well have a deterrent effect on this high-risk group. A federal program called Project Safe Neighborhoods was implemented during the late 1990s with federal-local cooperation in prosecuting such cases as a key element.

"Felon in possession" laws are an example of "focused" or "targeted" deterrence. Those who have already been convicted of a felony most certainly constitute a relatively high-risk group (compared to the general public). The prominence of the federal prosecution strategy owed much to the publicity given to Project Exile in Richmond, Virginia. This partnership between local prosecutors and the US attorney was implemented in 1997, after which a number of ex-cons arrested for firearms possession were referred for federal prosecution and received hefty prison sentences. The subsequent drop in murder rates was widely credited to the deterrent effect of this program, although a careful look at the timing of the drop in gun murders suggests that claim is dubious at best.

On the other hand, an evaluation of Project Safe Neighborhoods in Chicago found evidence of a remarkably large deterrent effect in two high-violence neighborhoods. A key element of this effort was to personalize the threat of long prison sentences for felons in possession by use of notification sessions with small groups of convicts.

### Was the Brady Act Effective in Reducing Homicide and Suicide?

The Brady Handgun Violence Prevention Act, implemented in 1994, is the most prominent federal gun control law enacted since 1968. The evidence suggests that it had little effect on homicide rates, at least in the first few years. The likely explanation is that its regulations did not cover the kinds of transactions by which most criminals become armed.

James Brady, press secretary to President Reagan, was shot during an assassination attempt in March 1981. Together with his wife Sarah, Brady became a leader of the gun control movement, and through Handgun Control Inc. worked for seven years to achieve passage of the bill that bore his name. The first set of provisions was implemented in February 1994, requiring that licensed dealers conduct a background check and wait for five business days before transferring a handgun to a customer. Only 32 states were directly affected by these provisions, because the other 18 states and the District of Columbia already met the minimum requirements of the act. In effect these provisions created what social scientists call a "natural experiment," with 32 states in the "change" or "treatment" condition, and the 18 no-change states serving as "controls." After the Brady Act was implemented, economists Jens Ludwig and Philip Cook utilized this experiment-like setting to estimate the causal effect of the Brady Act on certain outcomes. Their article in the *Journal of the American Medical Association* found that average homicide rates in the "treatment" group and the "control" group followed almost exactly the same trajectories before 1994. Following implementation of the act, homicide rates declined, but equally so in the two groups, with no evident advantage for the newly regulated states.

Since the Brady Act provisions were limited to regulating sales by licensed dealers, the informal transactions by which almost all criminals get their guns were not directly affected. It is plausible that a more comprehensive law would have been more effective.

### What Is the "Private Sale Loophole," and What Would Be Gained from Closing It?

Federally licensed firearm dealers (FFLs) are required to conduct a background check to ensure that the would-be buyer is not a felon or otherwise barred from owning a firearm. The primary system for conducting these checks is the National Instant Criminal Background Check System (NICS). Mandated by the Brady Handgun Violence Prevention Act and launched by the FBI on November 30, 1998, NICS is used by dealers to quickly determine eligibility. The query either goes through a state agency, or, in 30 states, directly to the FBI, which maintains or has access to databases on criminal records, fugitives, illegal aliens, and those disqualified due to severe mental illness. Between 1998 and 2013, authorities conducted more than 180 million background checks (most for gun sales) and issued more than 2 million denials. The denial rate has been roughly 1.5% in recent years.

There is a loophole in this system, which is really more like a gaping barn door. Transactions that do not involve a licensed dealer are unregulated in most states. In states that lack their own regulations, private citizens can sell, loan, or give a firearm to anyone else, no questions asked, so long as they do not knowingly transfer a gun to someone prohibited from owning one. One national study (now rather dated) found that about 40% of all transactions did not involve a licensed dealer. The percentage is much higher for criminals. Most guns used in crime are acquired through informal channels—family members or friends, on the street, or by theft.

An obvious solution is to extend the background check requirement to private transactions. Six states impose that requirement for all firearms transactions, while ten others require checks for all handgun transactions. For example, since 1921 North Carolina has stipulated that before acquiring a handgun the buyer must get a permit from the local sheriff. California's regulation takes a somewhat different approach, requiring (since 1991) that all transactions be channeled through a licensed dealer, who is responsible for conducting the background check.

Following the Sandy Hook school massacre in 2012, a concerted effort led by President Obama was launched to persuade Congress to create a universal background check requirement, closing the private sale loophole nationwide. As of this writing, the effort has been unsuccessful, despite the overwhelming support of the American public.

A universal background check requirement would by no means eradicate gun crime, but it might reduce it, simply because some dangerous people—those disqualified from gun ownership—would find it more difficult to obtain a gun quickly when they wanted one. The benefits of this law could be counted in terms of lives saved in street crime, domestic violence, and suicides. Just how many lives would be saved presumably depends on how well the law is enforced.

But is a universal background check enforceable? California's system is complemented by a requirement that handguns be registered to their owner, which is useful in holding owners accountable when they decide to sell one. Even without a registration requirement, a universal background check system could be enforced in a variety of ways, including law enforcement oversight of gun shows and Internet sales and undercover "buy and bust" operations by the police. Whether the California system has been successful in reducing gun violence has not been established.

Another approach for giving teeth to the background check requirement is to improve the databases kept by the FBI. In recognition of this problem Congress established the National Criminal History Improvement Program (NCHIP) to provide grants and technical assistance to the states to improve the quality and immediate accessibility of criminal history records and related information. This federal investment resulted in a large increase in the criminal records accessible for background checks, thereby increasing the chance that a disqualified person would be identified as such through the NICS process. NCHIP has continued to provide modest funding for improving records and was supplemented in 2007 by a new program focused on helping states to incorporate mental health records into the NICS system. A few states have made large gains in this respect, but most do not yet have a reliable system in place for submitting relevant records on severe mental illness or drug abuse.

### How Effective Is the Federal Law That Disqualifies Perpetrators of Domestic Violence?

In 1993, the year before Congress passed the Violence Against Women Act (VAWA), the FBI counted about 1,400 homicides of adults by family members, either a man killing a woman (996 cases) or woman killing a man (381 cases). Most of these murders were by firearm (62%), and many were the culmination of a history of domestic violence. Research by Jacqueline Campbell and her associates has demonstrated that chronic domestic violence is five times more likely to result in death if a gun is available in the home. Thus a plausible approach to reducing intimate partner homicide is to remove guns from violent households. With that in mind, Congress in 1994 adopted a ban on firearms possession by anyone under a restraining order that protects an intimate partner or the partner's child. In 1996 the ban was extended to anyone with a

misdemeanor conviction for violence against an intimate partner (the Lautenberg Amendment). During the same decade a
number of states adopted parallel statutes that in some cases
went beyond the federal laws, for example by extending
gun possession bans to people under temporary (not just permanent) restraining orders. A number of these states permit or
require police to remove firearms from the scene when they are
called on a domestic violence case.

Several evaluations of these laws have found that state laws
that ban gun possession by those under a restraining order
have been somewhat effective in reducing intimate partner
homicide, with a best estimate of an 8% reduction. On the other
hand the state bans on domestic violence convicts appear to be
less effective. Enforcement of those laws has been hampered
by the difficulty of identifying disqualified people—criminal
record databases typically do not specify that a conviction for
misdemeanor violence involved an intimate partner.

Since 1993 intimate partner homicide has declined by about
one-third, with gun homicides leading the way. The federal
and state laws probably deserve credit for a portion of this
decline, but by no means all—other factors, including declining rates of marriage and cohabitation, get most of the credit.

### What Is the Evidence for Disqualifying Those with Violent Misdemeanors?

While there is broad consensus that violent criminals should
not be allowed to possess firearms, determining where to draw
the line is controversial. Federal law enumerates disqualifying characteristics, of which the most important in practice
is felony conviction. Yet a study of adult murder defendants
in Chicago found that only 43% of them had a felony conviction on their record. Similarly, a study of inmates sentenced
to prison for a firearms-related felony found that most of
them lacked any of the federal disqualifying characteristics
and could have purchased a gun legally prior to their current

offense. So there is a case for expanding the federal criteria for disqualification.

A natural next step would be to disqualify those convicted of violent crimes at the misdemeanor level. Compared with those with a clean record, gun buyers with a misdemeanor conviction for assault and battery, say, or for brandishing a weapon, have a greatly elevated risk of subsequent violence. With that in mind, California (and some other states) legislated a ban on gun possession for those with a violent misdemeanor on their record. (The disqualification extends for 10 years from time of conviction.) A study by Garen Wintemute and colleagues compared would-be gun buyers before and after the ban went into effect in 1991. They found that, after the ban went into effect, people with a violent record were less likely to reoffend than were their counterparts before the ban. That finding may surprise skeptics who assert that regulations of this sort have no effect in practice.

Are there other types of crime that should disqualify people from gun ownership? The Gun Control Act specifies that anyone who is an illegal user of a controlled substance (such as cocaine, heroin, or marijuana) is disqualified. Taken literally, this condition would disqualify more people than any of the other disqualifying criteria, since something like 22 million adults are current users of illicit substances. But in practice drug use is not a factor in screening gun buyers. To make the drug criterion operational, it would be helpful to make the law more specific, and that raises the question: Should it be enough to have a recent conviction for illicit drug possession? And what about a failed drug test for employment?

Another possibility of interest would be to disqualify habitual alcohol abusers from possession (or at least from concealed carrying). To make that dimension operational, the law could be amended to disqualify individuals who have accumulated several DUIs. (The disqualification in the case of drug or alcohol abuse could be of limited duration.) About 20 states do currently have a weaker restriction that bans possession while intoxicated.

### Should Disqualification as a Result of Criminal Record Be for Life?

A felony conviction and several other disqualifying conditions in the Gun Control Act bar firearms possession for life unless gun rights are restored. It was the Reagan-era Firearm Owners Protection Act (1986) that opened the door to restoration of gun rights. Today at least 11 states (Kansas, Ohio, Minnesota, Rhode Island, and others) restore rights automatically for nonviolent felons after they finish their sentences or soon thereafter. Even violent felons may petition the court to have their firearms rights restored in a number of states, and the process for doing so is often perfunctory, with many documented instances of serious crimes committed by ex-cons after restoration of rights.

It would make sense to approach this issue scientifically. Criminologists have long known that the likelihood of reoffending for ex-convicts declines over time. Similar to cancer survivors, the longer a convicted criminal maintains a clean record, the greater the chances that he will remain clean. Given enough years, it is possible to say that the ex-con is no more likely to be arrested than the average member of the community. In an actuarial sense, that is the point of "redemption"—a striking term coined by the dean of criminologists, Alfred Blumstein, and his associate Kiminori Nakamura. In their research on the subject, they identified the point of redemption at around 11 to 15 years for violent offenders, and slightly shorter times for drug or property offenders. Thus there is a scientific basis for considering convicted felons who have lived in the community for 15 years without an arrest to be good bets for restoration of gun rights.

The same issue arises with severe mental illness, which, like criminal careers or drug abuse, is not necessarily a permanent condition.

*What Are the Most Promising Strategies for Keeping Guns*
*Away from Those Who Are Dangerous to Themselves or Others*
*because of Mental Illness?*

The shooter in the Virginia Tech rampage of 2007, Seung-Hui Cho, had been diagnosed and treated for severe mental illness, but that fact was not in the public records accessible to gun dealers. As a result he was able to pass a NICS check and arm himself with the weapons he used to kill 32 people. The mental health aspects of this horrendous event were prominent in the political aftermath. As one result, Congress enacted a program to fund state-level efforts to improve their compilation and reporting of data on people disqualified due to severe mental illness. Virginia, Connecticut, and several other states have improved their reporting, but in many states reporting is still woefully incomplete. (The money comes with strings attached–states are required to adopt a procedure for restoring gun rights to those who are disqualified due to mental illness.)

The Gun Control Act bans gun possession by those who have been "adjudicated as a mental defective." That archaic terminology has been operationalized to include four categories of people for whom a court has ruled to be severely mentally ill: incompetent to stand trial; not guilty by reason of insanity; involuntarily committed to a mental institution; or subject to a conservatorship.

Connecticut provides a case study of the possibilities and limitations of the mental health disqualification. In 2007, Connecticut began compiling data on people who were disqualified due to severe mental illness and reporting to NICS. A careful study of administrative records over eight years in Connecticut found more than 23,000 cases in which someone was hospitalized for severe mental illness—schizophrenia, bipolar disorder, or major depression. As a whole, this group was at high risk of violence—39% were convicted of a violent crime during the eight years. But of this group, just 7% were disqualified as a result of their mental illness, since all the rest were voluntary self-commitments. The mental health disqualification had no statistical effect on the likelihood of their committing a violent crime prior to 2007, but after 2007, when Connecticut began submitting data to NICS, it was quite effective.

Thus for those mentally ill people whose only disqualification for gun possession is involuntary commitment, state reporting of records to NICS can make a real difference in forestalling violence. Nonetheless, the federal disqualification is of very limited scope, missing the great majority of people whose mental illness makes them a threat to themselves or others.

An alternative approach would be to focus on dangerousness rather than mental illness per se. If the court issues a restraining order on an individual, that should prompt an inquiry into whether that person is armed and if so lead to an appropriate intervention. In many cases, even before a court order is issued, there may be a need for a quick response to save lives. A typical scenario is that people contact the police to report family members or neighbors who are threatening to kill themselves or threatening others. If a gun is involved, removing that gun should be a high priority—but the authority to do so is limited in most states. Indiana is one exception. It has an innovative statute that allows the police, even if they lack a warrant, to seize weapons from individuals deemed dangerous. (The decision is reviewed by the court, and the owner can petition to have the gun returned.) In California, law enforcement must confiscate weapons found to be under the possession or control of any person who has been detained for a mental examination (usually a 72-hour hold) or who is prohibited from possession of firearms by reason of a mental disorder. Law enforcement must retain custody of the firearm and notify the individual of the procedure for its return.

### Do State Authorities Seek to Disarm Newly Disqualified People?

The Gun Control Act sets the national standard on who is disqualified from possessing a firearm. That standard is reproduced, in whole or part, by the laws of many states. People who are newly indicted or convicted of a felony, or committed to a mental institution, are no longer legally entitled to possess a firearm, and it seems logical that they would be ordered to give up any in their possession. But only a handful of states, (e.g., Massachusetts and Connecticut) have legislated a process by which newly disqualified people are to get rid of their firearms, with a timeline for compliance.

Of course any disqualified person whom the police find with a gun can be prosecuted. The federal "felon in possession" law specifies a long prison term.

### Do Sentencing Enhancements Reduce Gun Use in Violent Crime?

About half of the states have legislation that stipulates a longer sentence for someone who is convicted of assault or robbery with a gun than with a less lethal weapon. These sentencing enhancements, most of which were adopted in the 1970s and 1980s, were intended to reduce firearms use in violence; either criminals would be induced to desist from violence, or to substitute another weapon. Legal scholar David Abrams of the University of Pennsylvania Law School found that the introduction of enhancements in several states had the effect of reducing gun robberies an average of 5%, with no effect on nongun robberies.

### Is Targeted Policing against Guns Productive?

Yes. Illegal carrying and its deadly consequences can be reduced through focused police efforts to get guns off the street. That is especially important for reducing violent crime; at least 46% of murders and most robberies are committed in public places.

The best known of the focused-deterrence strategies to reduce illicit gun use is Boston's Operation Ceasefire. Beginning in 1995, an interagency working group composed of Harvard University researchers, members of the Boston Police Department, and other criminal justice agencies conducted research and analysis on Boston's youth violence problem and launched a carefully designed program to reduce youth violence. Their research showed that the problem of youth violence in Boston was concentrated among a small number of serially offending gang-involved youth. The key intervention was for the police to make gang members believe that gun use by any one member of the gang would result in a crackdown on all members. (Most of them were vulnerable to more stringent enforcement since they had outstanding warrants, traffic tickets, or other legal problems.) The intent was for each gang to have an incentive to discourage gunplay by its members.

A key element of the strategy was the delivery of a personalized message to a small target audience regarding what kind of behavior would provoke a law enforcement response. This "retail deterrence" message was delivered by talking to gang members on the street, handing out fliers in the hot-spot areas explaining the enforcement actions, and organizing forums between violent gang members and members of the interagency working group. The youth homicide rate plunged in Boston following the intervention. Evaluation efforts have focused on whether Ceasefire should get the credit for this sharp reduction. Several replications of this general approach have been evaluated, with generally positive results.

Over the past two decades, police have recognized that crime and violence are highly concentrated in particular neighborhoods, even specific blocks within cities, and have adjusted their strategies accordingly. Concentrating police activities in the high-crime areas ("hot spots") can be an efficient use of available police personnel. While one could imagine this tactic would simply displace crime to other neighborhoods, it rarely happens in practice. Evidence from directed-patrol programs in Indianapolis and Pittsburgh, as well as two cities in Colombia, suggests the effectiveness of this approach in reducing serious crime.

Targeted policing has become religion for New York City's Police Department, which conducted 700,000 stops in 2011 alone—mostly young men of color. While the yield with respect to confiscated guns has been low, police officials claim (and it is reasonable to believe) that this tactic has had a deterrent effect on illicit carrying and gun use in crime. We know that New York City enjoyed an extraordinary and sustained drop in violence after the early 1990s, and that drop was associated with a number of policing innovations. It is difficult to sort out the separate contribution of the stop-and-frisk policy. Of course this policy places a considerable strain on police-community relations and has been challenged for the apparent racial profiling.

The potential effectiveness of targeted patrols against illicit carrying depends on the regulatory environment. If carrying a concealed gun does not require a permit (as is true in five states), then the goal of "getting guns off the street" is unattainable.

### How Effective Are Hunting Regulations on Firearms Safety?

Hunters handle and occasionally discharge lethal weapons. The risk of injury was brought to the public's attention in 2006, when Vice President Dick Cheney shot Harry Whittington, a 78-year-old Texas attorney, while they were on a quail hunt. Because it appeared at the time that Whittington was not seriously injured, the event was good for laughs in some quarters. Of course, some of us remember Tom Lehrer singing "The Hunting Song" with the lyric "I went and shot the maximum the game laws would allow, two game wardens, seven hunters, and a cow." But hunter safety is in fact serious business.

Licensing requirements for hunters are intended to reduce accidents by ensuring that hunters know the regulations on hunting and know how to handle their weapon safely. These requirements are imposed by states and, as with concealed-carry permits, tend to differ widely among states. Typical requirements include enrolling in a hunter education course for 10 hours, passing a written test, and completing a "field day," which may include a live-fire exercise and even a marksmanship requirement. In some cases the requirements for a hunting license are a good deal more stringent than the requirements for carrying a concealed handgun; Vermont and Wyoming, for example, have *no* requirements for carrying concealed, but do require that hunters enroll in a training course and be licensed. One might ask why competence in handling a firearm is more important in the fields and forests than on the city streets. As Congressman Mike Thompson (D-CA), a hunter, observed: "Federal law prohibits me from having more than three shells in my shotgun when I'm duck hunting. So federal law provides more protection for the ducks than it does for citizens."

In any event, the number of hunting accidents has declined over time and fatal accidents are quite rare. In New York State, for example, the steady decline in gun accidents far outpaced the general decline in hunting. The number of accidental shootings averaged 137 in the 1960s and just 30 in the 2000s. In 2012 there were just 24 shootings statewide (13 self-inflicted), 2 of them fatal.

If it is true that training requirements have enhanced hunter safety over the last few decades, that fact would surely be relevant to the consideration of appropriate requirements for other uses of firearms.

# 8

# GUNS AND GUN CONTROL
# IN HISTORY

## Is There a Uniquely American Gun Culture?

Yes. We know of no other country where firearms are as plentiful and as inextricably linked to individual identity and popular values as they are in the United States. Citizens of other
nations possess and use guns, to be sure, and some of these gun
owners associate their firearms with symbolic meaning. But
no country imbues private possession with larger social, historical, and political significance to the extent that the United
States does. If a gun culture rivaling America's existed somewhere, we are confident that someone would have noticed.

It's hard to describe what a "gun culture" looks like in practice, but we like political scientist Robert Spitzer's definition:

> the long-term sentimental attachment of many Americans
> to the gun, founded on the presence and proliferation
> of guns since the earliest days of the country; the con-
> nection between personal weapons ownership and the
> country's early struggle for survival and independence
> followed by the country's frontier experience; and the
> cultural mythology that has grown up about the gun in
> both frontier and modern life, as reflected in books, mov-
> ies, folklore, and other forms of popular expression.

In a famous 1970 essay, "America as a Gun Culture," the historian Richard Hofstadter defined the culture a bit more darkly: The United States, he said, "is the only industrial nation in which the possession of rifles, shotguns, and handguns is lawfully prevalent among large numbers of its population. It is the only such nation that has been impelled in recent years to agonize at length about its own disposition toward violence and to set up a commission to examine it, the only nation so attached to the supposed 'right' to bear arms that its laws abet assassins, professional criminals, berserk murderers, and political terrorists at the expense of the orderly population."

American gun culture might be more fruitfully thought of as several overlapping subcultures, as Spitzer notes. One subculture is oriented around hunting and other shooting sports. As we noted in chapter 1, gun-oriented recreation is prevalent, particularly in rural areas, where it often is a core feature of family life. For boys in particular, the gift of a first gun traditionally has served as a rite of passage, though that practice is fading amid urbanization and the decline of hunting.

A second subculture, what Spitzer calls the "militia/frontier ethos," remains prominent in American society and politics and is often what we think of when we hear the term "gun culture." The militia/frontier subculture takes its inspiration from American history and the mythology that has developed around it. In this perspective, citizen militias of privately armed men won American independence from tyrannical King George, and rugged rifle-toting settlers finished the job of nation building by conquering the frontier. Brave individualists made America, and they did so with firearms. Historians accept this account up to a point, but as we discuss below, they also find considerable hype and oversimplification in the retelling. But no matter. To those who view guns as pivotal to American greatness, the lessons of history are ignored at the nation's peril. Relatively unfettered access to firearms is equally relevant today as it was in 1776, for guns allow everyday citizens to serve as a vigilant counterpoise to creeping tyranny.

This traditional, even patriotic perspective has morphed into an "insurrectionist" ideology embraced not just by fringe elements but also by leaders of some pro-gun organizations. For example, the Coalition to Stop Gun Violence maintains an "insurrectionism timeline" featuring more than 200 statements and actions by private individuals, media personalities, elected officials, and advocacy groups supporting a war against the government or other forms of political violence. The militia/frontier subculture has birthed a *sub*-subculture of armed men and women who believe that private action against government "tyranny" is both justifiable and inevitable.

Although the notion of American gun culture resonates with people across the ideological spectrum, scholars struggle with what the term "culture" means in practice and how to measure it. One common understanding is that culture encompasses symbols, stories, rituals, and worldviews that everyday citizens draw on to engage in politics.

*Symbols.* When Americans want to win a political argument, they are wont to invoke the Constitution and the rights it protects. These rights have practical legal import as well as symbolic value. For pro-gun advocates, the Second Amendment's "right to keep and bear arms" has long served as a rhetorical anchor. And the Constitution is a powerful tool: Even though most Americans favor gun control, around half nevertheless believe that laws limiting gun ownership infringe on the right to bear arms.

*Stories.* History texts, popular fiction, movies, and marketers lionize guns and have done so for more than 150 years. From iconic tales of musket-bearing minutemen at Lexington and Concord, to Buffalo Bill Cody's fabulously successful Wild West shows, to Laura Ingalls Wilder's best-selling "Little House" children's series, to postwar John Wayne westerns, to immigrant tales such as *The Godfather* and *The Sopranos*—guns figure prominently in the story of America. The storytelling about American history may contribute as much as history itself to the creation of the American gun culture.

*Rituals.* Family life and rites of passage, particularly in rural areas, often revolve around shooting sports. Hunting season signifies not just a time of year but also an opportunity to strengthen one's ties to family and community traditions. Studies have found that hunting typically begins at a young age and that kids are initiated by members of the immediate family. Even today, as hunting is declining in America, schools in some rural areas are closed on the first day of hunting season. The parental practice of acculturating kids to guns caused alarm in some quarters, even decades ago. In a definitive account of homicide in the United States, sociologist Harrington Brearley[1] in the 1930s noted that sales of toy revolvers was booming, leading children to "lurk in ambush and in sport hold up pedestrians" and to kill "song birds and household pets, meanwhile endangering the lives of bystanders and becoming accustomed to the reckless use of firearms."

*Worldviews.* Advocacy groups skillfully link guns to American values of liberty and equality, an association that simply does not resonate to the same extent in other democracies. The National Rifle Association refers to the Second Amendment right to keep and bear arms as "America's first freedom" because it protects all the other freedoms. The NRA's major donors are inducted into the "Ring of Freedom." Its annual conventions are festooned with flags and other cultural symbols. It refers to itself as "America's longest standing civil rights organization." Studies have found that attitudes toward guns reflect larger worldviews about individual versus collective responsibility. Even after accounting for gun ownership and other factors, people with a dim view of government's role in solving problems are more likely to embrace gun rights than are people more favorable to public approaches.

A variant on the "gun culture" argument concerns the belief that violence, particularly involving guns, solves problems. This theme has come up mostly in the context of the American

South, where observers going back to Charles Dickens have suggested that citizens seem to be unusually quick to draw their weapons, particularly where questions of honor are concerned. That culture is probably a contributing factor to American gun violence, though not the overriding one.

Guns are central to the American experience, but they don't define it. While on average Americans are probably more tolerant of guns in public life than are citizens of other advanced democracies, many Americans are also troubled by the sentimental attachment to firearms and wish that stricter gun laws were in place. What most people think of as the American "gun culture"—passionate, highly politically engaged gun owners who believe that firearms do more good than harm and that most law-abiding people should own them—is actually a relatively small subculture of, at most, 5% of the adult population.[2] But that translates into upwards of 10 million people willing to e-mail and call their elected officials and show up at their town hall meetings.

### Where Does the Gun Culture Come From?

The gun culture has its roots in lived experience magnified by mass marketing and media.

The historical antecedents are true enough. From the earliest settlements, guns have had important practical functions. As the historians Lee Kennett and James Anderson have observed, "Survival dictated that old social distinctions of arms ownership give way to the practical necessities of creating a new colony." Virginia moved early on to require all men to be armed, and citizen militias formed in the 1620s in response to Native American attacks. Laws encouraged men to hunt to sharpen their marksmanship skills.

The American Revolution owed its success in part to civic-minded men—the militia—who took up arms against a despot and then served as reinforcements for the Continental army. Anywhere from 175,000 to 500,000 men served in the militia during this period. As Kennett and Anderson note, "The militiaman symbolized the nation—crude, unorganized, undisciplined, but ready to protect his rights."

Moving westward in the post-Revolutionary period, American frontiersmen required firearms to hunt, ward off threatening wildlife, and vanquish Native Americans, cattle rustlers, and pugnacious troublemakers in mining camps and other untamed surroundings. In areas with little if any organized law enforcement, private individuals relied on themselves for protection. Prominent citizens often had to band together in vigilante groups to chase down outlaws holding up stagecoaches, banks, railroads, and mine offices, while gun-slinging sheriffs, such as the legendary Bat Masterson, tried to keep law and order in town.

The federal government and firearms makers encouraged the arming of the frontier. Congress legalized the firearms trade with Native Americans in 1834 and used rifles as inducements for them to move westward in the 1840s. The US government began handing out surplus guns to settlers in 1849. In the middle decades of the nineteenth century, the marketing genius Samuel Colt created a line of affordable firearms and promoted them with "a system of myths, symbols, stagecraft, and distribution that has been mimicked by generations of industrial mass marketers and has rarely been improved upon."[3] Celebrity spokesmen were key: Colt deployed the famous artist and adventurer George Catlin, as well as a who's who of Mexican-American War heroes to advertise his wares; manufacturers Remington and Winchester sent expert marksmen around the country to stage shooting exhibitions.

In his history of the Winchester rifle, Harold Williamson suggested that "firearms, the axe, and the plow were the three cornerstones upon which the pioneer Americans built this nation. Of the three, firearms were the most dramatic and appealed most to popular imagination." However, historians have argued that the heroic militiaman and his gun were far less effective than children's stories would have us believe, and the frontier far less of a firearms free-for-all than we think. For historical embellishment of guns and their place in American history, we can thank entrepreneurial fiction writers, movie-makers, showmen, political advocates, and even gun makers.

Children's textbooks portray the "minutemen" and other colonial musket bearers as a ragtag force that, through quintessentially American grit and ingenuity, beat back a well-disciplined, more heavily armed British army. In real-ity, the Continental Congress quickly realized that citizen militias were not up to the task of fighting a prolonged war and created a standing army under the command of George Washington, a Virginia militia leader. Although the militia had achieved notable victories, Washington's complaints about the militia reflected the general belief that citizen soldiers could not replace a professional army. Without considerable help from European allies, most notably the French, the American Revolution might have turned out differently.

The narrative of the frontier gun culture, while surely con-taining more than a grain of truth, also owes a great deal to popular entertainment. Historians looking at homicide statis-tics have found that even places synonymous with Wild West violence had relatively few murders—the cattle town of Dodge City, Kansas, for example, averaged 1.5 per year. As the histo-rian Robert Dykstra notes, anyone "looking for true mayhem and big body counts should forget Little Bighorn, forget Wild Bill and Wyatt Earp, forget Dodge City. Instead, consider the lethal character of simply working on the railroad."

True, the cattle towns and mining camps of the Old West had some legendary gunslingers and their own brand of jus-tice, to say nothing of more firearms violence than the average prairie community of upstanding farmers and shopkeepers. But the popular image of the gun-soaked West owes much to mythologizing that began after the Civil War, when dime nov-els proliferated and Buffalo Bill Cody's legendary "Wild West" show traveled the country for decades dramatizing buffalo hunts, Indian battles, and Annie Oakley's marksmanship. As the cultural historian Richard Slotkin has observed, the show "was the most important commercial vehicle for the fabrication and transmission of the Myth of the Frontier."

By the dawn of the twentieth century, the frontier narrative had taken on new life on-screen. One of the earliest motion pictures, *The Great Train Robbery* (1903), featured western banditry. In the middle decades, the award-winning director John Ford popularized the western and brought the ultimate cowboy-actor John Wayne to stardom in *Stagecoach* (1939) and kept him there with *The Searchers* (1956) and *The Man Who Shot Liberty Valance* (1962). Clint Eastwood continued the glorification of the historic West with films such as *The Good, the Bad, and the Ugly* (1966), *The Outlaw Josie Wales* (1976), and *Unforgiven* (1992). Not to be upstaged, television fueled America's insatiable appetite for hero gunslingers in shows such as *The Wild Wild West*, *The Lone Ranger*, *Gunsmoke*, *The Rifleman*, *Wagon Train*, *Rawhide*, and *Bonanza*, which were replayed in syndication long after their initial run.

Gun rights advocacy groups have embraced this cultural iconography and made it relevant to a modern, urbanized, industrialized America. Listen to then-NRA president Charlton Heston—an actor whose oeuvre was ironically nearly devoid of westerns—addressing the association's 2000 annual convention:

> When freedom shivers in the cold shadow of true peril, it's always the patriots who first hear the call. When loss of liberty is looming, as it is now, the siren sounds first in the hearts of freedom's vanguard. The smoke in the air of our Concord bridges and Pearl Harbors is always smelled first by the farmers, who come from their simple homes to find the fire and fight—because they know that sacred stuff resides in that wooden stock and blued steel, something that gives the most common man the most uncommon of freedoms. When ordinary hands can

possess such an extraordinary instrument, that symbolizes the full measure of human dignity and liberty.

Heston ended the speech by hoisting a vintage rifle above his head and leveling a warning to presumptive Democratic presidential nominee Al Gore and other "divisive forces that would take freedom away." They would get his gun, he suggested, only by prying it "from my cold dead hands!"

Scholars have a different explanation for the staying power, even resurgence, of American gun culture. One account holds that it represents conservative white men's reaction to liberalism—an attempt to recapture "frontier masculinity" amid threats to status and identity posed by the "nanny state," feminism, and multiculturalism. Another account holds that the lionization of firearms isn't a reaction to an overweening state, but rather to a state that has failed to protect its citizens. The National Rifle Association and other pro-gun groups work both angles, mocking mothers and liberal "gun grabbers" who seek stricter firearms laws and portraying America as a land in which violent criminals are free to savage communities and anarchy is only one terrorist attack or natural disaster away.

### Was There Gun Control in Frontier America?

Yes—and in fact gun control goes back to America's earliest days.

In the Revolutionary era, citizen militias were responsible for the common defense, and the states had an interest in ensuring that citizen-soldiers were well prepared, which meant well regulated. State laws outlined who belonged to the militia—typically able-bodied white males in their prime years—and laid requirements of militia service. These requirements typically included maintaining private arms and turning out for periodic "musters" in which weapons were inspected and recorded on public rolls—what the legal historian Adam

Winkler terms "an early version of gun registration." And colonial governments conducted door-to-door inventories of privately owned weapons. When the Revolution arrived, colonial governments confiscated private weapons for use in the war effort.

In 1792 the new Congress adopted the Uniform Militia Act, requiring all free, able-bodied white male citizens under 45 to muster with a local militia and equip themselves "with a good musket or firelock." As Winkler notes, guns were private property with a public purpose. States and localities regulated the storage of gunpowder, prohibited the discharge of firearms in towns and cities, and in some cases prohibited militiamen from traveling to muster with a loaded weapon.

In the early nineteenth century, states inaugurated new forms of gun control in the form of bans on publicly carrying concealed weapons and on firing guns in certain places—so-called "time, place, and manner" restrictions. Kentucky and Louisiana banned the concealed carrying of firearms in 1813, and many states and territories followed throughout the century. One impetus for these laws was to curtail the practice of dueling, in which gentlemen challenged to a shootout those who had offended their honor, as well as to prevent impulsive acts of revenge. Judges upheld these bans. A Louisiana court, for example, supported the state's prerogative to curb citizens' use of concealed weapons to pursue "secret advantages and unmanly assassinations." Outside of the South, states concerned about the proliferation of concealable guns passed laws against traveling armed unless the individual had reason to fear imminent danger.

Even in the "Wild West," laws generally banned the carrying of weapons, except by law enforcement officers. Rather than leaving each man to his own, "Frontier towns handled guns the way a Boston restaurant today handles overcoats in winter," Winkler notes. "New arrivals were required to turn in their guns to authorities in exchange for something like a metal token. Certain places required people to check their guns at one of the major entry points to town or leave their weapons with their horses at the livery stables."

Early gun laws presaged the modern gun debate. In the "right hands," firearms were instruments of civic value; in the "wrong hands," they were instruments of unnecessary death. It was up to lawmakers and judges to decide how best to preserve the good while preventing the bad.

## Is Gun Control an Effort to Protect the Elite against Minorities and Immigrants?

Yes, no, and maybe. Throughout history, firearms regulations have been enacted in response to threats to public order. In some cases, the self-appointed guardians of the public order have targeted specific groups, either explicitly in the language of the law or effectively in its design and implementation. The laws have evolved over time, and their intent is often subject to inference and interpretation.

Consider African Americans. In the early period, even in the South, free African Americans were allowed to possess firearms and in some states to serve in the militia. Some laws carved out restrictions—for example, Virginia in 1680 banned both slaves and free African-Americans from carrying weapons. One legal scholar argues that the Second Amendment may have been intended, at least in part, to reassure the South that it could maintain militias to put down slave revolts. As the historians Robert Cottrol and Raymond Diamond note, blacks were more likely to be allowed to have a gun if whites deemed them loyal and reliable.

In the antebellum period, amid slave revolts and threats thereof, southern states began clamping down on the rights of free African Americans, including the right to possess firearms, and in some cases began regulating slaves' use of guns, previously the province of the master. In the three decades leading up to the Civil War, Delaware required free blacks to obtain a license to carry a gun; Maryland and Virginia prohibited the practice altogether; Georgia and Mississippi prohibited both carrying and owning; and Florida authorized white citizen patrols to confiscate guns from black homes. Several states incorporated right-to-bear-arms provisions in their state constitutions, but limited that protection to free white men. Free blacks were targeted because, according to Cottrol and Diamond, "they served as a bad example to slaves and because they might instigate or participate in a rebellion by their slave brethren." Meanwhile, Louisiana, Mississippi, South Carolina, and Texas passed laws aimed at restricting or barring slaves' handling of guns.

It is important to note that these clearly racially motivated laws were separate from other laws passed during the antebellum era that addressed the problem of concealed weapons.

After the Civil War, freedmen were at the center of policy debates over guns. The confederate states passed "Black Codes," including laws barring freedmen from carrying guns, but those laws were soon rendered unconstitutional by the Fourteenth Amendment, ratified in 1868. With full citizenship and equal protection for African Americans now enshrined in the US Constitution, states wishing to control freedmen's access to firearms would have had to try stealthier strategies. Modern gun rights supporters argue that states did so by banning the carrying or sales of the small, cheaply made pistols affordable to poor blacks; by exempting from gun restrictions service weapons that, in practice, were owned by white Confederate veterans; or by charging business taxes that would have made guns unaffordable to freedmen. States also empowered white citizen groups, including the Ku Klux Klan, by selectively enforcing gun laws and, in at least one state, exempting "special deputies" from the ban on pistol sales. African Americans seeking protection in the Second Amendment found none, for in 1875 the Supreme Court ruled in *U.S. v. Cruikshank* that the amendment applied only to acts of Congress, not vigilante groups or other usurpers of gun rights.

At the same time, during Reconstruction Republicans recruited freedmen to join citizen militias, which had once been restricted to whites. These militias not only served as a counterbalance to groups such as the KKK but also provided a way of organizing African Americans for citizenship.[4]

In the late nineteenth and early twentieth centuries, some observers believe, gun control was part of a larger effort to control "dangerous classes," which would include not only African Americans, but also southern and eastern European immigrants, labor organizers, and agrarian reformers. The nation's first handgun licensing law, enacted in New York in 1911, was part of a broader Progressive movement led by business and social elites, along with good-government reformers, in response to urban social disorder. The so-called Sullivan Law was a direct reaction to lawbreaking among the "dangerous classes," including Italian mobs and Chinese gangs—which at the time was a real problem. The law had been preceded by lesser efforts to regulate firearms in those communities, including canceling concealed pistol permits in Italian neighborhoods of New York City and barring aliens from having guns in public places. But the Sullivan Law had other precipitating factors: the shooting of the New York City mayor and a prominent author; extensive newspaper coverage of family violence; and, most obviously, a 50% jump in gun homicides in the prior year.

While there is consensus about the racial and ethnic roots of many gun laws enacted through the early part of the twentieth century, there is less agreement about efforts in the modern era. No doubt some gun laws have been enforced in a discriminatory fashion. For example, gun rights advocates have long complained that New York City issued handgun permits "only to the very wealthy, the politically powerful and the socially elite" and to those who guard their interests. For many decades, North Carolina's handgun permit law left it up to local sheriffs to determine whether the applicant was of "good moral character," an invitation for abuse in a state with a sad history of racial strife. In 1956, after his house was bombed, the Reverend Martin Luther King Jr. applied for a permit to carry a concealed weapon, but the Montgomery police chief used his discretion to deny the application.

In the 1960s, the Black Panther Party for Self-Defense, a radical wing of the civil rights movement, decided it was time to embrace firearms as tools of defiance and political empowerment. In much publicized acts of political theater, the Panthers strapped on fully loaded firearms and marched on the California State Capitol, in one case entering the assembly chamber during a legislative debate. A newspaper report at the time recounted, "It was one of the most amazing incidents in legislative history—a tumultuous, traveling group of grim-faced, silent young men with guns roaming the Capitol surrounded by reporters, television cameramen, stunned state police and watched by incredulous groups of visiting school children."[5] Shortly thereafter, the state enacted a law banning the carrying of loaded guns in public, adding a special provision that made the law effective immediately.

On the other hand, the impetus for, and the design and implementation of, modern gun laws make it hard to support charges of racism. The 1968 Gun Control Act was spurred by the back-to-back assassinations of Sen. Robert Kennedy and the Reverend Martin Luther King Jr. The first effort to regulate assault weapons, in 1989, came in response to a shooting of immigrant schoolchildren by a white assailant. Federal laws requiring licensed firearms dealers to run background checks on would-be buyers (1993) and banning certain types of assault weapons (1994) followed an epidemic of gun crime concentrated in urban neighborhoods, but the laws were designed and enforced without disparate racial impact and enjoyed support from civil rights organizations. Early efforts to expand background checks to private gun sales (for example, in Colorado and Oregon) came in response to shootings at predominantly white schools by white students. The most recent spate of gun reforms came in response to the shooting of 20 first-graders and six educators in a town straight out of a Norman Rockwell painting.

The history of guns and race is complicated, emotionally fraught, poorly documented, and subject to widely varying interpretations. Debates over guns and gun laws, particularly in earlier centuries, have been lost to history, and no doubt the individual and collective motives behind these laws were varied and often obfuscated. From what we do know, however, it's clear that gun ownership and gun regulation have been central to American efforts to maintain social order.

### How Have Laws Governing Carrying and Self-Defense Changed over Time?

It has become easier to carry guns legally in public and, as we note in chapter 6, to defend oneself without fearing jail time. Ironically, states that in the nineteenth century were strict on gun regulation are now among the most lenient.

Beginning in the early nineteenth century, many states passed laws banning the carrying of concealed handguns outside the home. The first in this category was Kentucky, in 1813, and by the late 1930s, 20 states had such bans.[6] Constitutional challenges were not uncommon, but courts nearly always upheld the laws.[7] Historically, legislatures and courts observed what amounted to a two-tiered system: Guns kept for public purposes, namely collective defense through militia service, enjoyed the highest level of constitutional protections (they could not be sold to pay taxes owed, for example), while those intended for private purposes, such as hunting or self-defense, were subject to state powers to promote public safety and health.

Bans or strong restrictions on carrying concealed firearms were adopted in every region of the nation. But real questions remain about whether citizens followed these laws and whether police enforced them. In a 1925 book on America's homicide problem, the author cites a South Carolina attorney general lamenting that the " 'deplorable custom' " of pistol carrying had turned the state into " 'an armed camp in time of peace.' " He remarked that " 'our young men and boys, black and white, rich and poor, seem to think that their outfit is not complete without a pistol,' " and that guns were routinely carried "at public meetings, on the streets, at social gatherings, even at dances, even at daily labor, and following the plough, and I add also even at church and prayer meeting."[8]

By the 1920s and 1930s, the laggard states had started to take concealed handguns seriously. "The trend of pistol legislation in the last ten to fifteen years has been toward stricter regulation," a legal commentator noted in 1938. "More and more it has been recognized that the possession of a pistol that can easily be concealed in the pocket furnishes a temptation which many young hoodlums are impotent to resist."[9] As he wrote, nearly every state that didn't bar carrying outright had passed a law requiring those who wished to carry a gun to obtain a permit from the local police chief or judge. By the late 1930s, 26 states had enacted licensing provisions. The National Rifle Association supported the licensing laws at the time, but in the latter decades of the twentieth century, the organization would mount a full-bore campaign against them on the grounds that they were unjustly restrictive, even discriminatory. At the time, however, legal experts had the opposite concern, that these laws were lax and easily evaded.

Thus, for most of American history, concealed carrying of guns was either prohibited or strictly regulated in all but one or two states. That all changed in the 1980s and 1990s, when the National Rifle Association made liberalization of these laws a top priority. In rapid succession, states have moved away from the early twentieth-century discretionary licensing system, known as "may issue," to a "shall issue" system in which law enforcement must grant a permit to anyone meeting basic legal requirements, such as not having been convicted of a felony, not abusing drugs or alcohol, and being of sound mental health.

The campaign to liberalize the laws that began in Florida in 1987 has been one of the National Rifle Association's biggest policy successes. Before 1977, only about one-fifth of states treated concealed carrying favorably (eight states had the liberal "shall issue" system, and one state did not require a license). By 2013, four-fifths of the states had adopted this liberalized posture (37 had shall-issue systems, and several others had abandoned licensing altogether for in-state use).[10]

In just one generation, lawmakers across the states have fundamentally upended public policy on packing heat. It's hard to think of such a sweeping change in law that has received so little public notice. Having largely succeeded in changing the concealed handgun laws, the NRA is now working to ensure that carriers licensed in one state may legally carry in another and in the end to secure a federal reciprocity law that would bind all states.

## Did Hitler's Gun Control Laws Cause the Holocaust?

If gun rights advocates have one refrain, it is that gun regulation will lead to gun confiscation, which will lead to tyranny. Exhibit A: Nazi Germany. Hitler disarmed the Jews, and then he murdered six million of them in one of history's greatest abominations. To gun rights supporters, the Holocaust has become a gruesome warning about the hidden threat behind even seemingly mild firearms control. As one pro-gun lawyer put it, "The record establishes that a well-meaning liberal republic would enact a gun control act that would later be highly useful to a dictatorship.... This dictatorship could, generally, disarm the people of the nation it governed and then disarm those of every nation it conquered."[11]

Because the putative linkage between gun control and tyranny, even genocide, rests largely on one historical case, it's important to get the history right. As one might expect, the story of Hitler, gun control, and the Holocaust contains core truths while drawing inferences that are at best debatable.

Although historians have written volumes about the Nazi period, they have paid little or no attention to the role of gun laws in facilitating Hitler's rise and reign—a fact that is either a terrible oversight or a telling omission. Instead, the argument that gun control facilitated Nazi terror emerged from the contemporary writings of American pro-gun lawyers and activists. Scholars and activists on the other side have answered with their own analysis. Remarkably, the two sides agree on the basic historical narrative, but they disagree on the inferences we should draw from the case.

The first point of agreement is that Germany was in the process of liberalizing its strict gun laws before Hitler came to power in 1933, and, with critical exceptions, he continued that trend. At the end of World War I, the parliament of the Weimar Republic banned gun possession and required that citizens surrender existing guns and ammunition. These laws remained in effect until 1928, when parliament relaxed the ban by allowing certain people to own, transfer, carry, and manufacture guns so long as the individual obtained a permit. To acquire a gun, regular citizens had to be of "undoubted reliability"; government and railway officials, as well as certain community leaders, were exempt from the permit requirement. The 1928 law also created a licensing system for manufacturing and sales. In 1938, Hitler further liberalized the law, removing rifles and shotguns from the permitting system and lowering the legal ownership age to 18. The law also exempted more groups from the permit system, including hunting license holders, additional government workers, and, importantly, Nazi Party members. As one legal scholar concluded, "The Nazis were relatively more pro-gun than the predecessor Weimar Republic."

However, the liberalization of gun laws did not apply to Germany's Jews. Hitler's 1938 law barred them from manufacturing guns or ammunition, although it did not explicitly ban them from obtaining a license to acquire or carry a firearm. After the law had been enacted, but before the implementing regulations had been formulated, a 17-year-old German Jewish refugee shot a German embassy worker in Paris. This event precipitated an immediate ban on Jews' acquiring, possessing, and carrying firearms, ammunition, or "cutting or stabbing weapons." Jews were ordered to surrender their weapons or be sent to a concentration camp for 20 years. During the infamous Kristallnacht, Nazi "wrecking crews" conducted massive raids on Jewish homes and businesses to search for weapons and arrest their owners. Thousands of homes, businesses, and synagogues were ransacked and destroyed. The mass extermination of Jews began not long thereafter.

So what are we to make of the connection between gun control and the Holocaust? And is the case relevant to firearms policymaking in the contemporary United States or other established democracies?

To gun rights scholars, the lesson is clear. When democracies require people to register their weapons, the government unwittingly creates a handy road map that can be appropriated by future dictators to guide them in disarming "enemies of the state" and thereby consolidating power. In his history of Weimar and Nazi gun laws, lawyer Stephen Halbrook presents evidence, for example, that local officials acting on the orders of Interior Minister Hermann Göring scrutinized firearms license lists to revoke permits of Jews and other political opponents. He speculates that these lists also may have been used to disarm or even arrest Jewish gun owners. But to Halbrook and other gun rights supporters, a larger lesson emerges from the Nazi era: that humanity is well served when nations have "an armed populace with a political culture of hallowed constitutional and natural rights that they are motivated to fight for."[12]

To those more sympathetic to gun control, the idea that regulation leads to genocide seems far-fetched, both in its particulars and as a larger cautionary tale. In the case of Nazi Germany, these critics argue, there is no way that a small, despised minority ever could have been a match for Hitler's well-armed storm troopers, police, and regular army, particularly in the absence of armed Gentiles willing to fight alongside the Jews. Even before the anti-Jewish gun control regulations, Hitler had suspended constitutional liberties, including freedom of speech and association; appropriated democratically organized shooting clubs; expanded search-and-seizure powers; ransacked the homes and offices of political enemies, including Jews; and used force to engineer the dissolution of parliament—facts that pro-gun writers don't dispute. Indeed, no direct evidence has been presented that the Nazis used a gun registry as a road map for raids on Jewish homes, which were often concentrated in Jewish quarters anyway and thus easily identified for mass sweeps.[13] In a context in which democracy had long since ceased to exist, "A right to keep and bear arms would have been as meaningless as other suppressed rights in the Third Reich."[14] If anything, one might argue that holes in gun laws helped Hitler to build up his private army, as Nazi Party members were exempt from the later permitting system.

The larger question is whether it's useful to invoke the Nazi experience as a cautionary tale for gun policy today. How you answer that question probably depends on whether you are fundamentally optimistic or pessimistic about democracy specifically and the human condition generally. Optimists can point out that modern states have longer liberal traditions and sturdier institutions for checking and sharing power than did the weak Weimar Republic, which lacked such popular norms and was beset from the start by internal strife and unable to stave off armed factions. Optimists can also note that roughly a dozen US states, to say nothing of many industrialized nations, have maintained gun registration or owner licensing, often for decades, while remaining thriving democracies. On the other hand, pessimists can point to countless state-sponsored atrocities as evidence that evil can erupt anywhere in our time—witness Bosnia or Rwanda. Given the alternative, it behooves freedom-loving individuals never to let their guard down.

Of course, there is a third possibility, satisfying to no one, which is that a well-armed and vigilant citizenry is unlikely to be any match for a well-trained and far more heavily armed military. Given advances in the technology of modern warfare, that observation may be even truer now than in the 1930s.

# 9

# PUBLIC OPINION AND POLITICAL PARTY POSITIONS ON GUNS

### Do Americans Want Stricter Gun Laws?

Public opinion experts have long observed that the United States has a gun control paradox: Most Americans favor a host of modest firearms regulations—sometimes overwhelmingly so—yet these regulations are not enacted into law. Four decades ago, one scholar went so far as to observe that "it is difficult to imagine any other issue on which Congress has been less responsive to public sentiment for a longer period of time," a frustration that many Americans voice today. Most answers to the paradox revolve around different levels of political mobilization: Gun owners are highly organized at all levels of government, and they make their voices heard, including at the ballot box. Conversely, gun control supporters are less well organized and, in some renditions, less focused and less intense. We believe that the organizational explanations are correct, and we address them later in this book. At the same time, opinion polls are a piece of the puzzle.

Do Americans support gun control laws? If you look at national opinion polls, the headline is yes. But degrees of support vary widely by policy question, as well as by gender, race, gun ownership status, and political party. And sometimes the poll findings are contradictory, indicating that most Americans probably do not understand the gun laws as well as they might think.

Many polls indicate that the vast majority of Americans— about 90%—support the laws we have now, or think they should be stricter. Specific proposals not on the books nationwide, such as requiring all gun buyers to undergo a background check, enjoy similarly commanding levels of support. Other proposals that the majority of Americans would like to see enacted include preventing people with mental illness from buying guns, creating a federal database to track gun sales, placing more armed guards in schools, and banning assault weapons and high-capacity ammunition magazines. In general, Americans are far more supportive of laws narrowly aimed at criminals and other dangerous people than of proposals targeting guns and ammo that "good guys" might want.

One proposal that has never enjoyed majority support (except in one possibly anomalous poll in 1959) is a ban on civilian handgun possession—which was a goal of gun reformers in the 1970s. In recent polls, fewer than 30% of Americans have supported such a provision. And, as we have noted, the Supreme Court has ruled that blanket handgun bans are unconstitutional.

In assessing whether most Americans support stricter gun laws, one immediately notices a contradiction. On the one hand, majorities of Americans—sometimes overwhelming majorities—favor specific proposals not currently on the books nationally or in most states, implying support for stricter gun laws. On the other hand, when asked the general question of whether they support stricter gun laws, far lower numbers say yes. Reading the polls, you would be forgiven for scratching your head: Americans want stricter gun laws, and they don't? One explanation for these contradictory findings is that Americans don't know what gun laws are currently on the books. Another possibility is that the gun lobby's narrative has sunk in and Americans are more likely now to equate "gun laws" with "gun bans." There is evidence for both interpretations.

It is a truism of American politics that most people don't know much about the policies governing them. People are busy with jobs and families, and they leave the governing to the experts. Firearms regulation is no exception. Take a recent experiment in which pollsters identified people who believe the government should enforce the laws already on the books before passing new laws—the NRA's standard position. The pollsters then asked those people whether federal law currently requires background checks on private sales, including those at gun shows. Nearly half got the answer wrong, and a tenth admitted they didn't know the rules. Large numbers also didn't know that assault weapons were legal in most states, or that people on the government's terrorist watch list can buy guns. As the pollsters concluded, "About 6 out of 10 people who believe we just need to do a better job of enforcing existing laws don't realize that those laws are far weaker than they think."[1]

Ignorance can lead to nonsensical findings. For example, in a 2012 poll 44% of Americans backed banning semiautomatic guns—a figure that seems quite high given that these guns constitute most firearms sold today and few Americans believe in banning mainstream weapons. Another poll found that more people backed a ban on semiautomatic weapons than on assault weapons—the opposite of what one would expect. We suspect that many survey respondents mistakenly thought semiautomatics were machine guns.

Besides not understanding the gun laws, many Americans may be reading general questions about gun control as synonymous, or close to synonymous, with gun bans. Two broadly consistent trends have unfolded over the past two decades: a plunge in the fraction of Americans who want stricter gun laws in the abstract (from 78% to 43%) and a concomitant rise in the fraction of people who think it's more important to protect gun rights than to control ownership (from 34% prioritizing rights in 1993 to 49% in 2012). Although there was an uptick in support for gun control after the Sandy Hook Elementary School shooting, the nation's long-term shift toward the gun rights position held, to the point where the country is almost exactly evenly divided. Over the past generation, the nation also moved away from support for handgun bans, which hovered at around 40% in the 1980s and 1990s, then dropped over the following decade to around 25%.

These questions—on support for gun control generally and handgun bans specifically—are the only gun policy questions that have shown significant movement over time. And their patterns are broadly similar. At the same time, support for specific, modest policy proposals has remained robust over time, or even strengthened. For example, in the 1990s and early 2000s, roughly 80% of Americans favored background checks on private gun sales; a slew of polls in the 2010s have put that number at 85% to 90% or more. The fraction supporting a ban on high-capacity magazines (generally defined as feeding devices holding more than 10 to 15 bullets) is about the same in the 2010s—in the 55% to 65% range in most polls—as it was in 1999 (67%). A tentative but defensible conclusion is that Americans are fine with firearms regulations that don't ban guns and will continue to voice their support as long as they don't "hear" gun ban in the pollster's question.

Looming beneath these muddled poll findings, of course, is the question of trust in government. Pollsters have long known that if questions imply a government role in gun control (which of course it would have), support for the proposal declines. A recent experiment by Gallup illustrated the dynamic: When asked whether they would vote for a law expanding background checks, 83% said yes; when asked whether the US Senate should have passed such a measure, support dropped nearly 20 points. People who opposed the Senate measure cited violation of the Second Amendment as their chief reason.

## Who Supports Gun Control, and Who Supports Gun Rights?

Not surprisingly, subgroups of Americans hold widely diverse views of gun control generally and of many specific proposals.

One of the most interesting developments over the past two decades is the growing gap between Democrats and Republicans on questions of gun policy. Indeed, the partisan gap—some 30 to 45 percentage points on general gun control questions—typically dwarfs differences across other demographic characteristics such as race, gender, and geography, and even the presence of a gun in the home. In the early 1990s, strong majorities of Democrats, independents, and Republicans believed that America needed stricter gun laws. Now only Democrats subscribe to that view. While their support has been declining, the widening gap has been driven by Republicans and independents, whose support for gun control broadly construed has plunged by more than half since the early 1990s. The party gap persists on specific policy questions—such as whether we should ban assault weapons—and is even more pronounced on questions of whether gun reforms would be effective (the view of most Democrats, but not Republicans) or whether gun control gives undue power to the government (the view of most Republicans and independents, but not most Democrats).

Views toward gun control also vary with individual characteristics that closely track political beliefs. So, for example, racial minorities are more likely than whites to support gun control (with a gap of about 20 to 25 points), women are more supportive than men (with a gap of about 10 to 20 points), and easterners are more sympathetic than are people from other parts of the country (with a gap of roughly 15 to 20 points). Requiring background checks of all gun buyers is one proposal supported by majorities of Republicans, southerners, westerners, and gun owners, all groups traditionally hostile to gun regulation.

Gun owners are more likely to be skeptical of new gun laws than are nonowners (about a 20-point gap). But even gun owners—and NRA-member households—overwhelmingly support one prominent gun control proposal, to expand the background check system to private sales. Other gun reforms, such as bans on military-style weapons or high-capacity magazines, are more divisive within gun-owning households, with NRA-member households considerably more skeptical than those without an NRA member.

However, lots of the personal characteristics associated with support for gun laws are also associated with one another—for example, women and Democrats tend to favor gun control, but women are also more likely than men to vote Democratic. These statistical correlations mean that it's hard to tell what's shaping public opinion and what's merely incidental. To sort out the separate effects of different factors, scholars use a statistical technique called regression analysis.

The authors' regression analysis of opinion on gun control reveals, not surprisingly, that household gun ownership is a strong predictor of support for gun rights. However, even *after* accounting for household gun ownership, political ideology and gender remain strong predictors of one's position on gun policy. All else being equal, Republicans and men are much more likely than Democrats and women to prioritize gun rights over gun control, meaning that there is something about partisanship and gender, having nothing to do with gun ownership, that orients people's views.[2] The findings are much the same on the question of whether mass shootings, in this case at the Sandy Hook school, reflect isolated acts or broader social problems. Men, Republicans, and those in gun-owning households were significantly more likely to view the event as an isolated act, while women, Democrats, and people without guns saw it as part of a larger phenomenon. Other significant predictors of pro-control sentiment, all else being equal, include Latino ethnicity and age (younger and older people are more pro-control than middle-aged people).

### Why Is the Issue of Guns and Gun Control So Emotional for Many People?

Because it touches on everything we hold dear: our lives and the lives of our family members and friends, our property, and our civic values. The deep emotions surrounding firearms may be a particularly American phenomenon, but it is a powerful one nonetheless.

### Do High-Profile Shootings Shift Public Opinion on Gun Policy?

Sometimes—but not by much, and the effects usually don't last long.

At any given time, most people have settled views on the question of gun control. So when we are looking for a shift—on this issue or any other hot-button issue—we would not expect to see much of one, even in the presence of signal events.

Two polling firms—Gallup and Pew—have regularly asked generic questions to gauge people's feelings about the gun issue. In several cases, the surveys have been fortuitously timed to capture opinion shortly before—and shortly after—mass shootings.

Gallup's survey—which asks whether laws governing firearms sales should be more strict, less strict, or kept as they are—registered a six-point bump in the "more strict" direction after the Columbine High School shooting in April 1999. But by December, support for stricter laws had retreated to its pre-Columbine level. Six months after the most deadly shooting in American history, at Virginia Tech in April 2007, support for stricter gun laws was actually *lower* than it had been six months before the event—meaning that, if the shooting of 50 students and professors moved Americans toward stricter gun laws, such sympathy did not last. There was an eight-point surge after the Tucson shooting in January 2011, but it had evaporated by the fall.

After the shootings at the Aurora, Colorado, theater (July 2012), at the Wisconsin Sikh temple (August 2012), and the

Sandy Hook school (December 2012), support for stricter gun laws surged 12 to 15 points. The Pew question—which asks whether it's more important to protect the right of Americans to own guns or to control gun ownership, showed less dramatic increases in pro-control sentiment after the 2012 shootings—roughly two points after the Aurora shooting and five points after Sandy Hook. It is too early to tell as of this writing (August 2013) whether these shifts will hold, or whether opinion will follow the normal pattern of returning to prior levels.

It's important to note, however, that these isolated pro-reform upticks are occurring against the backdrop of a pronounced, long-term shift toward protecting gun rights and leaving gun laws as they are.

### Where Do the Democratic and Republican Parties Stand on Gun Control?

By and large, Democrats favor stricter gun laws, while Republicans favor either keeping the laws the same or in some cases liberalizing them. The party divide on gun issues has grown stronger over time among both lawmakers and everyday citizens.

Not until 1968 did the two major parties first include positions on gun control in their platforms. The Republicans balanced competing concerns of controlling "indiscriminate availability" of guns with "safeguarding" gun rights for law-abiding citizens. The Democrats supported "passage and enforcement of effective" gun control laws. Thereafter, the party positions began to diverge. Beginning in the 1970s, Republican platforms increasingly emphasized support for the Second Amendment and the right of self-defense, as well as opposition to certain gun laws.

Meanwhile, the Democrats called for various new gun laws, including a ban on cheap pistols (1972, 1976); a waiting period on handgun purchases and a ban on assault weapons (1994); mandatory gun locks, gun owner licensing, and background checks on private sales (2000); and the continuation or renewal of the assault weapons ban and, again, expanded background checks (2004, 2008). In the 2004 campaign, fearful of the gun lobby—which had been widely credited (or blamed) with helping to defeat Al Gore in 2000—the Democrats began including language supporting Second Amendment rights.

The party positions on guns reflect each party's base: Republicans are strongest in the South and in rural areas, where gun ownership is widespread and reflective of strong traditions of individualism and distrust of government. Democrats are strongest in urban areas and among women and racial minorities, who either lack a gun-owning tradition or see the dangers up close. Not surprisingly, then, the partisan divide shows up in public opinion polls.

Political party affiliation is a strong predictor of one's position on gun control. And the divide between Republicans and Democrats has grown wider over time. Indeed, if you want to know someone's party affiliation, the best question to ask (besides "Who did you vote for in the last election?") is "Do you own a gun?" It turns out gun ownership is a better predictor of a person's political party than lots of other characteristics that often serve as pretty good signals, including whether a voter is gay, female, Latino, or southern.

Of course, within each party there are exceptions— Democrats who are fervent gun rights supporters and Republicans who are comfortable with stricter controls. In April 2013, the US Senate voted on a gun control measure, and four members of each party bucked their leadership. The four Democrats came from rural states with strong gun lobbies, the four Republicans represented what's left of the moderates and those who must win suburban votes.

### Does Support for Gun Control Cost Candidates Their Elections?

After the July 2012 massacre at a suburban Denver movie theater, Colorado's legislature passed and the governor signed a package of new gun control laws. Within three months, angry gun owners had gathered enough signatures to force recall elections for two Democrats who had supported the legislation. Three months later, the lawmakers were out of a job. A third Democratic lawmaker resigned in the midst of a recall effort.

To many people the events in Colorado underscored the conventional political wisdom that casting a pro-gun control vote is politically suicidal. In swing districts or during low-turnout elections, as with the Colorado recall, that judgment may well be correct. However, the larger body of evidence is considerably less compelling.

Consider exhibit A: the Democrats' drubbing in the 1994 midterm elections. The NRA's Wayne LaPierre and Bill Clinton don't agree on much, but they are convinced that gun control flipped the House of Representatives to the Republicans in 1994. The argument is that the NRA, its members, and gun owners generally were angered by two federal gun laws—the Brady background check bill (1993) and the federal assault weapons ban (1994)—passed in the 103rd Congress. As President Clinton lamented in his 1995 State of the Union address, several members of Congress who had supported the assault weapons law "aren't here tonight because they voted for it."

Social scientists decided to test Clinton's hypothesis by looking at how a newly invigorated GOP, led by firebrand Georgia congressman Newt Gingrich, picked up more than 50 seats and retook control of the House of Representatives after four decades in the minority. These same social scientists also looked at 1996, in which Congress members were again up for election. The thrust of their findings: Even after accounting for local idiosyncrasies and broader political trends, having the support of the NRA probably helped, but only in 1994 and only if the candidate was a Republican challenger. On average, the NRA endorsement provided a two-percentage-point boost to these candidates. Having lots of NRA members active in the district also helped challengers generally, but again only in 1994. In 1996, the NRA had no statistically discernible impact.

The liberal journalist Paul Waldman also attempted to answer the $64,000 question of whether the NRA swung the House of Representatives to Republican control in the 1994 election. He noted that, if an NRA endorsement boosted Republican challengers by two points, it could have decided, at most, a dozen especially close races. However, even if the NRA had stayed out of the races, and all had gone to the Democrats, the GOP still would have won control of the House. In short, the NRA may have helped elect a few new Republicans, but it didn't deliver the House to the GOP. That is good news to gun control advocates, but not all that reassuring to however many members of the 103rd Congress lost their seats because they favored stricter gun laws.

Exhibit B for the proposition that gun votes swing elections is Al Gore. If he had won his home state of Tennessee in 2000, as the Clinton-Gore ticket had in 1996, he would have become the forty-third US president—and the term "hanging chads" never would have entered the lexicon. But in the real world, Gore lost Tennessee by nearly four percentage points. Was the six-point drop owing to angry gun owners who felt betrayed by passage of new federal gun laws in the first administration and a new push in 1999 to 2000 after the shootings at Columbine High and other public schools?

No scholar has a definitive answer, but a reasonable interpretation is that gun rights may have been a part of a constellation of intertwined cultural issues moving southern whites away from the Democrats, whom conservative advocacy groups had increasingly identified as naive and arrogant elites with an unhealthy faith in the federal government.[3] Tennessee had voted for Republican presidential candidates in the 1980s but, along with other border states, it had returned to the Democratic fold in the 1990s with the all-southern Clinton-Gore ticket. Clinton seemed more authentically southern—he was a poor kid from an Arkansas town called Hope—while Gore was the Harvard-educated son of a US senator and had spent most of his life in Washington. The gun-owning, traditionally Democratic states of Tennessee (and for that matter, West Virginia) turned on Gore in 2000, but other states with pronounced gun cultures went for him, notably Pennsylvania and Michigan. On the other hand, in the run-up to the presidential election, the Clinton-Gore administration *had* been pushing for a new round of gun control laws.

In recent years, gun control advocates and sympathetic journalists have sought to dispel what they see as the "myth of NRA dominance." Their message: Although memories of 1994 and 2000 may loom large in politicians' memories, gun regulation isn't so toxic now. A review of NRA endorsements in the 2004 to 2010 congressional election cycles found that they made a small difference in the share of the vote the endorsee received, but only in the small fraction of cases where the NRA endorsed Republican challengers. By this analysis, out of more than 1,000 endorsements, the boost provided by the NRA was large enough to determine the outcome in only four races—a significant achievement for any one interest group, but hardly proof of political omnipotence.

A nonpartisan analysis of the 2012 election, in which Barack Obama was reelected president and the Democrats picked up seats in both houses of Congress, underscored earlier findings that the NRA doesn't do well when the political winds are blowing leftward. Of the roughly $11 million that the NRA's political action committee spent to swing the 2012 congressional and presidential elections, less than 1% went to the winning candidate. That was a bad showing even when compared to other conservative groups, such as Americans for Tax Reform (with 57% going to the victor) and the National Republican Congressional Committee (32%).

And while the gun rights forces can point to their success in recalling the two Colorado lawmakers in 2013, gun control supporters can point to their victory just a few months before in a special election for a Chicago-area congressional seat. In that case a gun control supporter came from behind to beat the gun-friendly favorite in the Democratic primary and went on to win handily in the general election.

Thus, a candidate's position on gun policy can influence the outcome of an election in certain circumstances—when the candidate is in a swing district, for example, or when turnout is expected to be low. Evidence that the gun issue has decided major elections is far less compelling. Ultimately, however, these questions may be of little more than academic concern. The vast majority of lawmakers will never face a risky gun vote, as they serve increasingly homogeneous districts and tend to agree with their constituents' views. In the rare case when a lawmaker might have to cast a tough vote, he or she is likely to be swayed far more by cautionary tales—Al Gore or the Colorado recall—than by systematic evidence with uncertain implications. The perception of the gun lobby's invincibility looms large, and in politics perception is reality.

# 10

# THE GUN RIGHTS MOVEMENT

## What Is the Gun Rights Movement?

The gun rights movement consists of several hundred local, state, and national organizations that seek to promote a positive view of firearms in public life and to prevent and remove restrictions on their ownership and use. Generally speaking, you can think of the gun rights movement as being an interlocking set of actors:

**National and state membership organizations** that do a substantial amount of policy advocacy, whether lobbying, mobilizing individuals for direct action, or communicating with the media. Prominent examples include the National Rifle Association (NRA) and the Virginia Citizens Defense League.

**Think tanks and researchers** who conduct studies on policy issues and sponsor lawsuits to overturn gun control laws. Prominent think tanks include the Independence Institute and the Second Amendment Foundation, and key advocate-lawyers include David Kopel, Don B. Kates, and Stephen Halbrook.

**Gun safety and training organizations, sport-shooting associations, and gun shops** whose primary mission is not political but which bring gun aficionados together to reinforce worldviews and communicate about policy and politics.

**Gun manufacturers, distributors, and retailers**, which are represented by the National Shooting Sports Foundation, based in Newtown, Connecticut. Compared to many other big businesses, such as defense and healthcare, the gun industry per se is not an especially significant political player, leading critics to contend that the NRA does the industry's bidding, or that the industry is beholden to the NRA.

**Political action committees, such as the National Rifle Association of America Political Victory Fund and the Gun Owners of America Political Victory Fund,** that raise money to finance candidates for public office.

**Unaffiliated activists,** including libertarian sheriffs and private individuals who challenge gun laws. For example, several hundred sheriffs have vowed not to enforce any federal gun laws that they consider unconstitutional.

The National Rifle Association, founded in 1871, is the oldest and dominant organization in the gun rights movement. Headquartered in a Washington, DC, suburb, the NRA also enjoys the head seat at the table when major firearms legislation is under consideration and is the go-to organization for reporters seeking comment on all matters relating to gun policy. The organization claims 4.5 million members, but a more reliable estimate is about 3.4 million; either way, it is one of the largest pressure groups in the country.[1] It recently has taken to calling itself "America's longest-standing civil rights organization."

What we call the NRA is actually three organizations: a political advocacy organization of several million members; a charitable foundation that develops gun safety education programs and provides grants to hundreds of gun clubs and ranges around the country; and a political action committee, which gives money to candidates. The largest of these three is the membership association, the National Rifle Association, which had a budget of $230 million in 2011. The NRA Foundation is only about one-tenth that size, $27 million. The PAC, known as the NRA Political Victory Fund, spent about $16 million in the 2012 election cycle.

The NRA has multiple missions: to "protect and defend the US Constitution"; "to promote public safety, law and order, and the national defense"; "to train law enforcement agencies"; "to train civilians in marksmanship"; "to foster and promote the shooting sports"; and "to promote hunter safety." That the political mission comes first is no accident. Although founded to improve civilian marksmanship in the wake of Union troops' lackluster performance in the Civil War, the NRA has become increasingly concerned with politics, particularly after gun control rose on the congressional agenda in the 1960s. At the group's 1977 national convention, a hard-line faction took control of the board, and its willingness to work with lawmakers on gun reform—however mild—began to dissipate.

Even if the NRA is the best-known gun rights group, the movement is much broader. Other national gun rights groups are smaller, but they fill niches that the large organization does not and sometimes serve as a burr in its saddle. Gun Owners of America calls itself the "no compromise gun lobby," a not-so-subtle dig at the NRA, and manages to make a lot of noise in lawmakers' offices when gun control legislation is on the agenda. The National Association for Gun Rights likewise believes the NRA has sold out to Washington and uses its modest budget to "assist the growing movement of state-level grassroots gun rights organizations." The Citizens Committee for the Right to Keep and Bear Arms made waves in 2013 by signaling support for a bill in Congress to expand background checks—heresy in the gun rights movement.

Gun owner organizations exist in every state. Many originated as "rifle and pistol associations" in the latter decades of the nineteenth century and the first decades of the twentieth to promote the shooting sports. Beginning in the 1990s, however, more explicitly political grassroots groups have sprung up in at least 28 states. These groups often emphasize their "no compromise" stance toward gun policy and evoke patriotic values—"citizens defense," constitutional rights, freedoms—in their names and mission statements. Several of these groups are oriented around promoting what they see as a positive role for guns, for example by advocating for laws allowing people to carry firearms in public and for greater social acceptance of the practice.

Around the fringes of the gun rights movement is the patriot movement. Motivated by different threats—taxes, secularism, multiculturalism, globalization, gun control—"patriot," militia, and "sovereign citizen" groups agree on one thing: The federal government has run afoul of the Constitution, and at any moment citizens may need to lead an armed insurrection to restore the system that God and the founders intended. Mainstream gun rights groups have an uneasy relationship with the patriot movement. The two movements' philosophy and rhetoric can sound similar, but gun rights groups work within the system of laws to achieve their ends and risk undermining their legitimacy if they associate too closely with actors on the fringe. Gun control advocates have warned, however, of the increasingly strident antigovernment, insurrectionist positions voiced by representatives of mainstream gun rights groups.

### Why Is the Gun Lobby So Strong?

In surveys of Washington political insiders, the National Rifle Association routinely ranks as one of the most powerful interest groups. In public opinion polls, even those taken right after a mass shooting, the NRA enjoys broad public approval. Indeed, immediately after the Sandy Hook school shooting, only about a third of Americans thought the NRA had too much influence over the nation's gun laws. A Democratic congressional staffer, speaking to a reporter on condition of anonymity, bemoaned, "We do absolutely anything they [the NRA] ask and we NEVER cross them . . . Pandering to the NRA is probably the worst part of my job."[2]

The main source of the NRA's power is its committed membership base of somewhere around 3.4 million gun owners. In the American system, with its many points of political access and relatively weak political parties, dedicated citizen groups pushing very specific ideas often prevail, especially when their opposition is spread out and unorganized. What's more, in an era in which membership has come to mean little more than sending a check to Washington, the NRA and allied gun rights groups stand out in their ability to generate true grassroots engagement—getting members to show up at lawmakers' town hall meetings, contact elected officials, write letters to the editor, harass opponents, and cast their votes based on a candidate's gun rights positions. Although money is the mother's milk of politics, it is not the primary source of the gun lobby's power (and, as we noted in chapter 9, may not be particularly effectively spent).

So if the gun lobby's success is due to its members' engagement, how does the lobby pull it off? And why have opponents had difficulty ginning up an equal and opposite force to neutralize the pro-gun side? The answer is that the gun rights movement has certain built-in advantages that its leaders have leveraged with strategies that are especially well suited to succeeding in American politics.

The first key to the gun lobby's success is its structure: With national, state, and local organizations, it can apply pressure on lawmakers at all three levels of government. When legislation comes up in Congress, the national lobbyists are on the scene. NRA-affiliated sportsmen's organizations and independent political groups do the same in state capitols, augmenting lobbying with grassroots activities such as protests. Finally, in most localities there are gun shows, gun shops, shooting ranges, and other venues where individuals can meet and share information. Although few states allow cities or counties to do much by way of gun control, locally rooted activists are available should the need arise. The gun lobby also is positioned to apply pressure across the three branches of government, with lobbyists working on the legislative branch, lawyers taking pro-gun cases to court, and technical experts and lobbyists weighing in on regulations promulgated by the executive branch. In short, the gun lobby succeeds in part because its structure mirrors that of government.

The second key to the gun lobby's power is the mix of incentives that it can offer to potential members. Here the gun lobby has a distinct advantage over its opponents. First, it can offer tangible things of value that people will join the organization just to receive—in the NRA's case, items such as magazines with useful information, discounts on everything from hotels to hearing aids, even a wine club membership. The NRA and other gun groups also can offer honors or respect bestowed on individuals by virtue of their membership, as well as the sense of bonhomie and fellowship that one experiences when sharing experiences with others. Gun rights groups nurture gun-owner solidarity by holding shooting events and bestowing marksmanship honors and recruiting members in places where gun hobbyists socialize, such as shooting clubs and gun shops. A third membership inducement that groups can offer is the sense of meaning and satisfaction we get when we work for a cause we hold dear. Gun groups have leveraged our need to be part of something larger than ourselves by connecting gun ownership and use to widely held understandings of American history and values. Although the American belief system contains contradictions—for example, between individualism and populism—gun rights advocates have sampled and combined core American values to promote the idea that guns contribute to the public good.

With all these incentives to offer, the NRA has attracted a lot of members, and the income that comes from member dues— some $102 million in 2011—finances a panoply of programs that enhance the association's political clout. These programs include developing and disseminating authoritative research and talking points for lawmakers, orchestrating grassroots and inside-the-Beltway lobbying, communicating with members, and influencing elections.[3]

Although the gun lobby is suspicious, even contemptuous, of the federal government, one longtime scholar of gun politics has observed that "the NRA probably owes its existence to its long-term, intimate association with government subsidies and other forms of support."[4] Throughout the twentieth century, the US government's civilian marksmanship program directly subsidized the NRA and its state affiliates. The War Department and its successor, the Department of Defense, provided guns and ammunition to rifle clubs, supported rifle range operations and instruction, and sold military surplus weapons at rock-bottom prices. Until 1979, one had to be an NRA member to buy the surplus guns, meaning that the government was providing a tangible incentive for gun aficionados to join. As an internal NRA report concluded in 1971, the association's "phenomenal growth...to more than one million members was made possible primarily by the Defense Department." Even today, the federal government provides special concessions that help the NRA, including permission to build target ranges on federal land, which is not subject to local zoning laws.

### Are Gun Rights Supporters More Intense Than Gun Control Supporters?

For decades social scientists have pointed to the "gun control paradox," which in its simplified form holds that "most people want stronger gun laws but rarely get them." Gun rights advocates would object to that framing—see our discussion of "20,000 gun laws" in chapter 6—but the paradox contains a timeless truth.

The traditional resolution to the gun control paradox concerns intensity. Yes, people support gun control, but they don't feel that strongly about it, and even if they do, they care about a lot of other issues too and aren't willing to make guns the single issue that they advocate for and cast their votes on. On the other hand, gun rights supporters are passionate, relentless, single-issue voters who will stop at nothing to prevent passage of stronger gun laws. Although combined into a single narrative, these are two different propositions. In our opinion there is strong evidence for the latter, that gun rights advocates care a lot, and mixed evidence for the former, that gun reform advocates don't care all that much.

Advocates for gun rights have two built-in advantages not unique to this issue. The first is that, in a political system with many choke points, it's easier to block a proposal than it is to push something through. The second is that people respond more vigorously to threats of loss than they do to the prospect of gains, particularly if those gains are theoretical or off in the future. Both of these general principles tilt the political playing field in favor of gun rights groups.

But gun owner groups have had influence beyond what such general theories of political advantage would suggest. Beyond blocking proposals to strengthen gun laws nationally and in some states, the gun rights movement has skillfully pushed an affirmative strategy to enact new laws relaxing the old ones. In so doing, the movement has taken advantage of regular opportunities for activists to meet face-to-face—in gun shops and on gun ranges, for example—and a smorgasbord of cultural values and historical allegories that create a sense of shared citizen identity among hobbyists. As we discuss in the next chapter, gun control supporters face more built-in barriers to finding one another, creating politically powerful collective identities, and overcoming the built-in barriers to enacting social regulation of any form.

So what do we make of the argument that gun owners get their way because they care more and consequently participate more than do their opponents? As noted above, it's important not to confuse different issues. In this case, there's lots of evidence that gun owners participate more around the gun issue than their opponents. There's less evidence that gun owners care more—or, to be more precise, that gun control supporters don't care much. In our opinion, some of the perceived intensity gap is about differences in organization and in perceived ability to effect change.

Two recent surveys illustrate the point. In the week after the Sandy Hook shooting, the Pew Research Center asked people how strongly they felt about their position on gun policy. Among those who thought it was more important to control gun ownership, 42% felt strongly about the matter, compared to 37% of those who felt it was more important to protect gun rights. A month after the shooting, the basic pattern held. Several months later, Pew sought to figure out how many people are truly single-issue gun voters. In that poll, 41% of gun rights supporters claimed to be single-issue voters, meaning they would refuse to support a candidate who disagreed with them on gun policy but agreed with them on other issues. On the gun control side, the comparable figure was 31%. Adjusting for the fact that there are more gun control supporters in the population, we find—as did a similar study three decades before—that the number of single-issue voters on each side is more balanced than the conventional wisdom would suggest (20% of the population claims to vote on a pro-gun basis, compared to 16% on a pro-control basis).

The more significant gap is not in intensity, but in action. In a 1978 poll, scholars Howard Schuman and Stanley Presser found that compared to pro-control supporters, gun rights advocates were three times as likely to have taken some action on the issue, such as writing a letter or giving money. Even when correcting for the fact that there were more pro-control supporters, nearly two-thirds of all letter writers and donors were from the pro-gun rights side. A 2013 poll reached a similar conclusion: Gun rights supporters were almost twice as likely as gun control supporters ever to have given money, contacted a public official, expressed an opinion on a social networking site, or signed a petition on the gun issue. Even zeroing in on participation within the six months after the

Sandy Hook shooting, the gun rights side still had a significant activist advantage, although the percentage of gun control supporters who had contacted a public official or signed a petition was very close to the percentage of gun rights advocates who had done so. We conclude, as did other scholars in the late 1970s, that the polls provide evidence of "an efficient lobby against gun control legislation, which is able to activate adherents whenever necessary."[5]

Although polls are a blunt instrument for measuring political engagement, the findings are broadly consistent over time: It's not intensity per se that favors the gun rights movement but rather its ability to translate passion into action. Perhaps more importantly, lawmakers' votes and election outcomes are often decided at the margins, meaning that a few especially loud, focused activist efforts can have outsized influence not detectable from national polls. One of the interesting findings from a recent Pew survey is that single-issue gun voting seems to be concentrated among conservative Republicans. As the GOP has moved rightward, moderate Republicans and even establishment conservatives increasingly must fear a primary election challenge. In such circumstances, particularly engaged constituency groups have disproportionate influence, given that they may determine the outcome of low-turnout primary elections. Elected officials know that gun rights supporters, who see each other regularly and keep abreast of ongoing developments, will be a consistent presence and for that reason must be taken into account even when gun policy is not in the headlines.

### How Has the NRA Shaped Gun Control Policy?

Profoundly, and its influence stems in large part from its structure. The national media focuses on the NRA's hold over Congress, but the group's influence is as strong at the state level, where many recent successes have occurred.

As of late 2013, the NRA had not lost a major battle over federal gun control legislation in nearly two decades. In 1994

Congress passed and President Clinton signed legislation banning the future manufacture of certain types of assault weapons
and high-capacity magazines for civilian use, but gun policy
enacted thereafter was friendly to gun rights. In the mid-1990s,
the NRA worked its congressional connections to effectively
halt government-sponsored research on the public health
consequences of firearms. In 2005, the organization secured
a federal law largely immunizing gun makers, distributors,
and dealers from a broad range of lawsuits, undermining one
of the gun control lobby's most promising strategies. In 2007,
after the Virginia Tech tragedy, Congress passed a law to help
states enter records of prohibited purchasers into the national
background check system. Although some gun rights groups
balked, the NRA shaped the legislation and extracted numerous concessions to make it a "win for American gun owners."
In 2009, gun groups won passage of legislation lifting the ban
on loaded guns in National Parks. In addition to this string
of victories, the NRA and its allies staved off congressional
proposals to reinstate the assault weapons ban and to require
background checks on most private gun sales. Although the
NRA did not get all that it wants—for example, a federal law
that would force states to accept each other's concealed weapons permits—the organization was successful at preventing
further gun restrictions.

At the state level, the NRA, its affiliates, and independent
gun rights advocacy groups have worked methodically on a
series of issue campaigns to deregulate firearms. We touched
on several of these campaigns in chapter 6. They include
securing preemption laws in most states, thereby limiting or
eliminating the authority of local governments to regulate
firearms; passing state laws barring lawsuits against the gun
industry before Congress did so nationally; eliminating local
law enforcement agencies' discretion in determining who can
be licensed to carry a concealed weapon; protecting shooting
ranges from lawsuits or other actions brought by annoyed
neighbors; removing restrictions on guns in bars, on campuses,

and in other public spaces; and securing reciprocity laws that allow concealed-carry license holders to holster their guns in other states.

These campaigns owe their success to a combination of smart strategy, the disproportionate representation of rural interests in many state legislatures, and the ease with which gun owners can be located and organized for political action. The upshot of these efforts is that guns have a more prominent place in public life today than they did 50 or 100 years ago.

### Does the NRA Represent the Firearms Industry?

The question is a matter of interpretation, but as a practical matter the answer may not matter much.

The NRA has long prided itself on being an authentic grass-roots membership organization that "is not affiliated with any firearm or ammunition manufacturers or with any businesses that deal in guns and ammunition." In recent years, gun control advocates and liberal journalists have challenged that statement. Their evidence:

- In 1999, when the gun industry was facing lawsuits from cities and victims, the NRA's then-president, Charlton Heston, told gun industry executives at their large annual trade show, "Your fight has become our fight." The NRA then made its top legislative priority passage of a federal law immunizing the gun industry; the measure was enacted in 2005. Such intervention was necessary, observers note, because the gun industry's official trade association, the National Shooting Sports Foundation, had nowhere near the NRA's political muscle.
- After the immunity law was enacted, the NRA introduced a corporate giving program that has reaped rewards from gun and ammunition manufacturers and dealers. Between 2005 and 2011, according to one report, the gun industry contributed somewhere between

$15 million and $39 million through the NRA's "Ring of Freedom" corporate sponsorship program. Some gun makers allow customers to "round up" their gun purchase to the nearest dollar, with the extra money—several million dollars in recent years—going to the NRA's political advocacy arm.

- Several gun industry executives serve on the NRA's 76-member board, including one as second vice president (as of this writing).
- Having the NRA take the lead on the political front serves the gun industry's bottom-line interests. Most obviously, the industry benefits when gun rights groups generate fear of firearm confiscation and gun owners respond by stocking up. Profits are higher when the industry doesn't have to spend money on political fights and when fewer regulations are in place. What's more, the widely respected NRA can insulate the industry from political heat when its products are misused—say, in a school massacre.

If you are persuaded by this evidence, the question is, what does it mean? To NRA critics, it means the organization will take positions primarily to shore up corporate profits, even if those positions are at odds with mainstream gun owners' views. Here is Mark Kelly, who became a gun control activist after the shooting of his wife, Rep. Gabrielle Giffords (D-AZ), writing an op-ed coinciding with the NRA's 2013 convention in Houston: "The NRA leadership's top priority is to make sure the corporations that make guns and ammunition continue to turn huge profits. Their top priority isn't you, the NRA member."

But it's not clear that the views of the industry are really more extreme than the views of the NRA's base (in fact, the opposite is probably true). And the larger suggestion—that the NRA is working for the gun industry—has its skeptics. If anything, say insiders, the NRA runs the show and the industry goes along because it fears the NRA's wrath and because their interests are largely aligned anyway.

Political scientist Robert Spitzer has observed that at least since the early twentieth century a "'revolving door' commonly existed between personnel in the NRA and the weapons industry."[6] And for decades the NRA has carried political water for the gun industry, which didn't have a lobbyist until 1989. In the 1990s, when gun manufacturers attempted to compromise with the Clinton administration, the NRA penalized them for stepping out of line. Since then, the industry has been content to continue supporting the NRA financially—by advertising in its magazines, contributing to its corporate fundraising program, and selling NRA memberships in gun shops—while deferring to the association on the handling of policy questions and political controversies. As reporter Paul Barrett, author of a book on the Glock company, wrote, "The companies that make and market firearms might prefer a softer tone, but they rarely complain publicly about NRA fear mongering because it's good for business."[7]

For gun control groups, however, there may be strategic reasons to play up NRA-industry ties. As longtime gun control advocate Josh Sugarmann noted, "I think it's much easier for policymakers to defend the NRA when they're perceived as efforts on behalf of gun owners. That equation changes dramatically when they're seen as defending the gun industry."

# 11

# THE GUN CONTROL MOVEMENT

## *What Is the Gun Control Movement?*

Like the gun rights movement, the gun control movement includes national, state, and local organizations, both those that are singularly devoted to the cause and allied organizations from the women's, religious, and minority communities that step in to help during major legislative battles. And like the gun rights movement, gun control groups use an array of educational, lobbying, and electoral strategies to advance their cause. However, historically the gun control movement has lacked the energized grassroots membership and steady financial resources that their opponents enjoy. Indeed, a 2006 scholarly history went so far as to argue that by any reasonable standard there was no real gun control movement in America. That may be changing.

Unlike a lot of other issues, civil rights for example, gun control has not relied on a mass movement from below to secure many key laws. In the 1930s, when Congress enacted restrictions on machine guns and created a federal licensing scheme for dealers, the key player was the US attorney general, though women's groups testified and mobilized their members in favor of those foundation-setting laws. The landmark gun control laws of the late 1960s, including the Gun Control Act of 1968, were the handiwork of key Congress members and President Johnson, though a short-lived "Emergency Committee for Gun Control" generated thousands of letters from concerned citizens in support of the bill.

The institutional gun control lobby really began to form amid the handgun-crime wave of the early 1970s. Between 1974 and 1976, six state gun control groups and five national organizations were established, including two that would go on to lead the movement in the decades to come: the National Council to Control Handguns (later renamed Handgun Control Inc. and now called the Brady Campaign to Prevent Gun Violence) and the National Coalition to Ban Handguns (now called the Coalition to Stop Gun Violence). The Brady group is a membership association that traditionally has relied primarily on contributions from the public that tend to flow most heavily in response to high-profile acts of gun violence; the Coalition was founded by the Methodist Church as an association of women's, labor, and religious groups and today also includes individual members.

The gun control universe expanded during the gun violence epidemic of the 1980s and 1990s. The Violence Policy Center was founded in 1988 to conduct research useful to gun control advocates. During the 1990s, 46 state groups were formed to pursue educational and legislative strategies to reduce gun violence; many of these groups arose in response to citizens' concerns about gun violence involving youths. After a spate of school shootings in the late 1990s, women formed the Million Mom March to stage protests and lobby for gun control; they later became part of the Brady Campaign. However, the resources of the gun control lobby never have come close to those of the National Rifle Association. One study estimated that the combined membership of state and national gun control groups in the early 2000s was about 7% of that of the NRA. The combined revenues of the Coalition and the Brady Campaign (and their respective educational arms) likewise totaled about 7% of the NRA's revenues in 2001.

These longtime gun control advocacy groups are still far smaller than the NRA, but in the 2000s, they were joined by a 600-pound gorilla: New York City Mayor Michael Bloomberg, whose personal wealth is estimated at $27 billion and who has made gun reform a key priority in his capacity both as an elected official and as a philanthropist. In 2006, Mayor Bloomberg, along with Mayor Thomas Menino of Boston, founded Mayors Against Illegal Guns (MAIG), a research and political advocacy organization that has become the de facto chief strategist of the gun control movement. The organization counts more than 1,000 mayors among its membership.

Two other recent developments may help the gun control movement begin to level the playing field against its better-funded, better-organized opponents. The first development is the decision by gun control advocates to focus on elections. In past years, the Brady Campaign's PAC has given a few contributions here and there, but the organization never had the resources to be a power player. Sensing a void, Mayor Bloomberg has begun using his Independence USA "super PAC" to unseat NRA-friendly candidates and fund the candidacies of gun control supporters. In a 2013 special election for a Chicago congressional seat, Bloomberg's PAC contributed more than $2 million, helping an underdog candidate sail to victory over a better-known opponent.

Paralleling Bloomberg's efforts are those of Gabrielle Giffords, the Arizona congresswoman who was shot in the head and nearly killed at a constituent event outside a Tucson grocery store in 2011. Along with her husband, the former astronaut Mark Kelly, Giffords founded Americans for Responsible Solutions, a super PAC and a lobbying group whose goal is to raise millions to influence the 2014 midterm elections and beyond. As longtime gun owners and self-identified Second Amendment supporters, Giffords and Kelly are also lobbying personally, appearing in the media, and sponsoring television ads in favor of stricter national gun laws. Within the first six months of its existence, the Giffords-Kelly super PAC had raised almost as much as its NRA counterpart.

The second significant development within the gun control movement is the decision to engage family members and survivors of gun violence as full-time lobbyists, media spokespeople, and grassroots advocates. Although victims and family members had always played a key role at the local and state levels—often they were the founders of grassroots gun violence prevention groups—they generally did not maintain a high-profile presence on the national stage. Some notable exceptions included Sarah Brady, whose husband, James, was severely wounded in the 1981 assassination attempt on President Reagan; Tom Mauser, whose son, Daniel, was killed in the 1999 Columbine High School shootings; and Mary Leigh Blek, a Southern California activist whose son was murdered and who became chair of the Million Mom March organization. With the mass shooting at Virginia Tech, the number of survivors and family members advocating for gun control increased manyfold. The Virginia Tech families were key to passage of the 2007 federal legislation to improve the national background check system, and many have continued to be active on other gun reform measures at both the state and national levels. After the recent mass shootings in Tucson, Aurora, and Newtown, more and more victims and family members have joined the cause, in many cases as fulltime employees of national gun control groups. These survivors and family members have also found each other, creating a supportive advocacy network that spans different shootings.

### Why Is the Gun Control Movement Relatively Weak?

Although gun control groups have had some notable victories, including enactment of a federal background check law in 1993, the movement historically has struggled to raise the money and mobilize the sustained, grassroots engagement enjoyed by the gun rights movement. This asymmetry may be the real gun control paradox: Americans favor stronger gun laws but historically have not mobilized very noticeably to achieve that goal.

One set of challenges is built into the issue itself. As we noted earlier, an axiom of politics holds that it's easier to block legislative proposals than to get them passed. While opponents simply have to agree that they don't like a proposal, supporters of new policies have to agree on what they would like done. Historically, gun control leaders have disagreed among themselves, sometimes bitterly, over which policy option would be most effective, while the gun rights movement has been unified around the notion that having fewer gun laws is better than having more. The general public—whose consent gun control advocates presumably must court—also has lacked consensus on how best to prevent firearms violence: Should we put more police in schools? Spend more on mental health screening and treatment? Reduce the depiction of violence in the media? Ban assault weapons? Polls suggest there is no single, overwhelmingly supported approach. Recently, something like a consensus has begun to form, within the gun control movement and the general public, about the priority of expanding background checks to most or all gun sales.

A second challenge is that gun control belongs to a broader category of social regulatory policies, which restrict individual liberties in the perceived interest of the public good. To people whose behavior is regulated by these policies, they have moralizing overtones, with the government telling individuals how to live their lives. In a political culture prioritizing personal autonomy, such regulations are often difficult to enact. This challenge is compounded in the realm of gun control, which has been successfully branded as a threat to American values.

Gun control groups also face the challenge of promoting what economists call a public good, in this case, a society free of gun violence. Because people benefit from a public good regardless of whether they helped to achieve it, they have a tendency to withhold their time and money and "free ride" on the contributions of others. One way to overcome this problem is to offer incentives for people to join, as we discussed earlier in this book. While gun rights groups can offer all sorts of incentives for members—glossy magazines, opportunities to have fun at the firing range, the feeling of supporting the cause of liberty—gun control groups must rely primarily on altruistic incentives, which work well for a relatively small number of especially civic-minded people but are the least effective at mobilizing en masse. For this reason, groups advocating for public goods have chronic problems sustaining mass memberships. The twin challenges of enacting social regulation and organizing around public goods are compounded in the case of gun control, where the connection between the specific policy and its effects may not be visible immediately.

So gun control groups start off with some built-in disadvantages that afflict movements for other types of reforms as well. But the gun control movement has its own unique challenges. For one, its core constituency—people who have suffered from gun violence or live in fear of it—often lack what political scientists call "civic resources." Many survivors and family members live in low income communities and lack time, money, and powerful networks that are useful in movement building; many would-be advocates also are emotionally depleted by their experience. Likewise, the gun control movement traditionally has been ambivalent about organizing at the grass roots and pursuing the sort of incremental, state-to-state strategy for which movements are well suited. Although this perspective is evolving, for the first few decades of their existence national gun control groups focused on passing strict federal legislation on the theory that, with guns and "bad guys" moving easily across jurisdictions, local or state policies would be ineffective. The gun control movement has also struggled to find powerful frameworks to inspire people to join, though it has had success in mobilizing women with arguments centered on children's safety. A prominent example is Moms Demand Action for Gun Sense in America, which an Indiana mother of five began as a Facebook page the day after the Sandy Hook school shooting; within months the organization counted more than 100,000 grassroots supporters and activist chapters in every state. As of this writing, the mothers' group had announced plans to merge with the mayors' group, a marriage that would combine grassroots intensity with big money.

One of the greatest challenges, however, has been that the gun control movement faces an implacable, well-funded, and occasionally threatening foe. (Gun rights supporters have been known to show up at gun control meetings legally carrying loaded weapons and to threaten sexual violence against mothers supporting gun reform—such tactics have acquired a name, "the hassle factor.") The gun rights movement has millions of supporters delivering a very disciplined message, that gun control is futile at best and un-American at worst, and that message has gained traction among the public and many lawmakers over the last two decades. When activists are literally and figuratively outgunned, it's tempting to get discouraged and move on to other causes where political engagement is more likely to bear fruit. Interestingly, many of the gun control movement's state and local leaders have been at their jobs for a long time, showing no signs of retreat, but activism among the movement's foot soldiers has been harder to sustain.

### What Happens after a High-Profile Shooting?

If it happens in England or Australia, lawmakers enact sweeping gun control laws. In the United States, however, the outcomes are more variable.

High-profile shootings such as assassinations and massacres in seemingly safe spaces often move a public policy issue onto the public agenda and provide an opportunity to debate and possibly enact legislation. However, the window of opportunity is often narrow, as attention by the public, media, and lawmakers tends to shift quickly.

The political scientist Robert Spitzer has observed that high-profile shootings often provoke a cycle of outrage, action, and reaction. An especially shocking shooting sparks an outpouring of popular emotion and demands for change; lawmakers respond by considering stricter gun laws and sometimes passing them; and gun rights advocates respond by mustering resources and activists to fight these efforts. The challenge for gun control advocates is to keep the attention of the media, the public, and policymakers focused for as long as possible; for gun rights supporters, the goal is to influence the terms of debate, or to change the subject entirely. As we discussed in chapter 8, mass shootings don't change many people's opinions about the wisdom of gun control. But they do intensify the emotional urgency felt by those supporting stronger laws and the threat experienced by those who oppose such regulations.

For gun control supporters, continued media coverage is critical. A study of the Columbine High School shooting found that the national media (specifically, the *New York Times*) followed the story for a month before yielding space to other news events. Media coverage of school shootings unfolds in terms that are favorable to gun control advocates, who seek to frame individual incidents as part of broader problems that government has an obligation to address. Over time media stories about school shootings come to focus on the societal implications and future remedies or actions to be taken.

However, just because gun control advocates hope that policy change emerges from tragedies, and just because the media gravitate to this story angle, lawmakers don't necessarily oblige. In some cases—say, the assassination of President Kennedy in 1963 or the 2011 shooting of a congresswoman, a federal judge, and 17 others at a Tucson shopping center—high-profile gun violence provokes no policy change. In other cases, high-profile events may contribute to policy change already under consideration or on its way. In rare cases, such shootings prove to be the driving force behind new gun laws, but only in circumstances that are otherwise politically hospitable.

At the federal level, when high-profile shootings make a difference in public policy, they do so as catalysts for legislative action already under consideration—providing the proverbial straw that broke the camel's back. Take the case of the landmark federal gun control laws enacted in 1968, the Omnibus Crime Control and Safe Streets Act and the Gun Control Act. Key provisions had been under consideration for five years. The assassination of Robert F. Kennedy may have provided the final spur to the House to pass the omnibus bill and to the Johnson administration to push for introduction of the Gun Control Act, a more sweeping bill. But other factors were at work, including rioting and general social disorder, rising fear of crime, broad public support for gun control, and a sympathetic Congress and president. Contrast this outcome with the aftermath of the near assassination of President Reagan in 1981. At that time, the political conditions were less favorable toward gun reform, and no new federal laws were enacted. The modest federal background check bill bearing the name of Reagan's gravely wounded press secretary, James Brady, did not pass until 12 years later, when Democrats controlled the White House and Congress.

High-profile shootings are more likely to lead directly to policy change at the state level. After shootings at a high school in Springfield, Oregon, and a year later in Littleton, Colorado, activists got popular referenda on the ballot in those states to close the gun show loophole by requiring background checks on private sales at those events. Both measures passed handily. The Sandy Hook shootings provided the impetus to pass stronger gun laws in a handful of states. Again, terrible shootings aren't enough; they must be accompanied by favorable political conditions. Mass shootings in gun-friendly states (at schools in Mississippi and Kentucky in 1997 and Arkansas in 1998) often provoke no legislative response. By and large, the states that strengthened their firearms laws after the Sandy Hook shooting already had comparatively strong gun laws and weak gun rights lobbies. (And some states actually relaxed their gun laws after Sandy Hook.) Widely publicized shootings are important, but they are not all that's important.

## *Do the Media Favor Gun Control?*

Gun rights advocates and gun-friendly scholars have long complained that the media are allied against firearms owners and in favor of gun control. These critics charge that reporters approach firearms issues with a preconceived story line— guns are bad—and omit data or arguments at odds with that presumption. Another charge is that reporters tend to write about guns in ways that needlessly frighten the public—for example, by characterizing random upticks in shootings as out-of-control epidemics or by leaving the erroneous impression that machine guns are often used in crime. Finally, these critics provide evidence, some of it open to interpretation, that the media treat the pro-control cause more favorably, in both tone and amount of coverage, than they treat the gun rights cause and gun owners. Whatever organizational advantages the NRA may have, these authors argue, the pro-control groups have an almost monolithically sympathetic media establishment on their side, significantly leveling the political playing field.

While most work on media coverage of gun issues rests on anecdotes or small samples of news reporting, their general conclusion—that the media favor gun control—is consistent with a wider body of research on media norms and incentives. One of the most consistent findings is that the media play up conflict and drama, of which gun crime is an example, to generate ratings. As the saying goes, "If it bleeds, it leads." Thus one would expect large-scale violence, whether crime waves or mass shootings, to attract more attention than isolated cases of defensive gun use. A long-term study of network news stories on two major gun reforms—the Brady background check law and the assault weapons ban—found that the media's dominant framework centered on a "culture of violence" particularly in inner cities, a theme the study found was also promoted by gun control groups. Needless to say, stories about gun misuse do not put firearms in a positive light.

Gun rights advocates assert that media bias is rooted in the worldviews and political ideology of reporters, whom numerous studies have found to be overwhelmingly Democrats. In reality, any media slant is probably rooted in something much more mundane: the bottom line. The big agenda-setting newspapers in New York and Washington operate in localities with pro-control readerships and relatively weak gun cultures. The network news may skew in the same direction as it tries to attract female viewers, who are both pro-control and coveted by advertisers because women make household buying decisions.

Although some studies have documented a liberal, reformist slant in the traditional mainstream media, and logically that bias should favor gun control, there are reasons not to take the case too far. For example, one of the most-cited, recent studies documenting liberal media bias suggests that, in the area of gun policy, the bias may go the other way. Counting mainstream media mentions of think tanks and interest groups, the study found that the NRA was the tenth most cited organization generally, with more than five times as many citations as its rival, Handgun Control Inc. (which ranked 46th). Clearly, on gun policy the NRA is reporters' go-to organization. Similarly, the study of 1990s national gun control debates mentioned above found no media bias in favor of gun control or gun rights.

A final caveat is in order. Even if the mainstream media demonstrate bias toward gun control, these outlets no longer monopolize the market for information. With the proliferation of niche outlets on the Web, the "narrowcasting" of cable news, and the growth of social media, Americans are freer than ever to choose their news by seeking out sources suited to their political sensibilities. In such a wide-open media environment, bias by any single media outlet may not matter as much as it once did.

# 12

# WHAT SORTS OF GUN POLICIES MIGHT BE POLITICALLY ACCEPTABLE GOING FORWARD?

Every question about guns, gun violence, or gun policy is contentious. Basic facts—the annual number of gun transactions or even the number of guns in private hands—are not known with any precision. Estimates of the costs and consequences of our nation's gun laws are hotly disputed. Disparate beliefs about whether widespread gun possession is a guarantor of freedom and personal safety, or on the contrary a leading cause of early death and neighborhood decline, fuel acrimonious debates at family gatherings, online, and in the halls of government.

A commentator noted four decades ago that Americans were engaged in a great American gun war. That war has shown no signs of abating. Indeed, by some measures the politics of guns has intensified in recent years, raising questions about how we might proceed as a diverse, participatory democracy toward our common goal of reducing firearms violence.

In 2008, when the US Supreme Court found a constitutional right to keep a gun in the home, some commentators thought the ruling might open a new path forward on firearms policy. Fundamental gun rights having been secured, the reasoning went, the "slippery slope" argument was off the table, and America could at last craft careful, consensus-based regulations and other interventions to reduce unnecessary injury and death. Alas, such hopes were not fulfilled. Since the Court's landmark ruling, no gun legislation has passed at the national level, even after the spate of mass shootings that culminated with the murder of 20 children at Sandy Hook Elementary School. A few states enacted stronger regulations, but in most states the pro-gun lobby continued to hold sway.

Indeed, for the last three decades the trend has been toward weaker state and local regulation. The most dramatic change has been to loosen the restrictions on concealed carrying of firearms. Thirty years ago many states banned private citizens from carrying concealed, or restricted the privilege to those who were able to persuade the authorities of their trustworthiness and need for a gun. Now concealed carry is either unregulated (in five states) or legal for anyone with a permit—and in most states, law enforcement is denied any discretion in issuing those permits to applicants who meet the minimum criteria. At the same time state legislatures have been stripping away the restrictions on just where guns can be carried; the widespread enactment of state preemption laws (which blocked the cities from regulating "place and manner" of gun carrying) has been coupled with an easing of state bans on guns in locations such as bars, public buildings, universities, parades, polling places, and so forth. The *Heller* decision has, if anything, accelerated this trend.

The widespread deregulation of guns in America has been supported by an ethos of self-reliance together with much-touted (but suspect) research findings that can be summed up by the slogan "An armed society is a polite society." In this view the answer to crime, and indeed to mass shootings, is not government restriction on gun possession and carrying. The answer is more guns in more places more of the time. Carrying a gun is not only prudent (given the limited ability of the police to protect us) but also a public service. Indeed, half the states have adopted "stand your ground" laws that legitimize and offer legal protection for the private use of deadly force against someone who is perceived as threatening. This movement, and the accompanying rhetoric, is remarkable in part because it is such a departure from the norms that prevailed during the twentieth century and before. Even a frontier cow town like Dodge City banned firearms within city limits.

Of course not everyone is convinced that more guns in more places will ensure greater safety. Indeed, most Americans favor specific proposals to keep guns away from potentially dangerous people, including the 90% who support universal background checks. The push to permit gun carrying most everywhere meets with resistance. And a handful of states, including California and New York (all together including one-quarter of the U.S. population), have promulgated regulations of gun design, transactions, possession, and use that go well beyond the federal requirement.

The politics of gun regulation has become more closely aligned with party politics. Registered Republicans tend to prefer weaker gun laws, while registered Democrats prefer more stringent laws. The states with the strictest laws are all blue.

The 2010s constitute an especially partisan era, and guns help define the conflict. In such political circumstances, what might we do to reduce needless gun violence while protecting the rights of firearm owners? We see several promising approaches that, while likely to attract some controversy—all proposals involving firearms violence do—are well suited to balancing different interests while advancing shared goals.

*Technology.* In cases where policy fixes are unlikely, technological fixes show promise—birth control helped end infanticide, and nicotine-replacement products have reduced smoking. For several decades gun violence prevention advocates have urged the development of "personalized" guns, which could only be fired by the owner. For example, a gun can be engineered so that it will only fire when near an electronic key of the sort used to unlock vehicle doors (the radio frequency identification technology). Personalized guns wouldn't reduce violence by reckless or criminal owners, but they would cut down on household diversion to young children who find a loaded handgun in their parents' bedroom, to youths who want to "borrow" a household gun to show off to their friends or worse (as when Adam Lanza took his mother's firearms to murder children and educators at the Sandy Hook School), and to suicidal members of the household for whom a gun poses a deadly temptation. Furthermore, if it were sufficiently difficult to overcome the personalized locking mechanism, smart guns would be of reduced value to thieves.

Smart guns are in production but not yet sold in the United States. It is hard to see why pro-gun advocates would resist allowing buyers with this option when and if it has been proven sufficiently reliable—freedom of choice should include the freedom to buy a gun that does not expose household members to unnecessary risks.

*Policing.* Most gun assaults occur out in public. The guns that are involved in robberies and shootings are necessarily transported away from the home. A traditional goal of urban policing has been to "get the guns off the street," or at least to discourage youths, gang members, and other very dangerous people from carrying. In jurisdictions that take guns seriously, most notably New York City, police have made a practice of stopping people they have "reasonable suspicion" to believe are engaged in criminal behavior, such as carrying an illegal weapon. This practice may well deter illegal carrying of guns but places a heavy burden on individual privacy and police-community relations. If the selection of "suspects" appears to be influenced by their race, it is likely unconstitutional as well.

Still, law enforcement agencies are necessarily on the front lines in reducing gun violence. In addition to (or in place of) targeted patrols against illicit carrying, there are a variety of tactics available for discouraging illicit gun transactions, and for giving assaults with guns priority in the courts. The famous intervention run by the Boston Police Department known as Operation Ceasefire (beginning in 1996) used a creative "retail deterrence" strategy, informing gang members in person that gunplay would not be tolerated and that any indication of gun use by a member of a gang would single that gang out for special attention by the police.

It is also important for judges to cooperate in the view that illicit gun carrying is a serious offense so that they do not routinely dismiss such cases as "victimless." After all, most DUI cases are "victimless" in the same sense that there are no immediate victims, but without question reducing DUI—and illicit carrying—will save lives.

*Mental health.* Most people with mental disorders, even serious ones, do not shoot other people, and many of the warning signs that become clear in retrospect—withdrawal and delusions, for example—occur in the nonviolent population as well. Yet we know that certain types of mental illness put people at elevated risk for committing violence. How to identify and intervene with those especially at-risk people, while not stigmatizing those with mental illness or unnecessarily infringing on individual freedom, constitutes a vital challenge. Recent mass shootings have brought mental health experts and gun violence prevention advocates together to forge sensible approaches.

Current federal law disqualifies those who have been involuntarily committed to a mental institution, or who in some other context have been ruled mentally incompetent by a judge. That disqualification can only be effectively implemented in the handful of states that make mental health records available for NICS checks. Further, those provisions miss the great bulk of people with severe mental illness, including those who may have been voluntarily hospitalized. An alternative approach could be designed to remove guns from individuals who make specific threats and are deemed dangerous to themselves or others due to mental illness. In practice this approach would provide some protection for violence-prone individuals and their family and friends. A quick-response option of this sort should be coupled with a process to restore gun rights when the danger has dissipated.

In this regard it is worth emphasizing that for most Americans who die every year from gunfire, the wound is self-inflicted. Having thoughts of suicide has considerable overlap with mental illness, and the likelihood that such thoughts will result in death is greatly exacerbated when a firearm is handy. Taking steps to keep guns out of the hands of people who are prone to suicide is a task that begins at home and includes teachers, counselors, and others who may be in touch with the individual. Training and sensible protocols for responding to threats can make a difference in this regard.

*Respecting guns.* Government policies can influence behavior, but they become far more effective if they receive social support. Sometimes regulations make unhealthy or unsafe behaviors more problematic, and then social influence does the rest—creating and reinforcing positive norms to make prudent choices. Deaths due to drunk driving have declined because legal penalties are steeper, but also because most people no longer think it's okay to "have one for the road." Cigarette taxes and antismoking ordinances have reduced the number of people who light up, but quitting is also a product of individual will reinforced by community approbation.

It is our sense that traditional norms among hunters and other sportsmen have been very respectful of the harm that guns can do, embracing best practice in storing, handling, and discharging firearms. This perspective recognizes that guns can end up doing great harm even when possessed by a generally law-abiding adult—especially one who is careless, or tends to drink too much, or has a hot temper, or who has no training in handling a firearm. A view that respects the dangers posed by a firearm does not deny the pleasures of gun sports and collecting, or even the peace of mind that some gain by having a gun handy for self-defense. In dealing with cars, alcohol, medical procedures, and much else, we seek the right balance between risks and benefits—both in government policy and in what we teach our kids and say to our friends. Finding that balanced approach for firearms has not been easy, but it is our hope that there's still a possibility of a reasoned discussion based on the best available information.

That aspiration was the motivation for this book.

# NOTES

## Chapter 1

1. The Geneva Declaration reports that armed violence kills approximately 526,000 people each year. While this figure reflects armed violence by all weapons, the majority of lethal violence is committed with firearms.
2. This is based on the percentage of suicides committed with guns (an excellent proxy for prevalence of gun ownership).
3. DeConde 2001, 49–50.
4. In some cases the end of the barrel is sawed off to make the gun more easily concealed. Such weapons must be registered with the federal government under the National Firearms Act of 1934.

## Chapter 2

1. There were an average of 1 million residential burglaries per year, 2003–2007. Assuming 3% involved self-defense with a gun provides the answer.
2. The exceptions are Vermont, Arizona, Alaska, Arkansas, and Wyoming.
3. Baum 2010.
4. Ibid.
5. Ibid.

6. General Social Survey data show a rise during the 1980s and 1990s in the fraction of women who "definitely" don't think guns belong in the home.

7. The 1999 National Gun Policy Survey found that 30% of people who supported the right of any trained, noncriminal adult to get a concealed-carry permit changed their position once told that these gun owners would then be free to bring their handguns into stores, restaurants, and other public places.

8. Tarrance Group and Mellman, Lazarus & Lake/*U.S. News & World Report*, May 16–18, 1994 (1,000 telephone interviews of a national adult sample); Tarrance Group/American Firearms Council, July 21–23, 1996 (1,004 telephone interviews of a national sample of registered voters).

9. "Why Own a Gun? Protection Is Now Top Reason," Pew Research Center for the People and the Press, 2013.

10. Polsby and Kates 1997, 1238.

11. The Farleigh-Dickinson University's PublicMind Poll reached 863 registered voters by telephone (landline and cell) and had a margin of error of 3.4 percentage points.

12. As Polsby and Kates (1997, 1240) note, gun owners and gun control advocates "are inclined to make very different guesses about how much potential for evil to ascribe to the government of the United States."

### Chapter 3

1. The classification of gunshot deaths as "unintentional" in the Vital Statistics Registry is unreliable. Harvard researchers Catherine Barber and David Hemenway have found that there are numerous false positives and false negatives in this classification, and that to some extent they balance out.

2. Wolfgang 1958, 83.

3. Associated Press 1927.

4. Bjelopera et al. 2013, 10.

5. Vossekuil et al. 2002, 11–12.

6. Sanger-Katz 2013 (quoting University of Virginia Professor John Monahan).

7. Cook and Ludwig 2000.

**Chapter 4**

1. It is no surprise that not all scholars are on board with this finding. In his book *More Guns, Less Crime*, John Lott (2000) reports an analysis that finds that an increase in gun prevalence is associated with a reduced murder rate. In that study Lott uses a measure of gun prevalence that has not been validated and is of dubious validity (see Cook and Ludwig 2006). His aberrant finding is an example of an important but unsurprising lesson, that the analytical details, such as just what index of gun prevalence is used, can have a large effect on the results.

2. Redfield 2000 [1880], 17.

3. We thank Professor Matthew Miller of Harvard University for sharing these data with us. Data compiled from various sources, including the Small Arms Survey and national statistics bureaus.

**Chapter 5**

1. Corchado 2008.

2. Original tabulations from the 2004 survey. The data are available online from the Bureau of Justice Statistics. We limit the analysis to the 676 respondents who had not been in prison very long—sentenced after January 1, 2002—which should improve accuracy of recall. That limitation also makes the results more representative of currently active criminals. The problem with the full sample is that the prison population itself includes many who committed serious crimes decades earlier and received long sentences.

**Chapter 6**

1. As of this writing, state officials were deciding whether to appeal the ruling to the Supreme Court.

2. We thank Professor Joseph Blocher of Duke Law School for pointing us to this standard. For a discussion of scholarly attempts to articulate the proper standard, see Cornell and Kozuskanich 2013.

3. With respect to these groups, the 1968 Gun Control Act had barred sales only by federally licensed dealers. The 1986 law barred sales to these groups by all persons.

4. This is likely a low estimate, as eight states either did not or could not supply the information, or do not have a licensing scheme.

5. A January 27, 2000, NRA-ILA "Fact Sheet" claims that New York City seized guns from a Staten Island man who maintained his assault weapons after the ban went into effect, but according to the fact sheet, the police found the man not through a registry but through his public declaration that he would not comply with the law.

6. A couple of bills to raise firearm or ammunition taxes were introduced in Congress in the early 1990s but went nowhere.

7. North Carolina passed a law after this summary was compiled; we have excluded Wisconsin from the list, as universities appear to have a fairly straightforward way of working around its strictures.

### Chapter 8

1. Brearley 1932, 75.

2. Hosley 1999, 54.

3. A May 2013 Pew poll found that 48% of Americans prioritized gun rights over gun control, and 11% of them had contacted a public official within the past six months. This period included the first five months after the Sandy Hook school massacre, when new gun control legislation loomed and gun rights groups were mobilizing their members—and hence provides a good chance to measure the scope of the politically engaged gun owner subculture. A quick calculation suggests that this subculture constitutes 4% to 5% (0.11 × 0.48) of American adults. However, we take this to

be an upper-bound estimate, as people tend to overreport socially desirable practices (such as civic engagement), and such bias is amplified when the relevant sample population is small and the activity uncommon.

4. We thank Professor Saul Cornell for this observation.

5. Rankin 1967.

6. These laws made exceptions for law enforcement officers, travelers, and people who had been threatened. One state (New Mexico) limited the ban to "settlements." See Warner 1938, 539 n. 26.

7. One exception was Idaho's law, which was held unconstitutional in 1902.

8. Hoffman 1925, 31.

9. Warner 1938, 532.

10. The figure refers to the permitting process for in-state residents; a few "shall issue" states use the "may issue" system for out-of-state applicants. Rhode Island has a dual system; here it is counted as a "shall issue" state. The figure also reflects the movement of Illinois to the "shall issue" column, from the "no issue" column.

11. Halbrook 2000, 531.

12. Halbrook 2013, 218.

13. Halbrook (2000) suggests that the registry was "quite useful" (493) to Hitler's regime and "facilitated" repressive measures (502). The same author later goes further, stating that the Nazis "disarmed Berlin's Jews using the Weimar firearm registration records" (Halbrook 2006, 121). However, he provides no direct evidence for these assertions.

14. Horwitz and Anderson 2009, 152.

## Chapter 9

1. Benenson and Connolly 2013.

2. We thank Emily Tiry for doing this regression analysis, and we thank Scott Keeter at the Pew Center for People & the Press for

releasing the data. The analysis is based on Pew's gun policy survey conducted December 17–19, 2012.

3. See, for example, Grossback and Hammack 2003 on how these trends intersected in the traditionally Democratic state of West Virginia.

## Chapter 10

1. The 3.4 million figure is based on audited circulation figures for the NRA's three magazines on June 30, 2103. A choice of magazine comes free with membership. Reporters looking into the NRA's more expansive membership claims have found evidence that they are exaggerated, a practice not unheard of among nonprofit organizations.

2. Cherlin 2012.

3. Lorelei Kelly (2013) has argued that the NRA's influence has grown as Congress's capacity for generating policy expertise, benefiting from institutional memory and information sharing, and thinking long term have eroded.

4. Spitzer 2012, 91.

5. Schuman and Presser 1981, 46.

6. Spitzer 2012, 94

7. Barrett 2013.

# REFERENCES

*Chapter 1*

1993. "1991 National Survey of Fishing, Hunting, and Wildlife-Associated Recreation." Washington, DC: US Department of the Interior, US Department of Commerce.

2012. "2011 National Survey of Fishing, Hunting, and Wildlife-Associated Recreation." Washington, DC: US Department of the Interior, US Fish and Wildlife Service, US Department of Commerce, US Census Bureau.

2013. "First-Time Gun Buyers: A Study of Consumers That Purchased Their First Firearm in 2012." Newtown, CT: National Shooting Sports Foundation.

2013, February 12. "Gun Purchases under Obama's Presidency Four Times the Number of Babies Born." *Huffington Post*.

Associated Press. 2013, April 29. "Sturm, Ruger & Co. Profit Jumps 53 Percent as Gun Sales Surge."

Azrael, Deborah, Philip J. Cook, and Matthew Miller. 2004. "State and Local Prevalence of Firearms Ownership: Measurement, Structure, and Trends." *Journal of Quantitative Criminology* 20(1), 43–62.

Bear, James A. n.d. "Some Jefferson Ideas on Exercise, Guns and Game." Monticello Research Report.

Boyd, Julian Parks, ed. 1953. *The Papers of Thomas Jefferson*. Princeton, NJ: Princeton University Press.

Brauer, Jurgen. 2013. "The US Firearms Industry: Production and Supply." Geneva: Small Arms Survey, Graduate Institute of International and Development Studies.

Bureau of Alcohol, Tobacco, and Firearms. 2000. *Commerce in Firearms in the United States.* Washington, DC: US Department of the Treasury.

Bureau of Alcohol, Tobacco, Firearms, and Explosives. 2013. "Firearms Commerce in the United States: Annual Statistical Update 2013." Washington, DC: US Department of Justice.

Centers for Disease Control and Prevention. 2013, April 2. "National Suicide Statistics at a Glance: Case Fatality Rate among Persons Ages 10 Years and Older for Males and Females Separately, and by Selected Mechanism for Both Sexes Combined, United States, 2005–2009."

Centers for Disease Control and Prevention, National Center for Health Statistics. 2013. Compressed Mortality File 1999–2010.

Centers for Disease Control and Prevention, National Center for Injury Prevention and Control. 2013. Web-Based Injury Statistics Query and Reporting System (WISQARS).

Committee on Priorities for a Public Health Research Agenda to Reduce the Threat of Firearm-Related Violence. 2013. *Priorities for Research to Reduce the Threat of Firearm-Related Violence.* Edited by A. I. Leshner, B. M. Altevogt, A. F. Lee, M. A. McCoy, and P. W. Kelley. Washington, DC: National Academies Press.

Cook, Philip J. 1991. "The Technology of Personal Violence." *Crime and Justice: An Annual Review of Research* 14, 1–71.

Cook, Philip J., Wendy Cukier, and Keith Krause. 2009. "The Illicit Firearms Trade in North America." *Criminology and Criminal Justice* 9(3), 265–86.

Cook, Philip J., and Jens Ludwig. 1996. *Guns in America: Results of a Comprehensive National Survey on Firearms Ownership and Use.* Washington, DC: Police Foundation.

DeConde, Alexander. 2001. *Gun Violence in America: The Struggle for Control.* Boston: Northeastern University Press.

Geneva Declaration Secretariat. 2011. "Trends and Patterns of Lethal Violence." In *Global Burden of Armed Violence 2011: Lethal Encounters*, edited by Keith Krause, Robert Muggah, and Elisabeth Gilgen, 43–86. New York: Cambridge University Press.

Greene, Mark. 2013. "A Review of Gun Safety Technologies." Washington, DC: National Institute of Justice, US Department of Justice.

Hepburn, Lisa, Matthew Miller, Deborah Azrael, and David Hemenway. 2007. "The U.S. Gun Stock: Results from the 2004 National Firearms Survey." *Injury Prevention* 13(1), 15–9.

Hoyert, Donna L., and Jiaquan Xu. 2012. "Deaths: Preliminary Data for 2011." *National Vital Statistics Reports* 61(6), 1–65.

Kennett, Lee, and James LaVerne Anderson. 1975. *The Gun in America: The Origins of a National Dilemma*. Westport, CT: Greenwood Press.

Klevens, R. Monina, Jonathan R. Edwards, Chesley L. Richards, Teresa C. Horan, Robert P. Gaynes, Daniel A. Pollock, and Denise M. Cardo. 2007. "Estimating Health Care-Associated Infections and Deaths in US Hospitals, 2002." *Public Health Reports* 122(2), 160–6.

Krouse, William J. 2012. "Gun Control Legislation." Congressional Research Service.

La Jeunesse, William. 2012, December 18. "Gun Sales Surge after Connecticut Massacre." *Fox News*.

Lizotte, Alan J., David J. Bordua, and Carolyn S. White. 1981. "Firearms Ownership for Sport and Protection: Two Not So Divergent Models." *American Sociological Review* 46(4), 499–503.

McDougal, Topher, David A. Shirk, Rogert Muggah, and John H. Patterson. 2013. "The Way of the Gun: Estimating Firearms Traffic across the U.S.-Mexico Border." University of San Diego Trans-Border Institute and the Igarapé Institute.

Pew Research Center for the People and the Press. 2013. "Why Own a Gun? Protection Is Now Top Reason."

Planty, Michael, and Jennifer L. Truman. 2013. "Firearm Violence, 1993–2011." Washington, DC: Bureau of Justice Statistics, US Department of Justice.

Sheley, Joseph F., and James D. Wright. 1995. *In the Line of Fire: Youth, Guns, and Violence in Urban America*. Hawthorne, NY: Aldine de Gruyter.

Spitzer, Robert J. 2012. *The Politics of Gun Control*. Boulder, CO: Paradigm.

Stedman, Richard C., and Thomas A. Heberlein. 2001. "Hunting and Rural Socialization: Contingent Effects of the Rural Setting on Hunting Participation." *Rural Sociology* 66(4), 599–617.

US Department of Transportation, National Highway Traffic Safety Administration. 2010. "Highlights of the 2009 Motor Vehicle Crashes."

US Department of Energy. 2010. "Table 8.2 Vehicles and Vehicle-Miles Per Capita, 1950–2010." *Transportation Energy Data Book*. Oak Ridge, TN: Oak Ridge National Laboratory.

Velasco, Schuyler. n.d. "US Gun Industry Is Thriving. Seven Key Figures." *Christian Science Monitor*.

Violence Policy Center. 2011. "A Shrinking Minority: The Continuing Decline of Gun Ownership in America."

Wright, James D., Jana L. Jasinski, and Drew N. Lanier. 2012. "Crime, Punishment and Social Disorder: Crime Rates and Trends in Public Opinion over More Than Three Decades." In *Social Trends in American Life: Findings from the General Social Survey since 1972*, edited by Peter V. Marsden, 146–73. Princeton, NJ: Princeton University Press.

Wright, James D., and Peter H. Rossi. 1986. *Armed and Considered Dangerous: A Survey of Felons and Their Firearms* New York: Aldine de Gruyter.

*Chapter 2*

2012. "States' Laws and Requirements for Concealed Carry Permits Vary across the Nation." Washington, DC: US Government Accountability Office.

Aneja, Abhay, John J. Donohue III, and Alexandria Zhang. 2012. "The Impact of Right to Carry Laws and the NRC Report: The Latest

Lessons for the Empirical Evaluation of Law and Policy." Working Paper. Cambridge, MA: National Bureau of Economic Research.

Ayres, Ian, and John J. Donohue III. 2009. "More Guns, Less Crime Fails Again: The Latest Evidence from 1977–2006." *Econ Journal Watch* 6(2), 218–38.

Baum, Dan. 2010, August. "Happiness Is a Worn Gun: My Concealed Weapon and Me." *Harper's*, 29–38.

Bogus, Carl T. 2008. "Heller and Insurrectionism." *Syracuse Law Review* 59(2), 253–65.

Carlson, Jennifer. 2013. "Clinging to Their Guns: The New Politics of Gun Carry in Everyday Life." Unpublished.

Catalano, Shannan. 2010. "National Crime Victimization Survey Special Report: Victimization During Household Burglary." Washington, DC: US Department of Justice, Office of Justice Programs, Bureau of Justice Statistics.

Cook, Philip J., and Jens Ludwig. 2003. "Guns and Burglary." In *Evaluating Gun Policy: Effects on Crime and Violence*, edited by Jens Ludwig and Philip J. Cook, 74–118. Washington, DC: Brookings Institution Press.

——. 1996. *Guns in America: Results of a Comprehensive National Survey on Firearms Ownership and Use.* Washington, DC: Police Foundation.

Cook, Philip J., Jens Ludwig, and David Hemenway. 1997. "The Gun Debate's New Mythical Number: How Many Defensive Uses Per Year?" *Journal of Policy Analysis and Management* 16(3), 463–9.

Cook, Philip J., Mark H. Moore, and Anthony A. Braga. 2002. "Gun Control." In *Crime: Public Policies for Crime Control*, edited by James Q. Wilson and Joan Petersilia, 291–329. Oakland, CA: ICS Press.

*District of Columbia v. Heller.* 554 U.S. 570 (2008).

Donohue, John J., III. 2003. "The Impact of Concealed-Carry Laws." In *Evaluating Gun Policy: Effects on Crime and Violence*, edited by Jens Ludwig and Philip J. Cook, 287–324. Washington, DC: Brookings Institution Press.

Florida Department of Agriculture and Consumer Services Division of Licensing. 2013. "Concealed Weapon or Firearm License Holder Profile."

Goss, Kristin A., and Theda Skocpol. 2006. "Changing Agendas: The Impact of Feminism on American Politics." In *Gender and Social Capital*, edited by Brenda O'Neill and Elisabeth Gidengil, 323–56. New York: Routledge.

Hemenway, David. 1997a. "The Myth of Millions of Annual Self-Defense Gun Uses: A Case Study of Survey Overestimates of Rare Events." *Chance* 10(3), 6–10.

——. 1997b. "Survey Research and Self-Defense Gun Use: An Explanation of Extreme Overestimates." *Journal of Criminal Law and Criminology* 87(4), 1430–45.

——. 2011. "Risks and Benefits of a Gun in the Home." *American Journal of Lifestyle Medicine* 5(6), 502–11.

Hemenway, David, Deborah Azrael, and Matthew Miller. 2000. "Gun Use in the United States: Results from Two National Surveys." *Injury Prevention* 6(4), 263–7.

Hill, Jeffrey M. 1997. "The Impact of Liberalized Concealed Weapon Statutes on Rates of Violent Crime." Public Policy thesis, Duke University.

Horwitz, Joshua, and Casey Anderson. 2009. *Guns, Democracy, and the Insurrectionist Idea*. Ann Arbor: University of Michigan Press.

Kleck, Gary. 1997. *Targeting Guns: Firearms and Their Control*. Hawthorne, NY: Aldine de Gruyter.

Kleck, Gary, and Marc G. Gertz. 1995. "Armed Resistance to Crime: The Prevalence and Nature of Self-Defense with a Gun." *Journal of Criminal Law and Criminology* 86(1), 150–87.

Kopel, David B. 2001. "Lawyers, Guns, and Burglars." *Arizona Law Review* 43(2), 345–68.

Lott, John R. 2000. *More Guns, Less Crime: Understanding Crime and Gun Control Laws*. 2nd ed. Chicago: University of Chicago Press.

Lott, John R., Jr., and David B. Mustard. 1997. "Crime, Deterrence, and Right-to-Carry Concealed Handguns." *Journal of Legal Studies* 26(1), 1–68.

*Moore v. Madigan*, 708 F.3d 901 (7th Cir. 2013).

Newport, Frank. 2013, May 27. "Views in U.S. That Gov't Is Too Powerful Show Little Change." Gallup Organization.

Pew Research Center for the People and the Press. 2012. "After Newtown, Modest Change in Opinion About Gun Control."

———. 2013. "Gun Control: Key Data Points from Pew Research."

———. 2013. "Why Own a Gun? Protection Is Now Top Reason."

Polsby, Daniel D., and Don B. Kates, Jr. 1997. "Of Holocausts and Gun Control." *Washington University Law Quarterly* 75(3), 1237–75.

Rhodin, Tony. 2013, May 1. "Armed Revolution Might Be Coming in Next Few Years, 44 Percent of Republicans Say in National Poll." *Express-Times* (Lehigh Valley, PA).

Robuck-Mangum, G. 1997. "Concealed Weapon Permit Holders in North Carolina: A Descriptive Study of Handgun-Carrying Behavior." Master's thesis, University of North Carolina, School of Public Health.

Tark, Jongyeon, and Gary Kleck. 2004. "Resisting Crime: The Effects of Victim Action on the Outcomes of Crimes." *Criminology* 42(4), 861–910.

Wellford, Charles F., John V. Pepper, and Carol V. Petrie, eds. 2004. *Firearms and Violence: A Critical Review*. Washington, DC: National Academies Press.

*Chapter 3*

2012, August 24. "A History of Mass Shootings in the US since Columbine." *The Telegraph*.

1927, May 20. "School Dynamiter First Slew Wife." *New York Times*. 3.

Abrams, David S. 2011. "Estimating the Deterrent Effect of Incarceration Using Sentencing Enhancements." University of Pennsylvania, Institute for Law and Economics Research Paper.

Associated Press. 2012, July 20. "The Deadliest Mass Shootings around the World." *Huffington Post*.

——. 1927, May 19. "Survivors Tell of Explosion." *New York Times.*

Barber, Catherine, and David Hemenway. 2011. "Too Many or Too Few Unintentional Firearm Deaths in Official U.S. Mortality Data?" *Accident Analysis & Prevention* 43(3), 724–31.

Behavioral Analysis Unit, National Center for the Analysis of Violent Crime. 2008. "Serial Murder: Multi-disciplinary Perspectives for Investigators." Edited by R. J. Morton and M. A. Hilts. United States Department of Justice, Federal Bureau of Investigation.

Bjelopera, Jerome, Erin Bagalman, Sarah W. Caldwell, Kristin M. Finklea, and Gail McCallion. 2013. "Public Mass Shootings in the United States: Selected Implications for Federal Public Health and Safety Policy." Washington, DC: Congressional Research Service.

Blair, J. Pete, and M. Hunter Martaindale. 2013. "United States Active Shooter Events from 2000 to 2010: Training and Equipment Implications." Texas State University.

Campbell, Jacquelyn C., Daniel Webster, Jane Koziol-McLain, Carolyn Block, Doris Campbell, Mary Ann Curry, Faye Gary, Nancy Glass, Judith McFarlane, and Carolyn Sachs. 2003. "Risk Factors for Femicide in Abusive Relationships: Results from a Multisite Case Control Study." *American Journal of Public Health* 93(7), 1089–97.

Centers for Disease Control and Prevention, National Center for Injury Prevention and Control. n.d. Web-Based Injury Statistics Query and Reporting System (WISQARS).

Columbine Review Commission. 2001. "The Report of Governor Bill Owens' Columbine Review Commission."

Cook, Philip J. 1980. "Reducing Injury and Death Rates in Robbery." *Policy Analysis* 6(1), 21–45.

——. 1985. "The Case of the Missing Victims: Gunshot Woundings in the National Crime Survey." *Journal of Quantitative Criminology* 1(1), 91–102.

——. 1987. "Robbery Violence." *Journal of Criminal Law and Criminology* 78(2), 357–76.

———. 2009. "Crime Control in the City: A Research-Based Briefing on Public and Private Measures." *Cityscape* 11(1), 53–79.

Cook, Philip J., Wendy Cukier, and Keith Krause. 2009. "The Illicit Firearms Trade in North America." *Criminology and Criminal Justice* 9(3), 265–86.

Cook, Philip J., and John H. Laub. 2002. "After the Epidemic: Recent Trends in Youth Violence in the United States." *Crime and Justice* 29, 1–37.

Cook, Philip J., Bruce A. Lawrence, Jens Ludwig, and Ted R. Miller. 1999. "The Medical Costs of Gunshot Injuries in the United States." *Journal of the American Medical Association* 282(5), 447–54.

Cook, Philip J., and Jens Ludwig. 2002. "The Costs of Gun Violence against Children." *Future of Children* 12(2), 86–99.

———. 2000. *Gun Violence: The Real Costs.* New York: Oxford University Press.

Fields, Gary, and Cameron McWhirter. 2012, December 8. "In Medical Triumph, Homicides Fall Despite Soaring Gun Violence." *Wall Street Journal.*

Follman, Mark, Gavin Aronsen, and Deanna Pan. 2013, February 27. "A Guide to Mass Shootings in America." *Mother Jones.*

Fox, James Alan. 2012, August 6. "No Increase in Mass Shootings." *Boston Globe.*

Kleck, Gary, and Karen McElrath. 1991. "The Effects of Weaponry on Human Violence." *Social Forces* 69(3), 669–92.

Loftin, Colin, and David McDowall. 1984. "The Deterrent Effects of the Florida Felony Firearm Law." *Journal of Criminal Law and Criminology* 75(1), 250–9.

———. 1981. "'One with a Gun Gets You Two': Mandatory Sentencing and Firearms Violence in Detroit." *Annals of the American Academy of Political and Social Science* 455(1), 150–67.

Mayors Against Illegal Guns. 2013. "Analysis of Recent Mass Shootings."

McConville, Ben, and Jill Lawless. 2012, December 18. "Gun Control Laws around the World Spurred by Mass Shootings." *Huffington Post.*

Miller, Matthew, Catherine Barber, Richard A. White, and Deborah Azrael. 2013, August 23 (advanced online access). "Firearms and suicide in the United States: Is risk independent of underlying suicidal behavior?" *American Journal of Epidemiology*.

Miller, Matthew, and David Hemenway. 2008. "Guns and Suicide in the United States." *New England Journal of Medicine* 359(10), 989–91.

Raphael, Lev. 2011, May 16. "America's Deadliest School Massacre Is the One You Never Heard Of." *Huffington Post*.

Richardson, Erin G., and David Hemenway. 2011. "Homicide, Suicide, and Unintentional Firearm Fatality: Comparing the United States with Other High-Income Countries, 2003." *Journal of Trauma and Acute Care Surgery* 70(1), 238–43.

Saltzman, Linda E., James A. Mercy, and Philip H. Rhodes. 1992. "Identification of Nonfatal Family and Intimate Assault Incidents in Police Data." *American Journal of Public Health* 82(7), 1018–20.

Sanger-Katz, Margot. 2013, January 24. "Why Improving Mental Health Would Do Little to End Gun Violence." *National Journal*.

US Department of Justice, Federal Bureau of Investigation. 2010. "Crime in the United States, by Selected Offenses, 2009."

Vernick, Jon S., and Lisa M. Hepburn. 2003. "State and Federal Gun Laws: Trends for 1970–99." In *Evaluating Gun Policy: Effects on Crime and Violence*, edited by Jens Ludwig and Philip J. Cook, 345–402. Washington, DC: Brookings Institution Press.

Virginia Tech Review Panel. 2007. "Mass Shootings at Virginia Tech April 16, 2007: Report of the Review Panel."

Vossekuil, Bryan, Robert A. Fein, Marisa Reddy, Randy Borum, and William Modzeleski. 2002, May. "The Final Report and Findings of the Safe School Initiative." Washington, DC: US Secret Service and US Department of Education.

Wolfgang, Marvin E. 1958. *Patterns in Criminal Homicide*. Philadelphia: University of Pennsylvania Press.

——. 1995. "A Tribute to a View I Have Opposed." *Journal of Criminal Law and Criminology* 86(1), 188–92.

Wright, James D., Peter Henry Rossi, and Kathleen Daly. 1983. *Under the Gun: Weapons, Crime, and Violence in America*. New York: Aldine de Gruyter.

Zimring, Franklin E. 1968. "Is Gun Control Likely to Reduce Violent Killings?" *University of Chicago Law Review* 35(4), 721–37.

———. 1972. "The Medium Is the Message: Firearm Caliber as a Determinant of Death from Assault." *Journal of Legal Studies* 1(1), 97–123.

Zimring, Franklin E., and Gordon Hawkins. 1997. *Crime Is Not the Problem: Lethal Violence in America*. New York: Oxford University Press.

*Chapter 4*

2012, December 21. "Remarks from the NRA Press Conference on Sandy Hook School Shooting, Delivered on Dec. 21, 2012 (Transcript)." *Washington Post*.

American Foundation for Suicide Prevention et al. n.d. "Reporting on Suicide: Recommendations for the Media."

Anderson, Elijah. 1994, May. "The Code of the Streets." *The Atlantic*, 80–94.

Arsenault-Lapierre, Geneviève, Caroline Kim, and Gustavo Turecki. 2004. "Psychiatric Diagnoses in 3275 Suicides: A Meta-Analysis." *BMC Psychiatry* 4(1), 37.

Associated Press. 2012, December 21. "Transcript: Statement by National Rifle Association's Wayne LaPierre, Dec. 21, 2012."

Azrael, Deborah, Philip J. Cook, and Matthew Miller. 2004. "State and Local Prevalence of Firearms Ownership: Measurement, Structure, and Trends." *Journal of Quantitative Criminology* 20(1), 43–62.

Blumenthal, Stephen, and Lawrence Bergner. 1973. "Suicide and Newspapers: A Replicated Study." *American Journal of Psychiatry* 130(4), 468–71.

Brearley, Harrington Cooper. 1932. *Homicide in the United States*. Chapel Hill: University of North Carolina Press.

*Brown v. Entertainment Merchants Association*. 564 U.S. ____ (2011).

Bureau of Justice Statistics. 2012, December 20. "Press Release: Serious Violent Crime against Youth Dropped 77 Percent from 1994 to 2010."

Butterfield, Fox. 1995. *All God's Children: The Bosket Family and the American Tradition of Violence*. New York: Knopf.

Cook, Philip J. 1979. "The Effect of Gun Availability on Robbery and Robbery Murder: A Cross Section Study of Fifty Cities." *Policy Studies Review Annual* 3, 743–81.

———. 1991. "The Technology of Personal Violence." *Crime and Justice: An Annual Review of Research* 14, 1–71.

Cook, Philip J., and Kristin A. Goss. 1996. *"A Selective Review of the Social-Contagion Literature."* Terry Sanford Institute Working Paper, Duke University.

Cook, Philip J., and Jens Ludwig. 2003. "Guns and Burglary." In *Evaluating Gun Policy: Effects on Crime and Violence*, edited by Jens Ludwig and Philip J. Cook, 74–118. Washington, DC: Brookings Institution Press.

———. 2004. "Does Gun Prevalence Affect Teen Gun Carrying after All?" *Criminology* 42(1), 27–54.

———. 2006. "Aiming for Evidence-Based Gun Policy." *Journal of Policy Analysis and Management* 25(3), 691–735.

Cook, Philip J., Jens Ludwig, and Anthony A. Braga. 2005. "Criminal Records of Homicide Offenders." *Journal of the American Medical Association* 294(5), 598–601.

Crump, C., K. Sundquist, M. A. Winkleby, and J. Sundquist. 2013. "Mental Disorders and Vulnerability to Homicidal Death: Swedish Nationwide Cohort Study." *British Medical Journal* 346(7898), art. no. f557.

DeLisi, Matt, Michael G. Vaughn, Douglas A. Gentile, Craig A. Anderson, and Jeffrey J. Shook. 2013. "Violent Video Games, Delinquency, and Youth Violence: New Evidence." *Youth Violence and Juvenile Justice* 11(2), 132–42.

Duggan, Mark. 2001. "More Guns, More Crime." *Journal of Political Economy* 109(5), 1086–114.

Etzersdorfer, Elmar, and Gernot Sonneck. 1998. "Preventing Suicide by Influencing Mass-Media Reporting. The Viennese Experience 1980–1996." *Archives of Suicide Research* 4(1), 67–74.

Fazel, Seena, and Martin Grann. 2006. "The Population Impact of Severe Mental Illness on Violent Crime." *American Journal of Psychiatry* 163(8), 1397–403.

Felson, Richard B., and Paul-Philippe Pare. 2010. "Firearms and Fisticuffs: Region, Race, and Adversary Effects on Homicide and Assault." *Social Science Research* 39(2), 272–84.

Fischer, David H. 1989. *Albion's Seed: Four British Folkways in America.* New York: Oxford University Press.

Fisher, Max. 2012, December 17. "Ten-Country Comparison Suggests There's Little or No Link between Video Games and Gun Murders." *Washington Post.*

Freedom Forum. 2000. "State of the First Amendment Survey." Archived at the Roper Center.

Gastil, Raymond D. 1971. "Homicide and a Regional Culture of Violence." *American Sociological Review* 36(3), 412–27.

Glaeser, Edward L., Bruce Sacerdote, and Jose A. Scheinkman. 1996. "Crime and Social Interactions." *Quarterly Journal of Economics* 111(2), 507–48.

Goldman, Russell. 2012, December 20. "Schools Face Threats Nationwide Following Sandy Hook Shooting." *ABC News.*

Gould, Madelyn S. 2001. "Suicide and the Media." *Annals of the New York Academy of Sciences* 932(1), 200–24.

Hackney, Sheldon. 1969. "Southern Violence." *American Historical Review* 74(3), 906–25.

Hamilton, James. 1998. *Channeling Violence: The Economic Market for Violent Television Programming.* Princeton, NJ: Princeton University Press.

Holden, Robert T. 1986. "The Contagiousness of Aircraft Hijacking." *American Journal of Sociology* 91(4), 874–904.

Holmes, Joseph L. 1929. "Crime and the Press." *Journal of the American Institute of Criminal Law and Criminology* 20(2), 246–93.

Huesmann, L. Rowell, Jessica Moise-Titus, Cheryl-Lynn Podolski, and Leonard D. Eron. 2003. "Longitudinal Relations between Children's

Exposure to TV Violence and Their Aggressive and Violent Behavior in Young Adulthood: 1977–1992." *Developmental Psychology* 39(2), 201–21.

Joyal, Christian C., Jean-Luc Dubreucq, Catherine Gendron, and Frederic Millaud. 2007. "Major Mental Disorders and Violence: A Critical Update." *Current Psychiatry Reviews* 3(1), 33–50.

Kleck, Gary, and E. B. Patterson. 1993. "The Impact of Gun Control and Gun Ownership Levels on Violence Rates." *Journal of Quantitative Criminology* 9(3), 249–87.

Lance, David. 1988. "Product Tampering." *FBI Law Enforcement Bulletin* 57(4), 20–3.

Le Bon, Gustave. 1896. *The Crowd: A Study of the Popular Mind.* New York: Macmillan.

Lee, Matthew R., William B. Bankston, Timothy C. Hayes, and Shaun A. Thomas. 2007. "Revisiting the Southern Culture of Violence." *Sociological Quarterly* 48(2), 253–75.

Loftin, Colin, and Robert H. Hill. 1974. "Regional Subculture and Homicide: An Examination of the Gastil-Hackney Thesis." *American Sociological Review* 39(5), 714–24.

Loftin, Colin, and David McDowall. 2003. "Regional Culture and Patterns of Homicide." *Homicide Studies* 7(4), 353–67.

Lott, John R. 2000. *More Guns, Less Crime*: Understanding Crime and Gun Control Laws. 2nd ed. Chicago: University of Chicago Press.

Messner, Steven F. 1986. "Television Violence and Violent Crime: An Aggregate Analysis." *Social Problems* 33(3), 218–35.

Mitchell, Alice Miller. 1929. *Children and Movies.* Chicago: University of Chicago Press.

Moffat, Steverson O., ed. 2003. "Bugs, Budgets, Mergers, and Fire: Disturbance Economics." Proceedings of the Southern Forest Economics Workers Annual Meeting, New Orleans, LA.

Morgan, N., D.A.G. Cook, C. E. Dorkins, and M. E. Doyle. 1995. "An Outbreak of Copycat Fire Raising." *British Journal of Medical Psychology* 68(4), 341–8.

Mortensen, P. B., E. Agerbo, T. Erikson, P. Qin, and N. Westergaard-Nielsen. 2000. "Psychiatric Illness and Risk Factors for Suicide in Denmark." *Lancet* 355(9197), 9–12.

Motto, Jerome A. 1970. "Newspaper Influence on Suicide: A Controlled Study." *Archives of General Psychiatry* 23(2), 143–8.

Nisbett, Richard E. 1993. "Violence and U.S. Regional Culture." *American Psychologist* 48(4), 441–9.

Nisbett, Richard E., and Dov Cohen. 1996. *Culture of Honor: The Psychology of Violence in the South.* Boulder, CO: Westview.

Paik, Haejung, and George Comstock. 1994. "The Effects of Television Violence on Antisocial Behavior: A Meta-Analysis 1." *Communication Research* 21(4), 516–46.

Phillips, David P., and Lundie L. Carstensen. 1986. "Clustering of Teenage Suicides after Television News Stories about Suicide." *New England Journal of Medicine* 315(11), 685–9.

Planty, Michael, and Jennifer L. Truman. 2013. "Firearm Violence, 1993–2011." Washington, DC: Bureau of Justice Statistics, US Department of Justice.

Redfield, H. V. 2000 [1880]. *Homicide, North and South.* Columbus: Ohio State University Press.

Roth, Randolph. 2009. *American Homicide.* Cambridge: Belknap Press of Harvard University Press.

Savage, Joanne. 2004. "Does Viewing Violent Media Really Cause Criminal Violence? A Methodological Review." *Aggression and Violent Behavior* 10(1), 99–128.

Savage, Joanne, and Christina Yancey. 2008. "The Effects of Media Violence Exposure on Criminal Aggression: A Meta-Analysis." *Criminal Justice and Behavior* 35(6), 772–91.

Sonneck, Gernot, Elmar Etzersdorfer, and Sibylle Nagel-Kuess. 1994. "Imitative Suicide on the Viennese Subway." *Social Science and Medicine* 38(3), 453–7.

Stack, Steven. 2005. "Suicide in the Media: A Quantitative Review of Studies Based on Nonfictional Stories." *Suicide and Life-Threatening Behavior* 35(2), 121–33.

Surette, Ray. 2012. "Cause or Catalyst: The Interaction of Real World and Media Crime Models." *American Journal of Criminal Justice*, 38(3), 392–409.

Swanson, Jeffrey W. 1994. "Mental Disorder, Substance Abuse, and Community Violence: An Epidemiological Approach." In *Violence and Mental Disorder: Developments in Risk Assessment*, edited by John Monahan and Henry J. Steadman, 101–36. Chicago: University of Chicago Press.

Swanson, J. W., C. E. Holzer, V. K. Ganju, and R. T. Jono. 1990. "Violence and Psychiatric Disorder in the Community: Evidence from the Epidemiologic Catchment Area Surveys." *Hospital and Community Psychiatry* 41(7), 761–70.

Swartz, Marvin S., Jeffrey W. Swanson, Virginia A. Hiday, Randy Borum, H. Ryan Wagner, and Barbara J. Burns. 1998. "Violence and Severe Mental Illness: The Effects of Substance Abuse and Nonadherence to Medication." *American Journal of Psychiatry* 155(2), 226–31.

Truman, Jennifer L., and Michael Planty. 2012. "Criminal Victimization, 2011." Washington, DC: US Department of Justice, Office of Justice Programs, Bureau of Justice Statistics.

Tufekci, Zeynep. 2012, December 19. "The Media Needs to Stop Inspiring Copycat Murders. Here's How." *The Atlantic*.

US Centers for Disease Control and Prevention. 2013. "FastStats: Assault or Homicide."

——. 2013. "FastStats: Suicide and Self-Inflicted Injury."

US Department of Justice, Bureau of Justice Statistics. 2007. "Survey of Inmates in State and Federal Correctional Facilities, 2004." Ann Arbor, MI: Inter-university Consortium for Political and Social Research.

Van Dorn, Richard, Jan Volavka, and Norman Johnson. 2012. "Mental Disorder and Violence: Is There a Relationship beyond Substance Use?" *Social Psychiatry and Psychiatric Epidemiology* 47(3), 487–503.

*Chapter 5*

2013, February. "ATF Fact Sheet: FFL Compliance Inspections." Washington, DC: Bureau of Alcohol, Tobacco, Firearms, and Explosives.

2013, April. "Review of ATF'S Federal Firearms Licensee Inspection Program." Washington, DC: US Department of Justice Office of the Inspector General.

2013. "Small Arms Manufacturing Industry in the U.S. And Its International Trade (2013 Q2 Edition)." Supplier Relations US, LLC.

Braga, Anthony A., and Peter L. Gagliardi. 2013. "Enforcing Federal Laws against Firearms Traffickers: Raising Operational Effectiveness by Lowering Enforcement Obstacles." In *Reducing Gun Violence in America*, edited by Daniel W. Webster and Jon S. Vernick, 143–54. Baltimore, MD: Johns Hopkins University Press.

Braga, Anthony A., Garen J. Wintemute, Glenn L. Pierce, Philip J. Cook, and Greg Ridgeway. 2012. "Interpreting the Empirical Evidence on Illegal Gun Market Dynamics." *Journal of Urban Health* 89(5), 779–93.

Brauer, Jurgen. 2013. "The US Firearms Industry: Production and Supply." Geneva: Small Arms Survey, Graduate Institute of International and Development Studies.

Bureau of Alcohol, Tobacco, and Firearms. 2000. *Commerce in Firearms in the United States*. Washington, DC: US Department of the Treasury.

Bureau of Alcohol, Tobacco, Firearms, and Explosives. 2013. *Firearms Commerce in the United States*: Annual Statistical Update 2013. Washington, DC: US Department of Justice.

Chu, Vivian S. 2012. "Internet Firearm and Ammunition Sales." Washington, DC: Congressional Research Service.

Cook, Philip J., and Anthony A. Braga. 2001. "Comprehensive Firearms Tracing: Strategic and Investigative Uses of New Data on Firearms Markets." *Arizona Law Review* 43(2), 277–309.

Cook, Philip J., Wendy Cukier, and Keith Krause. 2009. "The Illicit Firearms Trade in North America." *Criminology and Criminal Justice* 9(3), 265–86.

Cook, Philip J., and Jens Ludwig. 1996. *Guns in America: Results of a Comprehensive National Survey on Firearms Ownership and Use.* Washington, DC: Police Foundation.

Cook, Philip J., Jens Ludwig, Sudhir Venkatesh, and Anthony A. Braga. 2007. "Underground Gun Markets." *Economic Journal* 117(524), 588–618.

Cook, Philip J., Stephanie Molliconi, and Thomas B. Cole. 1995. "Regulating Gun Markets." *Journal of Criminal Law and Criminology* 86(1), 59–92.

Corchado, Alfredo. 2008, November 27. "Outgoing U.S. Ambassador to Mexico Lashes Out on Drug War." *Dallas Morning News.*

Diaz, Tom. 2013. *The Last Gun: How Changes in the Gun Industry Are Killing Americans and What It Will Take to Stop It.* New York: New Press.

Dube, Arindrajit, Oeindrila Dube, and Omar García-Ponce. 2013. "Cross-Border Spillover: US Gun Laws and Violence in Mexico." *American Political Science Review* 107(3), 397–417.

Mayors Against Illegal Guns. 2008. "The Movement of Illegal Guns in America: The Link between Gun Laws and Interstate Gun Trafficking."

Stewart, Scott. 2011, February 10. "Mexico's Gun Supply and the 90 Percent Myth." *Stratfor Global Intelligence.*

Sugarmann, Josh. 1992. *More Gun Dealers Than Gas Stations: A Study of Federally Licensed Firearms Dealers in America.* Washington, DC: Violence Policy Center.

US Department of Justice. Bureau of Justice Statistics. 2001. "Survey of Inmates in State and Federal Correctional Facilities, 1997." Ann Arbor, MI: Inter-university Consortium for Political and Social Research.

——. 2007. "Survey of Inmates in State and Federal Correctional Facilities, 2004." Ann Arbor, MI: Inter-university Consortium for Political and Social Research.

Violence Policy Center. 2007. "An Analysis of the Decline in Gun Dealers: 1994 to 2007."

——. 2011. "The Militarization of the U.S. Civilian Firearms Market."

Webster, Daniel W., Lorraine H. Freed, Shannon Frattaroli, and Moderna H. Wilson. 2002. "How Delinquent Youths Acquire Guns: Initial versus Most Recent Gun Acquisitions." *Journal of Urban Health* 79(1), 60–9.

Webster, Daniel W., Jon S. Vernick, and Maria T. Bulzacchelli. 2009. "Effects of State-Level Firearm Seller Accountability Policies on Firearm Trafficking." *Journal of Urban Health* 86(4), 525–37.

Webster, Daniel W., Jon S. Vernick, Emma E. McGinty, and Ted Alcorn. 2013. "Preventing the Diversion of Guns to Criminals through Effective Firearm Sales Laws." In *Reducing Gun Violence in America*, edited by Daniel W. Webster and Jon S. Vernick, 109–22. Baltimore, MD: Johns Hopkins University Press.

Wintemute, Garen J. 2007. "Gun Shows across a Multistate American Gun Market: Observational Evidence of the Effects of Regulatory Policies." *Injury Prevention* 13(3), 150–5.

——. 1994. *Ring of Fire: The Handgun Makers of Southern California*. Sacramento, CA: Violence Prevention Research Program.

Wintemute, Garen J., Philip J. Cook, and Mona A. Wright. 2005. "Risk Factors among Handgun Retailers for Frequent and Disproportionate Sales of Guns Used in Violent and Firearm-Related Crimes." *Injury Prevention* 11(6), 357–63.

*Chapter 6*

109th Congress of the United States of America. 2005. "S. 397 Protection of Lawful Commerce in Arms Act." Washington, DC.

Bade, Rachael. 2013, April 9. "Using Sales Taxes as a Gun Control Tool." *Politico*.

Brady Campaign to Prevent Gun Violence. 2011. "2011 State Rankings."

Bureau of Alcohol, Tobacco, Firearms, and Explosives. 2011. "Permanent Brady Permit Chart." Washington, DC: US Department of Justice.

Bureau of Justice Statistics. 1994. "Firearms and Crimes of Violence." Washington, DC: US Department of Justice.

Butterfield, Fox. 2000, April 3. "Massachusetts to Enforce Strict Gun Safety Laws." *New York Times*.

Cassidy, Warren. 1983, April. "Morton Grove: The Next Step." *American Rifleman*. 54.

Cheng, Cheng, and Mark Hoekstra. 2012. "Does Strengthening Self-Defense Law Deter Crime or Escalate Violence? Evidence from Castle Doctrine." Working Paper. Cambridge, MA: National Bureau of Economic Research.

Cook, Philip J., Jens Ludwig, and Adam M. Samaha. 2009. "Gun Control after *Heller*: Threats and Sideshows from a Social Welfare Perspective." *UCLA Law Review* 56(5), 1041–93.

Cooper, Alexia, and Erica L. Smith. 2011. "Homicide Trends in the United States, 1980–2008." Washington, DC: US Department of Justice, Bureau of Justice Statistics.

Cornell, Saul. 2006. *A Well-Regulated Militia: The Founding Fathers and the Origins of Gun Control in America*. New York: Oxford University Press.

Cornell, Saul, and Nathan Kozuskanich. 2013. "The Scholarly Landscape since *Heller*." In *The Second Amendment on Trial*, edited by Saul Cornell and Nathan Kozuskanich, 383–400. Amherst: University of Massachusetts Press.

*District of Columbia v. Heller*. 554 U.S. 570 (2008).

Fransden, Ronald J., Dave Naglich, Gene A. Lauver, and Allina D. Lee. 2013. "Background Checks for Firearm Transfers, 2012—Statistical Tables." Washington, DC: Bureau of Justice Statistics, US Department of Justice.

Friess, Steve. 2013, August 20. "How the NRA Built a Massive Secret Database of Gun Owners." *BuzzFeed*.

Goss, Kristin A. 2006. *Disarmed: The Missing Movement for Gun Control in America*. Princeton, NJ: Princeton University Press.

Hardy, David T. 1986. "The Firearms' Owners Protection Act: A Historical and Legal Perspective," *Cumberland Law Review* 17, 585–682.

Hemenway, David. 2006. *Private Guns, Public Health*. Ann Arbor: University of Michigan Press.

Henigan, Dennis A. 2009. *Lethal Logic: Exploding the Myths That Paralyze American Gun Policy*. Washington, DC: Potomac Books.

Hundley, Kris, Susan Taylor Martin, and Connie Humburg. 2012, June 1. "Florida 'Stand Your Ground' Law Yields Some Shocking Outcomes Depending on How Law Is Applied." *Tampa Bay Times*.

Kessler, Glenn. 2013, February 5. "The NRA's Fuzzy, Decades-Old Claim of '20,000' Gun Laws." *Washington Post*.

Krouse, William J. 2012. "Gun Control Legislation." Washington, DC: Congressional Research Service.

Law Center to Prevent Gun Violence. 2013. "Child Access Prevention Policy Summary."

———. 2012. "Design Safety Standards for Handguns Policy Summary."

———. 2012. "Federal Law on Background Checks."

———. 2012. "Gun Laws Matter 2012: Understanding the Link between Weak Laws and Gun Violence."

———. 2012. "Key Congressional Acts Related to Firearms."

———. 2012. "Locking Devices Policy Summary."

———. 2012. "Minimum Age to Purchase & Possess Firearms Policy Summary."

———. 2012. "Open Carrying Policy Summary."

———. 2013. "Post-*Heller* Litigation Summary."

———. 2012. "Private Sales Policy Summary (Universal Background Checks)."

Luo, Michael. 2011, November 13. "Felons Finding It Easy to Regain Gun Rights." *New York Times*.

Lytton, Timothy, ed. 2005. *Suing the Gun Industry: A Battle at the Crossroads of Gun Control and Mass Torts*. Ann Arbor: University of Michigan Press.

———. 2007. "Using Tort Litigation to Enhance Regulatory Policy Making: Evaluating Climate-Change Litigation in Light of Lessons from Gun-Industry and Clergy-Sexual-Abuse Lawsuits." *Texas Law Review* 86(7), 1837–76.

McClellan, Chandler B., and Erdal Tekin. 2012. "Stand Your Ground Laws and Homicides." Working Paper. Cambridge, MA: National Bureau of Economic Research.

*McDonald v. City of Chicago, Ill.* 130 S.Ct. 3020 (2010).

*Miller v. Texas.* 153 U.S. 535 (1894).

*Moore v. Madigan.* 708 F.3d 901 (7th Cir. 2013).

National Bank of Commerce in New York. 1919. "Federal Revenue Act of 1918: Complete Text with Reference Notes, Tables and Index."

National Conference of State Legislatures. 2013, July. "Guns on Campus: Overview."

NRA Institute for Legislative Action. 2007. "Compendium of State Laws Governing Firearms."

——. 2000, January 27. "Firearms Registration: New York City's Lesson."

Office of the Attorney General of Massachusetts. 2013. 940 CMR 16.00: Handgun Sales.

*Presser v. Illinois.* 116 U.S. 252 (1886).

Public Health Law Center. 2010. "Tobacco Control Litigation."

*Quilici v. Village of Morton Grove.* 695 F.2d 261 (1982).

Rosenthal, Lawrence E., and Adam Winkler. 2013. "The Scope of Regulatory Authority under the Second Amendment." In *Reducing Gun Violence in America*, edited by Daniel W. Webster and Jon S. Vernick, 225–36. Baltimore, MD: Johns Hopkins University Press.

Spitzer, Robert J. 2012. *The Politics of Gun Control*. Boulder, CO: Paradigm.

Stachelberg, Winnie, Arkadi Gerney, and Chelsea Parsons. 2013. "Blindfolded, and with One Hand Tied behind the Back." Center for American Progress.

Stolberg, Sheryl Gay. 2005, October 21. "Congress Passes New Legal Shield for Gun Industry." *New York Times*.

Timoney, John F. 2012, March 23. "Florida's Disastrous Self-Defense Law." Op-ed. *New York Times*.

*United States v. Lopez.* 514 U.S. 549 (1995).

*U.S. v. Cruikshank.* 92 U.S. 542 (1876).

*U.S. v. Miller.* 307 U.S. 174 (1939).

US Government Accountability Office. 2012, July. "Gun Control: States' Laws and Requirements for Concealed Carry Permits Vary across Nation." Washington, DC.

Vernick, Jon S., and Lisa M. Hepburn. 2003. "State and Federal Gun Laws: Trends for 1970–99." In *Evaluating Gun Policy: Effects on Crime and Violence*, edited by Jens Ludwig and Philip J. Cook, 345–402. Washington, DC: Brookings Institution Press.

Vernick, Jon S., and Julie Samia Mair. 2000. "State Laws Forbidding Municipalities from Suing the Firearm Industry: Will Firearm Immunity Laws Close the Courthouse Door?" *Journal of Health Care Law & Policy* 4(1), 126–46.

Vernick, Jon S., Lainie Rutkow, and Daniel A. Salmon. 2007. "Availability of Litigation as a Public Health Tool for Firearm Injury Prevention: Comparison of Guns, Vaccines, and Motor Vehicles." *American Journal of Public Health* 97(11), 1991–7.

Vizzard, William J. 2000. *Shots in the Dark: The Policy, Politics, and Symbolism of Gun Control*. Lanham, MD: Rowman & Littlefield.

Winkler, Adam. 2011. *Gunfight: The Battle over the Right to Bear Arms in America*. New York: Norton.

Zimring, Franklin E. 1975. "Firearms and Federal Law: The Gun Control Act of 1968." *Journal of Legal Studies* 4(1), 133–97.

Chapter 7

2012. "*Mother Jones'* Investigation: Assault Weapons and High-Capacity Magazines." *Mother Jones*.

Abrams, David S. 2011. "Estimating the Deterrent Effect of Incarceration Using Sentencing Enhancements." University of Pennsylvania, Institute for Law and Economics Research Paper.

Alpers, Philip. 2013. "The Big Melt: How One Democracy Changed after Scrapping a Third of Its Firearms." In *Reducing Gun Violence in America*, edited by Daniel W. Webster and Jon S. Vernick, 205–11. Baltimore, MD: Johns Hopkins University Press.

Azrael, Deborah, Philip J. Cook, and Matthew Miller. 2004. "State and Local Prevalence of Firearms Ownership: Measurement, Structure, and Trends." *Journal of Quantitative Criminology* 20(1), 43–62.

Baginski, Kenneth S. 2013. "2012 Hunting Safety Statistics." Albany: New York State Department of Environmental Conservation—Sportsman Education Program.

Blumstein, Alfred, and Kiminori Nakamura. 2009. "Redemption in the Presence of Widespread Criminal Background Checks." *Criminology* 47(2), 327–59.

Braga, Anthony A., David M. Kennedy, Elin J. Waring, and Anne M. Piehl. 2001. "Problem-Oriented Policing, Deterrence, and Youth Violence: An Evaluation of Boston's Operation Ceasefire." *Journal of Research in Crime and Delinquency* 38(3), 195–225.

Braga, Anthony A., and David L. Weisburd. 2012. "The Effects of Focused Deterrence Strategies on Crime: A Systematic Review and Meta-analysis of the Empirical Evidence." *Journal of Research in Crime and Delinquency* 49(3), 323–58.

Braga, Anthony A., and Garen J. Wintemute. 2013. "Improving the Potential Effectiveness of Gun Buyback Programs." *American Journal of Preventive Medicine* 45(5), 668–71.

Bureau of Alcohol, Tobacco, Firearms, and Explosives. 2012. "Firearm Types Recovered and Traced in the United States and Territories." Washington, DC: US Department of Justice.

Campbell, Jacquelyn C., Daniel Webster, Jane Koziol-McLain, Carolyn Block, Doris Campbell, Mary Ann Curry, Faye Gary, Nancy Glass, Judith McFarlane, and Carolyn Sachs. 2003. "Risk Factors for Femicide in Abusive Relationships: Results from a Multisite Case Control Study." *American Journal of Public Health* 93(7), 1089–97.

Centers for Disease Control and Prevention. 2013, April 2. "National Suicide Statistics at a Glance: Case Fatality Rate among Persons Ages 10 Years and Older for Males and Females Separately, and by Selected Mechanism for Both Sexes Combined, United States, 2005–2009."

Centers for Disease Control and Prevention, National Center for Injury Prevention and Control. n.d. National Violent Death Reporting System (NVDRS), Web-Based Injury Statistics Query and Reporting System (WISQARS).

Clarke, Ronald V., and David Weisburd. 1994. "Diffusion of Crime Control Benefits: Observations on the Reverse of Displacement." In *Crime Prevention Studies*, edited by Ronald V. Clarke, 165–84. Monsey, NY: Criminal Justice Press.

Cohen, Jacqueline, and Jens Ludwig. 2003. "Policing Crime Guns." In *Evaluating Gun Policy: Effects on Crime and Violence*, edited by Jens Ludwig and Philip J. Cook, 217–39. Washington, DC: Brookings Institution Press.

Cook, Philip J., and Anthony A. Braga. 2001. "Comprehensive Firearms Tracing: Strategic and Investigative Uses of New Data on Firearms Markets." *Arizona Law Review* 43(2), 277–309.

Cook, Philip J., and Jens Ludwig. 2006. "Aiming for Evidence-Based Gun Policy." *Journal of Policy Analysis and Management* 25(3), 691–735.

——. 1996. *Guns in America: Results of a Comprehensive National Survey on Firearms Ownership and Use*. Washington, DC: Police Foundation.

——. 2013. "The Limited Impact of the Brady Act: Evaluation and Implications." In *Reducing Gun Violence in America*, edited by Daniel W. Webster and Jon S. Vernick, 21–32. Baltimore, MD: Johns Hopkins University Press.

——. 2002. "Litigation as Regulation: Firearms." In *Regulation through Litigation*, edited by W. K. Viscusi, 67–93. Washington, DC: Brookings Institution Press.

Cook, Philip J., Jens Ludwig, and Anthony A. Braga. 2005. "Criminal Records of Homicide Offenders." *Journal of the American Medical Association* 294(5), 598–601.

Cook, Philip J., Jens Ludwig, Sudhir Venkatesh, and Anthony A. Braga. 2007. "Underground Gun Markets." *Economic Journal* 117(524), 588–618.

Dugan, Laura, Daniel S. Nagin, and Richard Rosenfeld. 1999. "Explaining the Decline in Intimate Partner Homicide: The Effects of Changing Domesticity, Women's Status, and Domestic Violence Resources." *Homicide Studies* 3(3), 187–214.

Fagan, Jeffrey. 2002. "Policing Guns and Youth Violence." *Future of Children* 12(2), 132–51.

Federal Bureau of Investigation. 2011. "Table 7: Offense Analysis, Crime in the United States 2011." Washington, DC: US Department of Justice.

Follman, Mark, Gavin Aronsen, Deanna Pan, and Maggie Caldwell. 2012, December 28. "US Mass Shootings, 1982–2012: Data from *Mother Jones'* Investigation." *Mother Jones.*

Kennedy, David M. 2011. *Don't Shoot: One Man, a Street Fellowship, and the End of Violence in Inner-City America.* New York: Bloomsbury.

Kennedy, David M., Anne M. Piehl, and Anthony A. Braga. 1996. "Youth Violence in Boston: Gun Markets, Serious Youth Offenders, and a Use-Reduction Strategy." *Law and Contemporary Problems* 59(1), 147–96.

Kleck, Gary. 2004. "Measures of Gun Ownership for Macro-Level Crime and Violence Research." *Journal of Research in Crime and Delinquency* 41(1), 3–36.

——. 1997. *Targeting Guns: Firearms and Their Control.* Hawthorne, NY: Aldine de Gruyter.

Knight, Brian G. 2011, September. "State Gun Policy and Cross-State Externalities: Evidence from Crime Gun Tracing." Working Paper. Cambridge, MA: National Bureau of Economic Research.

Koper, Christopher S. 2013. "America's Experience with the Federal Assault Weapons Ban, 1994–2004: Key Findings and Implications." In *Reducing Gun Violence in America*, edited by Daniel W. Webster and Jon S. Vernick, 157–71. Baltimore, MD: Johns Hopkins University Press.

——. 2004. "Updated Assessment of the Federal Assault Weapons Ban: Impacts on Gun Markets and Gun Violence, 1994–2003." National Institute of Justice, US Department of Justice.

Koper, Christopher S., and Evan Mayo-Wilson. 2006. "Police Crackdowns on Illegal Gun Carrying: A Systematic Review of Their Impact on Gun Crime." *Journal of Experimental Criminology* 2(2), 227–61.

Leitzel, J. 2003. "Comment." In *Evaluating Gun Policy: Effects on Crime and Violence*, edited by Jens Ludwig and Philip J. Cook, 145–56. Washington, DC: Brookings Institution.

Levitt, Steven D. 2004. "Understanding Why Crime Fell in the 1990's: Four Factors That Explain the Decline and Six That Do Not." *Journal of Economic Perspectives* 18(1), 163–90.

Levy, Pema. 2013, January 30. "Why Gun Control Backers Love to Talk about Duck Hunting." *TPM DC*.

Ludwig, Jens, and Philip J. Cook. 2000. "Homicide and Suicide Rates Associated with Implementation of the Brady Handgun Violence Prevention Act." *Journal of the American Medical Association* 284(5), 585–91.

Luo, Michael. 2011, November 13. "Felons Finding It Easy to Regain Gun Rights." *New York Times*.

Mayors Against Illegal Guns. 2011. "Fatal Gaps: How Missing Records in the Federal Background Check System Put Guns in the Hands of Killers."

——. "A Plan to Prevent Future Tragedies."

McGarrell, Edmund F., Steven M. Chermak, and Alexander Weiss. 2002. *Reducing Gun Violence: Evaluation of the Indianapolis Police Department's Directed Patrol Project*. US Department of Justice, Office of Justice Programs, National Institute of Justice.

McGarrell, Edmund F., Steven Chermak, Alexander Weiss, and Jeremy Wilson. 2001. "Reducing Firearms Violence through Directed Police Patrol." *Criminology and Public Policy* 1(1), 119–48.

Miller, Matthew, and David Hemenway. 2008. "Guns and Suicide in the United States." *New England Journal of Medicine* 359(10), 989–91.

——. 1999. "The Relationship between Firearms and Suicide: A Review of the Literature." *Aggression and Violent Behavior* 4(1), 59–75.

North, Michael J. 2013. "Gun Control in Great Britain after the Dunblane Shootings." In *Reducing Gun Violence in America*, edited by Daniel W. Webster and Jon S. Vernick, 185–93. Baltimore, MD: Johns Hopkins University Press.

Papachristos, Andrew V., Tracey L. Meares, and Jeffrey Fagan. 2007. "Attention Felons: Evaluating Project Safe Neighborhoods in Chicago." *Journal of Empirical Legal Studies* 4(2), 223–72.

Piehl, Anne M., Suzanne J. Cooper, Anthony A. Braga, and David M. Kennedy. 2003. "Testing for Structural Breaks in the Evaluation of Programs." *Review of Economics and Statistics* 85(3), 550–8.

Polsby, Daniel D. 1994, March. "The False Promise of Gun Control." *Atlantic Monthly*, 57–70.

Ramker, Gerard F. 2006. *Improving Criminal History Records for Background Checks, 2005*. Washington, DC: US Department of Justice, Office of Justice Programs, Bureau of Justice Statistics.

Raphael, Stephen, and Jens Ludwig. 2003. "Prison Sentence Enhancements: The Case of Project Exile." In *Evaluating Gun Policy: Effects on Crime and Violence*, edited by Jens Ludwig and Philip J. Cook, 251–86. Washington, DC: Brookings Institution Press.

Reuter, Peter, and Jenny Mouzos. 2003. "Australia: A Massive Buyback of Low-Risk Guns." In *Evaluating Gun Policy: Effects on Crime and Violence*, edited by Jens Ludwig and Philip J. Cook, 121–56. Washington, DC: Brookings Institution Press.

Romero, Michael P., Garen J. Wintemute, and Jon S. Vernick. 1998. "Characteristics of a Gun Exchange Program, and an Assessment of Potential Benefits." *Injury Prevention* 4(3), 206–10.

Rosenfeld, Richard. 1997. "Changing Relationships between Men and Women: A Note on the Decline in Intimate Partner Homicide." *Homicide Studies* 1(1), 72–83.

———. 1996. "Crime Prevention or Community Mobilization? The Dilemma of the Gun Buy-Back Program." In *Under Fire: Gun Buy-Backs, Exchanges and Amnesty Programs*, edited by Martha R Plotkin, 1–28. Washington, DC: Police Executive Research Forum.

Rosenfeld, Richard, Robert Fornango, and Eric Baumer. 2005. "Did Ceasefire, Compstat and Exile Reduce Homicide?" *Criminology and Public Policy* 4(3), 419–49.

Swanson, Jeffrey W., Allison Gilbert Robertson, Linda K. Frisman, Michael A. Norko, Hsiu-Ju Lin, Marvin S. Swartz, and Philip J. Cook. 2013. "Preventing Gun Violence Involving People with Serious Mental Illness." In *Reducing Gun Violence in America*, edited by Daniel W. Webster and Jon S. Vernick, 33–52. Baltimore, MD: Johns Hopkins University Press.

Vernick, Jon S., and Lisa M. Hepburn. 2003. "State and Federal Gun Laws: Trends for 1970–99." In *Evaluating Gun Policy: Effects on Crime and Violence*, edited by Jens Ludwig and Philip J. Cook, 345–402. Washington, DC: Brookings Institution Press.

Vigdor, Elizabeth R., and James A. Mercy. 2003. "Disarming Batterers: The Impact of Domestic Violence Firearm Laws." In *Evaluating Gun Policy: Effects on Crime and Violence*, edited by Jens Ludwig and Philip J. Cook, 157–201. Washington, DC: Brookings Institution Press.

———. 2006. "Do Laws Restricting Access to Firearms by Domestic Violence Offenders Prevent Intimate Partner Homicide?" *Evaluation Review* 30(3), 313–46.

Vittes, Katherine A., Jon S. Vernick, and Daniel W. Webster. 2013. "Legal Status and Source of Offenders' Firearms in States with the Least Stringent Criteria for Gun Ownership." *Injury Prevention* 19(1), 26–31.

Webster, Daniel W., Jon S. Vernick, and Maria T. Bulzacchelli. 2009. "Effects of State-Level Firearm Seller Accountability Policies on Firearm Trafficking." *Journal of Urban Health* 86(4), 525–37.

Webster, Daniel W., Jon S. Vernick, Emma E. McGinty, and Ted Alcorn. 2013. "Preventing the Diversion of Guns to Criminals through Effective Firearm Sales Laws." In *Reducing Gun Violence in America*, edited by Daniel W. Webster and Jon S. Vernick, 109–22. Baltimore, MD: Johns Hopkins University Press.

Weisburd, David L., Elizabeth R. Groff, and Sue-Ming Yang. 2012. *The Criminology of Place: Street Segments and Our Understanding of the Crime Problem*. New York: Oxford University Press.

Weisburd, David, and Cody W. Telep. 2011. "Spatial Displacement and Diffusion of Crime Control Benefits Revisited: New Evidence on Why Crime Doesn't Just Move around the Corner." In *The Reasoning Criminologist: Essays in Honour of Ronald V. Clarke*, edited by Nick Tilley and Graham Farrell, 142–59. New York: Routledge Press.

Wilson, James Q. 1994, March 20. "Just Take Away Their Guns." *New York Times Magazine*, 46–7.

Wintemute, G. J., C. M. Drake, J. J. Beaumont, M. A. Wright, and C. A. Parham. 1998. "Prior Misdemeanor Convictions as a Risk Factor for Later Violent and Firearm-Related Criminal Activity among Authorized Purchasers of Handguns." *Journal of the American Medical Association* 280(24), 2083–7.

Wintemute, Garen J. 2013. "Comprehensive Background Checks for Firearm Sales: Evidence from Gun Shows." In *Reducing Gun Violence in America*, edited by Daniel W. Webster and Jon S. Vernick, 95–107. Baltimore, MD: Johns Hopkins University Press.

Wintemute, Garen J., Mona A. Wright, Christiana M. Drake, and James J. Beaumont. 2001. "Subsequent Criminal Activity among Violent Misdemeanants Who Seek to Purchase Handguns." *Journal of the American Medical Association* 285(8), 1019–26.

Wright, James D. 1995. "Ten Essential Observations on Guns in America." *Society* 32(3), 63–8.

Zeoli, April M., and Daniel W. Webster. 2010. "Effects of Domestic Violence Policies, Alcohol Taxes and Police Staffing Levels on Intimate Partner Homicide in Large US Cities." *Injury Prevention* 16(2), 90–5.

Zeoli, April M., and Shannon Frattaroli. 2013. "Evidence for Optimism: Policies to Limit Batterers' Access to Guns." In *Reducing Gun Violence in America*, edited by Daniel W. Webster and Jon S. Vernick, 53–64. Baltimore, MD: Johns Hopkins University Press.

Zimring, Franklin E. 2011. *The City That Became Safe: New York's Lessons for Urban Crime and Its Control*. New York: Oxford University Press.

*Chapter 8*

Ayres, Ian, and John J. Donohue III. 1999. "Nondiscretionary Concealed Weapons Law: A Case Study of Statistics, Standards of Proof, and Public Policy." *American Law and Economics Review* 1(1), 436–70.

Bogus, Carl T. 1992. "Race, Riots, and Guns." *Southern California Law Review* 66, 1365–88.

Brearley, Harrington Cooper. 1932. *Homicide in the United States*. Chapel Hill: University of North Carolina Press.

Celinska, Katarzyna. 2007. "Individualism and Collectivism in America: The Case of Gun Ownership and Attitudes toward Gun Control." *Sociological Perspectives* 50(2), 229–47.

Churchill, Robert H. 2007. "Gun Regulation, the Police Power, and the Right to Keep Arms in Early America: The Legal Context of the Second Amendment." *Law and History Review* 25(1), 139–75.

Cook, Philip J., and Karen Hawley. 1981, Spring. "North Carolina's Pistol Permit Law: An Evaluation." *Popular Government* 46, 1–6.

Cornell, Saul. 2007. "Early American Gun Regulation and the Second Amendment: A Closer Look at the Evidence." *Law and History Review* 25(1), 197–204.

——. 2012. "The Right to Carry Firearms outside of the Home: Separating Historical Myths from Historical Realities." *Fordham Urban Law Journal* 39(5), 1695–726.

Cornell, Saul, and Nathan DeDino. 2004. "A Well Regulated Right: The Early American Origins of Gun Control." *Fordham Law Review* 73(2), 487–528.

Cottrol, Robert J., and Raymond T. Diamond. 1995. " 'Never Intended to Be Applied to the White Population': Firearms Regulation and Racial Disparity—the Redeemed South's Legacy to a National Jurisprudence? (Symposium on the Law of Freedom, Part 2)." *Chicago-Kent Law Review* 70(3), 1307–35.

Cramer, Clayton E. 1999. *Concealed Weapon Laws of the Early Republic: Dueling, Southern Violence, and Moral Reform.* Westport, CT: Praeger.

Cramer, Clayton E., and David B. Kopel. 1995. " 'Shall Issue': The New Wave of Concealed Handgun Permit Laws." *Tennessee Law Review* 62(3), 679–757.

DeConde, Alexander. 2001. *Gun Violence in America: The Struggle for Control.* Boston: Northeastern University Press.

Dykstra, Robert R. 1968. *The Cattle Towns.* New York: Knopf.

——. 1996. "Overdosing on Dodge City." *Western Historical Quarterly* 27(4), 505–14.

Halbrook, Stephen P. 2000. "Nazi Firearms Law and the Disarming of the German Jews." *Arizona Journal of International & Comparative Law* 17(3), 483–535.

____. 2013. *Gun Control in the Third Reich: Disarming the Jews and 'Enemies of the State.'* Oakland, CA: The Independent Institute.

Harcourt, Bernard E. 2004–5. "On Gun Registration, the NRA, Adolf Hitler, and Nazi Gun Laws: Exploding the Gun Culture Wars (a Call to Historians)." *Fordham Law Review* 73(2), 653–80.

Hoffman, Frederick L. 1925. *The Homicide Problem, a Paper by Frederick L. Hoffman.* Newark, NJ: Prudential Press.

Hofstadter, Richard. 1970, October. "America as a Gun Culture." *American Heritage* 21(6), 4–11, 82–85.

Horwitz, Joshua, and Casey Anderson. 2009. *Guns, Democracy, and the Insurrectionist Idea.* Ann Arbor: University of Michigan Press.

Hosley, William. 1999. "Guns, Gun Culture and the Peddling of Dreams." In *Guns in America: A Historical Reader,* edited by Jan E. Dizard, Robert

Merrill Muth, and Steve Andrews, Jr., 47–85. New York: New York University Press.

Kahan, Dan M., and Donald Braman. 2003. "More Statistics, Less Persuasion: A Cultural Theory of Gun-Risk Perceptions." *University of Pennsylvania Law Review* 151(4), 1291–327.

Kates, Don B. 1979. *Restricting Handguns: The Liberal Skeptics Speak Out.* Croton-on-Hudson, NY: North River Press.

Kennett, Lee, and James LaVerne Anderson. 1975. *The Gun in America: The Origins of a National Dilemma.* Westport, CT: Greenwood Press.

Lakoff, George. 2002. *Moral Politics: How Liberals and Conservatives Think.* Chicago: University of Chicago Press.

Melzer, Scott. 2009. *Gun Crusaders: The NRA's Culture War.* New York: New York University Press.

Pew Research Center for the People and the Press. 2013. "Why Own a Gun? Protection Is Now Top Reason."

Rankin, Jerry. 1967, May 3. "Heavily Armed Negro Group Walks into Assembly Chamber." *Los Angeles Times.*

Slotkin, Richard. 1998. *Gunfighter Nation: The Myth of the Frontier in Twentieth-Century America.* Norman: University of Oklahoma Press.

Spitzer, Robert J. 2004. "Don't Know Much about History, Politics, or Theory: A Comment." *Fordham Law Review* 73(2), 721–730.

——. 2012. *The Politics of Gun Control.* Boulder, CO: Paradigm.

Stedman, Richard C., and Thomas A. Heberlein. 2001. "Hunting and Rural Socialization: Contingent Effects of the Rural Setting on Hunting Participation." *Rural Sociology* 66(4), 599–617.

Swidler, Ann. 1986. "Culture in Action: Symbols and Strategies." *American Sociological Review* 51(2), 273–86.

Tahmassebi, Stefan B. 1991. "Gun Control and Racism." *George Mason University Civil Rights Law Journal* 2, 67–99.

Tonso, William R. 1985, December. "Gun Control: White Man's Law." *Reason* 17, 22–5.

US Government Accountability Office. 2012, July. "Gun Control: States' Laws and Requirements for Concealed Carry Permits Vary across Nation." Washington, DC.

Warner, Sam B. 1938. "The Uniform Pistol Act." *Journal of Criminal Law and Criminology (1931–1951)* 29(4), 529–54.

Whitney, Craig. 2012. *Living with Guns: A Liberal's Case for the Second Amendment.* New York: PublicAffairs.

Williamson, Harold F. 1952. *Winchester, the Gun That Won the West* Washington, DC: Combat Forces Press.

Winkler, Adam. 2011. *GunFight: The Battle over the Right to Bear Arms in America.* New York: Norton.

*Chapter 9*

2013. "Guns." Gallup Organization.

Benenson, Joel and Katie Connolly. 2013, April 6. "Don't Know Much about Gun Laws." Op-ed. *New York Times.*

Erskine, Hazel. 1972. "The Polls: Gun Control." *Public Opinion Quarterly* 36(3), 455–69.

Goss, Kristin A. 2006. *Disarmed: The Missing Movement for Gun Control in America.* Princeton, NJ: Princeton University Press.

Grossback, Lawrence, and Allan Hammock. 2003. "Overcoming One-Party Dominance: How Contextual Politics and West Virginia Helped Put George Bush in the White House." *Politics and Policy* 31(3), 406–31.

Jensen, Tom. 2013. "Red States Strongly Support Background Checks." Public Policy Polling.

Jones, Jeffrey M. 2011. "Record-Low 26% in U.S. Favor Handgun Ban." Gallup Organization.

Kenny, Christopher, Michael McBurnett, and David Bordua. 2004. "The Impact of Political Interests in the 1994 and 1996 Congressional Elections: The Role of the National Rifle Association." *British Journal of Political Science* 34(2), 331–44.

Mayors Against Illegal Guns. 2012. "Gun Owners Poll."

Newport, Frank. 2013. "Americans Wanted Gun Background Checks to Pass Senate." Gallup Organization.

Omero, Margie, et al. 2013. "What the Public Really Thinks about Guns." Washington, DC: Center for American Progress.

Pew Research Center for the People and the Press. 2012. "After Newtown, Modest Change in Opinion About Gun Control."

———. 2013. "Broad Support for Renewed Background Checks Bill, Skepticism about Its Chances."

———. 2013. "Gun Control: Key Data Points from Pew Research."

———. 2013. "In Gun Control Debate, Several Options Draw Majority Support."

———. 2013. "Why Own a Gun? Protection Is Now Top Reason."

Saad, Lydia. 2013. "Americans Back Obama's Proposals to Address Gun Violence." Gallup Organization.

Silver, Nate. 2012, December 18. "Party Identity in a Gun Cabinet." FiveThirtyEight. *New York Times.*

Spitzer, Robert J. 2012. *The Politics of Gun Control.* Boulder, CO: Paradigm.

Waldman, Paul. 2012. "The Myth of NRA Dominance Part II: Overrated Endorsements." ThinkProgress.

———. 2012. "The Myth of NRA Dominance Part III: Two Elections the NRA Did Not Win." ThinkProgress.

Young, Lindsay. 2012, December 18. "Outside Spenders' Return on Investment." Sunlight Foundation.

*Chapter 10*

"Eddie Eagle: What Is the Eddie Eagle GunSafe Program?" n.d. National Rifle Association.

"National Association for Gun Rights: About Us." n.d. National Association for Gun Rights.

2007. "Senate Passes NICS Improvement Act, House Concurs." National Rifle Association Institute for Legislative Action.

2013. *"National Rifle Assn Summary."* Washington, DC: Center for Responsive Politics.

Educational Fund to Stop Gun Violence. n.d. "Who Is the NRA Leadership?" (www.meetthenra.org/about).

Barrett, Paul M. 2013, March 14. "Why Gun Makers Fear the NRA." *Bloomberg Businessweek.*

Birnbaum, Jeffrey H., and Russell Newell. 2001, May 28. "Fat & Happy in D.C." *Fortune.*

Cherlin, Reid. 2012, July 24. "'We Do Absolutely Anything They Ask': How the NRA's Grading System Keeps Congress on Lockdown." *GQ.*

Diaz, Tom. 2013. *The Last Gun: How Changes in the Gun Industry Are Killing Americans and What It Will Take to Stop It.* New York: New Press.

Epstein, Aaron. 1979, May 14. "How Pentagon Boosted NRA." *Philadelphia Inquirer.*

Goss, Kristin A. 2006. *Disarmed: The Missing Movement for Gun Control in America.* Princeton, NJ: Princeton University Press.

Gun Owners of America. 2008, September 17. "About Gun Owners of America."

Hickey, Walter. 2013, January 16. "How the Gun Industry Funnels Tens of Millions of Dollars to the NRA." *Business Insider.*

Horwitz, Joshua, and Casey Anderson. 2009. *Guns, Democracy, and the Insurrectionist Idea.* Ann Arbor: University of Michigan Press.

Kelly, Lorelei. 2013, March 7. "How Groups Like the NRA Captured Congress—and How to Take It Back." *The Atlantic.*

Kelly, Mark. 2013, May 1. "NRA Leadership Should Refocus Its Priorities." *Houston Chronicle.*

Mann, Thomas E., and Norman J. Ornstein. 2012. *It's Even Worse Than It Looks: How the American Constitutional System Collided with the New Politics of Extremism.* New York: Basic Books.

Patterson, Kelly D., and Matthew M. Singer. 2006. "Targeting Success: The Enduring Power of the NRA." In *Interest Group Politics,* edited by Allan J. Cigler and Burdett A. Loomis, 37–64. Washington, DC: CQ Press.

Pew Research Center for the People and the Press. 2012. "After Newtown, Modest Change in Opinion About Gun Control."

——. 2013. "Broad Support for Renewed Background Checks Bill, Skepticism about Its Chances."

Schuman, Howard, and Stanley Presser. 1981. "The Attitude-Action Connection and the Issue of Gun Control." *Annals of the American Academy of Political and Social Science* 455, 40–7.

Spitzer, Robert J. 2012. *The Politics of Gun Control*. Boulder, CO: Paradigm.

Stone, Peter H., and Ben Hallman. 2013, January 11. "NRA Gun Control Crusade Reflects Firearms Industry Financial Ties." *Huffington Post*.

Violence Policy Center. 2011. "Blood Money: How the Gun Industry Bankrolls the NRA."

*Chapter 11*

"The World's Billionaires: Michael Bloomberg." 2013, September. *Forbes*.

Blumenthal, Paul. 2013, July 31. "Gabrielle Giffords Gun Control Super Pac Raises $6.5 Million." *Huffington Post*.

Callaghan, Karen, and Frauke Schnell. 2001. "Assessing the Democratic Debate: How the News Media Frame Elite Policy Discourse." *Political Communication* 18(2), 183–212.

Downs, Anthony. 1972. "Up and Down with Ecology: The Issue Attention Cycle." *Public Interest* 28(1), 38–50.

Downs, Douglas. 2002. "Representing Gun Owners: Frame Identification as Social Responsibility in News Media Discourse." *Written Communication* 19(1), 44–75.

Etten, Tamryn. 1991. "Gun Control and the Press: A Content Analysis of Newspaper Bias." Annual Meeting of the American Society of Criminology, San Francisco.

Gans, Herbert J. 1979. *Deciding What's News: A Study of CBS Evening News, NBC Nightly News, Newsweek, and Time*. New York: Pantheon.

Goss, Kristin A. 2006. *Disarmed: The Missing Movement for Gun Control in America*. Princeton, NJ: Princeton University Press.

Groseclose, Tim, and Jeffrey Milyo. 2005. "A Measure of Media Bias." *Quarterly Journal of Economics* 120(4), 1191–237.

Hamilton, James. 2004. *All the News That's Fit to Sell: How the Market Transforms Information into News*. Princeton, NJ: Princeton University Press.

Hsiang, Iris Chyi, and Maxwell McCombs. 2004. "Media Salience and the Process of Framing: Coverage of the Columbine School Shootings." *Journalism and Mass Communication Quarterly* 81(1), 22–35.

Jones, David R. 1968, July 7. "Gun Controls: Pressures to Disarm." *New York Times*.

Kingdon, John W. 2010. *Agendas, Alternatives, and Public Policies*. New York: Longman.

Kleck, Gary. 2001. "Modes of News Media Distortion." In *Armed: New Perspectives on Gun Control*, edited by Gary Kleck and Don B. Kates, 175–214. Amherst, NY: Prometheus Books.

Lott, John R. 2003. *The Bias against Guns: Why Almost Everything You've Heard about Gun Control Is Wrong*. New York: Regnery.

Moms Demand Action. "Moms Demand Action for Gun Sense in America" (momsdemandaction.org/about/).

Muschert, Glenn W., and Dawn Carr. 2006. "Media Salience and Frame Changing across Events: Coverage of Nine School Shootings, 1997–2001." *Journalism and Mass Communication Quarterly* 83(4), 747–66.

Newport, Frank. 2012, December 19. "To Stop Shootings, Americans Focus on Police, Mental Health." Gallup Politics.

Patrick, Brian Anse. 2002. *The National Rifle Association and the Media: The Motivating Force of Negative Coverage*. New York: Peter Lang.

Spitzer, Robert J. 2012. *The Politics of Gun Control*. Boulder, CO: Paradigm.

Sunlight Foundation Reporting Group. 2013. "Follow the Unlimited Money: Independence USA Pac, 2014 Cycle."

# INDEX